CATHERINE, KARMA, AND COMPLEX PTSD

Also by the author:

Along the Nile

Alternatives for Everyone

Cosmic Grandma Wisdom

Forgiveness Equals Fortune (co-authored with Liah Holtzman)

From the Depths of Thyme

Lemurian Way: Remembering your Essential Nature

Strangers in Paradise

Thymely Tales

Traveling on the River of Time

Twin Souls: A Karmic Love Story

Delphi and the Greek Warrior (coming out in 2019)

(All books are available on Amazon and Smashwords.com)

Visit the author's website: *thymelauren.wixsite.com/thymely-one*

CATHERINE, KARMA, and COMPLEX PTSD

Lauren O. Thyme

Lauren O. Thyme Publishing

2019

ISBN 978-0-9983446-8-3

Free image compliments of Pixabay
Ascension-1568162_960_720.jpg   JanBaby

Interior and Cover Design by Sue Stein

Contact Lauren O. Thyme:
Email: thyme.lauren@gmail.com
Facebook: Lauren O. Thyme
LaurenOThymeCreations.com

This book is dedicated to my beloved Aunt Edna
and counselor Pete Walker, author of
Complex PTSD: From Surviving to Thriving,
both of whom saved my life.

Contents

Chapter 1	The Beginning	9
Chapter 2	What are Past Lives and Karma?	19
Chapter 3	Catherine, Empress of Titania, and Philippe	23
Chapter 4	Lauren's Story	31
Chapter 5	Complex PTSD–Including Sexual Abuse and Incest	55
Chapter 6	Complex PTSD–Lauren, Catherine, The Empress and Philippe	75
Chapter 7	Astrology and Complex PTSD	79
Chapter 8	What is an Empath?	85
Chapter 9	Healing	97
Chapter 10	Conclusion	105
Acknowledgments and Gratitude		111

Appendix 1	Introduction to Appendix 1: Catherine	113
	Part 1	115
	Part 2	120
	Part 3	126
	Part 4	130
	Part 5	136
	Part 6	139
	Part 7	147
	Part 8	153
	Part 9	158
	Part 10	171
	Part 11	197

Appendix 2	Astrology	258
Appendix 3	How Strong is Your Pluto?	268
Appendix 4	Healing Modalities, Books, Workbooks, Websites	272
Appendix 5	Stages of Recovery	275
Appendix 6	Toolboxes for Recovery	288
Appendix 7	Voice Fighting	293
Appendix 8	Babaji Meditation, Babaji Lucid Dreaming	300
Appendix 9	How to Easily Get What You Want	312
Appendix 10	13 Steps for Managing an Emotional Flashback	318
Appendix 11	How to Reboot Yourself Using Sacred Feminine Consciousness (Sacred Healing)	321

CHAPTER 1

THE BEGINNING

"Take your broken heart and make it into art."
— Carrie Fisher

(Carrie was famous for playing Princess Leia in Star Wars.
She then created her famous one-woman comedy show on bipolar
disease which she suffered from and died as a consequence of it.)

Catherine, Karma and Complex PTSD is a genuine, factual account with scientific subtexts. The story line contains information of my childhood as Lauren, and my past lives. Also included is what I've learned about my karma, past and current lives, and complex PTSD, as these co-mingle in healing and understanding. I sometimes achieve a contemplative state, otherworldly, floating above and around my reality while my Higher Self gains epiphany. I live, as my deceased partner Paul used to say, in a naturally altered state, with little ego to hold me together, highly sensitive like the Princess and the Pea, with virtually no "skin" to protect myself. I have one foot on earth and the other in a transcendent space/time. That's on the good days. Other days I'm in a quagmire of despair, where volcanic emotions are whipped into a frenzy. I then hide away from others, indeed I often feel immense pain around people, and long for release from anguish.

This book is non-fiction, yet some parts read like fiction. Part of what is contained here are my memories, which I've gathered like a spiritual and psychological detective, a mystical high priestess, and a wounded child longing to be free. I also include methods of healing I've used.

My story is sadly too commonplace. My intention is not to fix blame, nor to have you feel sorry for me, to accuse me of being a victim, or to hate the perpetrators. Rather this book is offered for you to understand what, when, who, and with a little luck—why—my life has been as it is, often difficult, sometimes miraculous, while I try to mend my "broken heart."

In my opinion, nothing in life is accidental, coincidental, or by chance, but rather an awesome concurrence of cosmic events. Analytical psychologist C.G. Jung coined the word "synchronicity." Jung's belief was that, just as events may be connected by causality, they also may be connected by meaning. Thus, this book describes and elucidates many hundreds, thousands, or millions of bits of events and information into one holistic arrangement. As my Elders and David Bohm, a protégé of Einstein and a theoretical physicist, state, "Everything is connected to everything."

CATHERINE is a past life of mine, one of 102 past lives, all of which I remember in spectacular, kaleidoscopic detail. I chose my current lifetime as Lauren to finish karma from Catherine's life, to balance the disharmony I perpetrated as Catherine, and restore positive light, vibration, energy, and balance to my soul. I wrote the Catherine section of this book (Appendix 1) in 1988. Only now am I ready to finish the rest. Only now have I learned enough to explain coherently.

Although I entitle this work *Catherine, Karma and Complex PTSD*, I include a total of three of my past lives—Catherine, Philippe, and the Empress of Titania, who were each perpetrators of crimes, especially sexual crimes. During 65 years of remembering my past lives, as well as being a past life counselor during 50 of those years, my in depth research shows that being a perpetrator is far worse—karmically speaking—than being a victim or having a so-called neutral life.

In terms of **KARMA**, even though a person may appear cruel, evil and cold, psychopathic or psychotic, the soul/spirit cares deeply and wants the best for everyone. To hurt someone often creates deep regret, guilt, and shame. The Higher Self, which embodies the conscience, is most aggrieved at hurting another being. The soul then waits for a perfect opportunity in a specific lifetime to make amends. The Higher Self will find the appropriate lifetime to work out karma, and, if necessary, be a victim while repaying debts to those hurt from other lifetimes and to learn by experiencing. Often that life of contrition, repayment, and balance can be unrelentingly harsh and dreadfully painful.

The story of the ancient Egyptian Weighing of the Heart is a significant metaphor in this instance. In famous carvings, Anubis, a spiritual guide, has brought someone after death to have his heart weighed on a scale against Ma'at's Feather of Truth, while ibis-headed Thoth writes down the results. If one's heart is as light as Ma'at's feather, that soul would continue to the spirit world. If not, one was doomed to be devoured by Ammut and to return to earth, presumably to incarnate into another body, while continuing to experience karmic challenges and learning how to balance those appropriately.

COMPLEX POST TRAUMATIC STRESS DISORDER (C-PTSD)—
first coined by Judith Herman; also known as complex trauma) is a multifaceted, complicated psychological disorder similar to post-traumatic stress disorder—PTSD. Complex PTSD originates from repetitive, prolonged torment involving physical, sexual, mental, and/or emotional harm often accompanied by abandonment by a caregiver with an interpersonal relationship of uneven power dynamics, such as a parent, step-parent or adoptive parent. Lauren's soul decided to choose this lifetime including complex post-traumatic stress disorder in order to learn vital karmic lessons and to pay back karmic debts. Then as I'm learning, I share what I've learned with others.

As Lauren, the level of physical, emotional, sexual, and psychic pain has been daunting from birth, perhaps even in utero. I have worked tirelessly via dozens of methods and strategies to heal myself, as well as find happiness, forgiveness, and peace. These include: 42 years of traditional and non-traditional health care; 42 years of therapy and counseling using various psychological methods; 35 hypnosis sessions; 100 rebirthing sessions (conscious breathing); hundreds of various bodywork and massage sessions; spiritual and metaphysical classes and workshops; along with an ocean of pharmaceuticals, vitamins, herbs, supplements, and other health products. Also I attended years of 12-step programs—Alanon (friends and family of alcoholics), ACA (adult children of alcoholics), CoDa (co-dependents anonymous) and ISA (incest survivors anonymous), as well as reading, studying, meditating, contemplating, writing, traveling, and publishing my own books and articles. To reduce my misery was always the impetus behind the tireless work I carried out on myself. Pain compelled me to learn, uncover, forgive, and practice gratitude and compassion. Due to my extensive personal research, I also published a non-fiction book entitled *Alternatives for Everyone, A Guide to Non-traditional Health Care.*

Yet I have experienced miracles. I was granted many gifts and talents in this lifetime: writing, acting, lecturing, being a psychic, learning and practicing astrology, being a storyteller, and working with the Elders (a group of ascended masters). The spiritual part of me has always inexplicably felt protected and safe from harm.

The details of Catherine's, Philippe's, the Empress' and Lauren's lifetimes are distressing, yet revealing as a study of karma coupled with complex PTSD. I include them so you may satisfy your curiosity as well as to understand the numerous spiritual and dynamic synchronicities and connections between past lives and one's current lifetime. I hope that my revelations are of benefit to you—a survivor, a friend or relative of a survivor, or one who works professionally with survivors.

I entirely reveal myself to you because I am a High Priestess, a number 2, my personality and soul number according to the Alistair Crowley Thoth tarot, using my birth day and other numbers. The High Priestess is a "Service Job" which encompasses intuition, independence, self-trust, self-resourcefulness, receptivity, and assertiveness. Intuition is mental, emotional, spiritual, and physical. The High Priestess represents the journey homeward or return to self. As a High Priestess I share with you what I've gone through and learned in hopes it will be of advantage to you on your life's path.

How can I remember past lives? How do you remember yesterday? Last week? Last year? For me it's all the same. My memories are clear, expand in detail as time goes on, and even more powerfully when I meet specific people who have known me in other life times. Sometimes I feel "unstuck in time," similar to the character Billy Pilgrim in Kurt Vonnegut's book *Slaughter House Five*, in my current Lauren life with complex PTSD memories, as well as 102 past life memories. Recollections swirl through me a lot as if they are happening right now. When famous author Colin Wilson read and commented on my book *Along the Nile*, he said that it was hallucinogenic, as if he was "there" in the book. He was—because I am. All of it is for my healing, growth and evolution, so it is perfect. Not much fun, but perfect.

Conscious memories of my past lives began when I was 5 years old, after a 2nd suicide attempt trying to escape from my abusive, abandoning, molesting family. When I came out of my coma, I could hear the Elders and realized I was now highly psychic, as well as having an ability to remember past lives with ease. This shift into a highly spiritual and intuitive person is not unusual with those with near-death experiences. I immediately began assembling recollections of this life as Lauren as well as other lifetimes, like a massive jigsaw puzzle, while the process continues to this day. I believe there's no truth with a capital T. No reality with a capital R. Therefore, my life, past lives, and story are true and correct for me, make sense, and feel accurate. I believe that is all anyone can discern, discover, and comprehend.

OTHER MODALITIES TO CONSIDER

In addition to past lives, karma, and complex PTSD, I utilized other modalities to bring light to the darkness. These include astrology, as well my being a highly sensitive person, an empath, a conduit, and an INFJ, according Myers-Briggs Personality test. These all confirmed and clarified the penetrating sensitivity I live with.

I took a yearlong course in astrology in 1970-1971 and have been a practicing, professional astrologer ever since. Because it is an art as well as a science, I am always learning. Astrology is a language and a way of understanding myself, my personalities, traits, skills, challenges, past lives, and current events. I consider everyone's birth chart as a blueprint for what we are here to learn in our lifetime.

As a result of my intensive, lifelong studies and memories, I am a fatalist. I believe that I came here with a specific birth chart, parents, and a set of pre-determined circumstances and events that unrolled day-by-day, year-by-year, decade-by-decade. I learn through feeling, experiencing, remembering, understanding, and appreciating what all pieces of my lifetime puzzle mean. If anything, I came here to earth to learn forgiveness, especially towards those people and circumstances that seem unforgivable. I'm still learning and will continue until I depart this earthly plane.

I've altered the names of participants in my life. I have worked diligently at forgiveness of myself and others and hold no one—not even myself nor a higher power—to blame. I trust the universe will handle others' debts appropriately and have witnessed firsthand some of the heart-rending karma that others have paid. No one is bad. All participants are playing the roles they chose. I see my story as a perfect working out of my soul's evolution. The Elders tell me this is my last lifetime on earth, so perhaps that's why it has been multifaceted and tough, as I'm trying to finish all remaining karma and balance all relationships. Then I can go on to my next assignment.

Although I have practiced forgiveness towards many perpetrators, I still have to do the arduous work of healing myself, which has been a lifelong process. Whatever I've experienced has been worthwhile. I wouldn't change a single moment of my life. Through forgiveness, compassion, and understanding, I love myself as well as I love Catherine, Philippe, and the Empress of Titania.

Catherine, Karma and Complex PTSD is intended to inspire, contribute, encourage, soothe, and educate, especially for those who suffer, including friends, families, and relationships of victims. I'm grateful for this opportunity to share my path and triumphs with you and hope that it lightens your load. I especially address every soul who struggles to understand what on earth is going on in and around you. Your wounds are sacred wounds, leading you ever higher to a state of bliss and ascension, while healing your karma, making sense of your suffering, and gaining happiness, forgiveness, and peace.

You may think I'm brave (or perhaps foolish) to reveal so much of my history to you, some of which is shocking and embarrassing. I have vowed as part of my spiritual journey to share what I've learned in hopes it helps others to understand, have compassion, forgiveness, and healing, and perhaps to comprehend the complexity of their human/spiritual experience.

I'm also writing this book as a personal liberation so that I can release my life as it has been and how it came about. No one is able to comprehend me at the depth and breadth that I do, so it's only natural that I should explain it to myself (and you) in this format. Once I write about a subject, I am emancipated, at rest and peaceful, with no need to describe conditions any further.

I'm one of the lucky ones. Many who have faced similar challenges as I have are permanently bedridden, mentally ill, hospitalized, in jail or prison, an alcoholic, drug addict, isolated, a prostitute, or dead.

I am writing *Catherine, Karma and Complex PTSD* because I have empathy and compassion for those who suffer. If my book helps you in some small way, I celebrate.

As the Talmud says, "Whoever saves a life, it is considered as if he saved an entire world."

Let me be absolutely clear. I am *not* telling you, a survivor of any type of abuse in a current or past life including sexual abuse, that you deserve pain and suffering. No, you do not. It is not your fault. You are not to blame. You are innocent and guiltless. I ask the Higher Power's blessing for your healing and tranquility.

However, what I *am* saying is that I've struggled for most of my life to understand the full scope and reasons behind what, how, and why I have endured abuse and the emotional, physical, mental, and sexual torment that accompanied it. My desire is to release it. I have accumulated enough data in many different formats that my life makes sense and I can attain equanimity. Part of that data includes my past lives, astrology, psychology including the Myers–Briggs personality indicator, karma, and an all-encompassing spiritual decision to clean my soul's slate once and for all. To finish all my lifetimes and return to my spiritual home.

I have been a professional astrologer for over 40 years, a psychic since I was 5 years old, and have received many messages and explanations in my life from the Elders—intelligent, wise, loving, helpful, Higher Beings that are connected to me. Thus I can safely say that the information I have assembled makes sense to me in the broadest sense of spiritual, metaphysical, and psychological perception while I have forgiveness and compassion for myself and others— victims and perpetrators alike.

In spite of my exceedingly sensitive nature, both ingrained and acquired in my family, I have come to realize that my reactions and responses to my abusive environment were normal and healthy as a human being in my current as well as past lives. If one is traumatized, those kinds of reactions are to be expected. Only when the trauma is finished can one revisit oneself to shift those reactions that are now unhelpful—and to heal.

For myself and others I offer my stories, research, explanations, and methods of healing I've used with blessings and gratitude. I encourage your inspiration, liberation, and understanding of the cosmic system at work from my humble perspective.

This book contains 11 Appendices. You can read the main body of the book in an uninterrupted flow, then go to the in-depth, personal appendices that may interest you. Some of them are healing tools.

Appendix 1: Catherine (novelette)

Appendix 2: Lauren's astrological information

Appendix 3: Pluto questionnaire

Appendix 4: Books, authors, websites, and 12-step groups

Appendix 5: Stages of Recovery

Appendix 6: Toolboxes by Pete Walker; fighting the inner critic

Appendix 7: Voice fighting technique

Appendix 8: Babaji: Meditation methods and lucid dreaming

Appendix 9: How to write a God letter.

Appendix 10: 13 Steps for Managing an Emotional Flashback

Appendix 11: How to Reboot Yourself Using Sacred Feminine Consciousness (Sacred Healing)

I believe the Universe is essentially an amazing, kind, and transformative place.

I conclude with the wise words from my Elders who repeat to me an ongoing mantra: "Everything is perfect, no matter what it looks like, for the purpose of learning, growth, and evolution."

CHAPTER 2

WHAT ARE PAST LIVES and KARMA?

What are past lives? Loosely put, I use the term to describe other earthly experiences one has had in addition to one's current lifetime. Those experiences have occurred in varying epochs, countries, cultures, and races, and include one's soul experiencing both sexes in other lifetimes.

Why is it important to be concerned with past lives? Because in my experience, both personally and professionally, unhealed past lives, especially difficult ones, can shape your current life, affecting your relationships, health, finances, as well as mental and emotional states. Those unhealed lives beg to be remembered, understood, and released.

Time is not linear. According to quantum physicists, string theorists, metaphysicians, and spiritual teachers, time is different than what we have believed and understood. All lives, including one's current life, are happening in present time, what Eckhardt Tolle calls the "Now." Although I use the term "past lives," all thoughts, actions, behaviors, and feelings are occurring in present time.

One's current life can transform and improve when one works on healing problems and issues from those past lives. Past life traumas from another lifetime can be released, which then alters and enhances one's current lifetime.

Furthermore, your past lives can/will also change when you work on yourself in your current lifetime identity through conscious activities such as meditation, bodywork, prayer, and positive changes in thought and behavior—especially forgiveness and compassion. In other words because all lifetimes are operating in the now, lifetimes are fluid and interchangeable, and can be transformed purposefully.

I currently remember 102 lifetimes in detail, the memories starting when I was five years old. When I meet certain people, I can discern which lifetimes I knew them in, what our relationship was like, and what we are still working through together. Ultimately the goal seems to be forgiveness, peace, release, and balance. Having this knowledge and information helps me work through problems in myself and in my relationships.

After consulting for decades with other individuals on their past lives, an interesting aspect became clear. What is known as karma doesn't get created from what one does or doesn't do in a certain lifetime, but how one THINKS or FEELS about what he/she did or didn't do, as well as how one THINKS or FEELS about other people's actions or lack of action. This often results in guilt, anger, fear, blame, remorse, shame, and revenge in one's current lifetime.

At some point in its evolution the soul makes a decision to reverse or balance those erroneous assumptions, as well as to experience challenging issues relating to key individuals. Many times taking on the problems and deciding to upgrade one's soul results in tackling difficult lessons in one lifetime, analogous to going to a university to learn advanced curriculums. Thus the soul waits for an appropriate lifetime in which to work out a particular problem or problematic relationship. I've been a practicing astrologer for 45 years. I've concluded that the birth chart is a blueprint for the current life indicating challenges, talents, proclivities, obsessions, relationships, along with personality characteristics and defects. Thus the difficulties you experience are not wrong or bad in your chart. You have chosen obstacles and complications to achieve further knowledge and progress in the school of spiritual life.

A soul cannot learn everything in one short lifetime, so the soul chooses a few qualities to play with and learn about each time through hundreds or perhaps thousands of lifetimes.

Therefore, if a person has a problem, the soul has chosen that difficulty to learn and grow spiritually, as well as to heal and balance itself through understanding, forgiveness, and compassion for itself and others.

Although a soul may choose to lead a disruptive life, it does not mean that particular person is bad or evil. I don't believe in evil. A soul needs to have numerous experiences in order to grow and learn, which includes what we might consider "good" and "bad."

In my decades of work I notice that nowadays many souls are leading multiple lives in one lifetime—having many significant relationships, moving homes frequently, as well as having various jobs or careers. What I believe is happening is that time is speeding up on planet Earth and there is a lot to accomplish in a short amount of time. Our planet is going through interesting times.

Souls seem to travel through lifetimes in soul groups or soul families. Often a soul friend/family member will either assist another soul to weather a stormy lifetime or to create challenging situations to be worked out together.

You can think of yourself as a deep-sea diver, exploring the vast depths and infinite reaches of your soul's experiences. One's experience of clearing lifetimes can inform and heal your soul in its journey, to modify or even eliminate your current lifetime problems and expand positive events and attributes.

When you heal past life issues, you heal yourself. When you heal yourself, you heal your past life issues, which is a positive reinforcement loop for your soul's growth and evolution. That healing continues and expands in an endless spiral of spiritual improvement.

Do you worry that you might be making up stories and ideas about your past lives? Imagination is not fantasy or illusions, but our higher consciousness revealing itself to us. As the mystic, writer, poet, and artist William Blake said:

The imagination is not a state: it is the human existence itself.

Do you have to believe in past lives or reincarnation to benefit from this book? No, you don't. You can consider that what you learn are symbols and archetypes which describe and illuminate your current life."

Excerpt from Chapter 1 of my book Traveling on the River of Time © 2018, a do-it-yourself handbook for the exploration of past lives

Karma is often thought to be a debt "paid back" by experiencing the opposite side of one's behavior. If one has been a perpetrator, one may be obliged to return as a victim.

I'm convinced that I set up my current life to restore harmony and balance to my soul. I believe it was valuable for me to experience what being a perpetrator feels like and looks like in the guise of Catherine, along with Philippe and the Empress, and then to experience the other side as Lauren. Those three people were primarily sexual perpetrators, so the other side for me is to be the victim of sexual perpetrators, suffering challenging and aberrant sexual behavior from men, including incest, child molestation, sexual abuse, rape, and sexually dysfunctional relationships starting when I was eighteen months old and lasting for most of my 71 years.

CHAPTER 3

CATHERINE, EMPRESS OF TITANIA, and PHILIPPE

Catherine, approximately 1379 -1402 AD France

The following is a brief synopsis of Catherine's life. The entire novelette of *Catherine* can be found in Appendix 1.

Catherine's mother Antoinette was an herbalist, healer, and midwife in the village of Quimont. Antoinette mysteriously turned up pregnant and refused to reveal the identity of the father. The midwife suggested that Antoinette kill her baby Catherine, as Catherine had the mark of the devil on her face, but the loving mother refused.

She and her baby were shunned, despised and bullied by the town's people. Antoinette taught the lore of herbs to her daughter Catherine.

When Catherine was young, a child from the village showed up dead in the nearby Moselle River. Catherine was suspected.

At twelve Catherine seduced her mother's lover, Baron Jean duFont, a magistrate. He became obsessed with her and turned away his long-time lover Antoinette, Catherine's mother.

A band of actors, dancers, and gypsies arrived in Quimont and Catherine ran off with them. She got into trouble. Catherine's lover, Michel Lamont, was killed in a fight over her. She returned to Baron duFont for protection, a behavior she practiced for years. Michel's lover swore vengeance.

The following morning Catherine took herself and the Baron to Church. The priest turned out to be a former lover and duFont was humiliated.

The Sheriff of Roubaix paid a call to the Baron and claimed that Catherine had put a spell on Michel Lamont before he was murdered. The Baron bribed the Sheriff to keep silent about the murder and to avoid implicating Catherine.

The gypsy band returned and Catherine left with them again. Catherine danced and acted for the crowds. Francois of the Gypsies fell in love with Catherine while she toyed with him. Rene of the Gypsies was impressed with Catherine. Meanwhile Michel Lamont's lover Maxine plotted revenge.

After a street play, Catherine seduced a nobleman, the Duke of Casale Monterrato, known as Emilio Fialdini and became his mistress. The Duke was robbed and found dead. Rene of the Gypsies diverted attention away from Catherine with the Mayor. Then Rene helped Catherine escape on an old horse, and she traveled alone back to Quimont and the Baron.

A young boy in a small town fell in love with Catherine during her trek. She left in a carriage the boy had hired and returned to duFont, who joyously took her in. She became sick with a form of sexually transmitted disease when she arrived and overwintered with the Baron. In the spring it became apparent that she was going insane. DuFont took Catherine with him to a trial in Paris and they stayed in luxurious quarters.

At a party in Paris Catherine met Cardinal Malplaquet, two soldiers, and Colonel Pouissent. The two soldiers fought a duel over Catherine and one of them died. Colonel Pouissent sent the surviving soldier into battle after the second soldier died. The Colonel arrested Catherine and took her to his house, a virtual prisoner. He treated her cruelly.

Catherine seduced a guard then made her escape back to duFont in his Paris house. The Baron was now deathly ill with the same illness.

They traveled back to Quimont and Catherine arranged for her mother Antoinette to nurse the Baron back to wellness. He was healed but weak, and understood the severity of the illness.

Antoinette left again. When she arrived in Quimont, she discovered her family home had been mysteriously burned down.

Catherine ran away again.

Cardinal Malplaquet and Colonel Pouissent visited duFont, and ordered him to give up Catherine to them. They threatened duFont with imprisonment if he did not do what they asked. DuFont realized his wealth and power could not save him and agreed, in order to buy time for Catherine.

DuFont gave his servant, Pierre, who hated Catherine, a bag of coins, to find Catherine and take her somewhere safe. But first he asked Pierre to help him commit suicide, knowing that whatever fate had in store for him—losing Catherine, becoming sicker, or arrested and tortured—he will suffer. Pierre helped the Baron to commit suicide.

Afterwards Pierre set out to find Catherine. He found her cavorting with a group of men. He encouraged her to leave with him in his wagon and she did so, only to jump out and run away. Pierre watched her leave and he returned to Quimont. She found a group of vagabonds and joined them. Her appearance had coarsened and her manner had as well.

A pig farmer became interested in her, and left his wife and family to travel with her. But Catherine spurned him.

Maxine, Michel Lamont's lover, turned Catherine over to the authorities in the person of Colonel Pouissent. Catherine was arrested and put into prison, where she was tortured, charged with witchcraft, and eventually **executed**.

Empress of Titania, Atlantis, approximately 15,000 BCE

Chronologically my second lifetime on planet earth transpired in Atlantis after a stay in Lemuria, and is the second in my trilogy of being a perpetrator, along with Catherine and Philippe.

I had arrived in Atlantis after a lengthy stay in Lemuria and was still in possession of spiritual and metaphysical powers all Lemurian citizens were blessed with. I was born to a king and queen of a small area in Atlantis. The couple wasn't anything special, rather like a mayor of an insignificant town and his wife. However, for reasons I don't understand, (perhaps precognition) their advisers were afraid of me, even when I was a little child. They taught me everything they knew, but I was far more intelligent and quick than they were, with uncanny abilities. By the time I was around 10 or 12 years old, the advisors convinced my parents that I should be killed, because I was supposedly dangerous. My parents loved me and were kindly people, thus they weren't able to kill me outright. Instead of sentencing me to death, I was banished to the wilderness by myself, with no provisions. Human beings are social animals and don't do well by themselves, so to be exiled is like death. Not to mention I was still a youngster and didn't know how to fend for myself.

I wandered around in barren, empty grasslands for a few days but was then found by a hermit, a man who had spent many years living by himself practicing magic, herbs, and nature lore. He took me in and trained me well, appreciating my intellect and ability to learn. He was very knowledgeable about how to merge sexuality with magic, a potent mixture, and thus instructed me in those skills.

I was distraught, unhappy, and angry at my banishment. I felt unloved by my parents, their advisors, indeed the whole community and thirsted for my revenge. I appreciated the hermit's rescuing me, but often his ministrations were nothing short of sexual abuse. Since I had nowhere to go, I put up with his behavior, pretending to be compliant, but seethed inside with impotent rage.

After I had been with the hermit for several years, I discerned that I had learned all he had to teach me. While he was asleep, I cut off his testicles, so that he couldn't teach anyone else the same methods, and made my escape. This time I was more knowledgeable about the locale and eventually found my way to civilization. I came to an area known as Titania, quite a bit more metropolitan and populated than my birthplace.

The emperor of Titania was old and sickly. His son was young and healthy but rather simple, trusting, even slow. Within a short time I had seduced the Prince and we married. Once that was accomplished, I pushed him off a height to his death and made sure his father was eliminated as well. Thus I became the undisputed Empress of Titania.

If anyone dared to dispute me, I could kill them with the power of my mind, sometimes a whole number of them at once.

I came to an early demise by killing a lover who had the audacity to seek out the company of some other woman, and then stabbed myself to death.

Philippe of the Plague, France, approximately 1335 – 1353 AD

Philippe lived in France with his mother and older sister. His father was absent, the details being unclear. The father was dead, had abandoned the family, or perhaps was married to someone else. Philippe's family was poor and lived in a little house, attached to other little houses, perhaps apartments. The rooms were dark and dusty.

When Philippe was about eight years old he became ill with a fever. As a result his left arm became useless and hung limply at his side. His intelligence was stunted and he never fully matured.

When Philippe was about 11 or 12, a wealthy man became attracted to Philippe's mother and offered to marry her as well as care for the daughter. He emphatically did not want Philippe. Thus the mother and sister left in a crude wagon and moved to a different part of France, while Philippe was left to fend for himself. Philippe grew to be a large, strong man, even without the use of his left arm. He was hired to do manual labor and somehow survived. Because of his retardation and physical disability, girls and women were not attracted to him, and he stayed by himself most of the time. When he was about 16, plague broke out in his town. Philippe was hired to remove corpses from their homes, put the bodies in a wagon, and delivered them to the outskirts of town, where they were incinerated. Philippe had sexually matured but was unable to have a partner. Not even prostitutes were interested in him. So he surreptitiously began having sex with the dead bodies of women before he removed them from their homes. He was ashamed but couldn't stop himself.

One day as Philippe was ready to have sex with a corpse, he realized she was not yet dead. She began to scream and several men ran in to see Philippe ready to engage with her. The young man was arrested and brought before the Priest of the town. He was beaten, whipped, humiliated, and called names. The Priest then threatened Philippe to never again engage in such vile acts.

Sometime later, unable to stop himself, Philippe again had sex with a corpse. A helper came in to assist with the moving of the body and again Philippe was discovered. This time the priest ordered Philippe's good arm cut off. Thereupon Phillipe was unable to care for himself. He was shunned, reviled, and exiled from the town. He ate grass and bugs in the countryside, broke into henhouses and ate the newly laid eggs. Winter came upon him and he died of the elements. He was 18.

Karma—the soul of all three of these individuals regrets the participation in the overpowering of other people, using sexuality in harmful ways, hurting and sometimes killing individuals—all Pluto issues. I explain Pluto issues below. Although these three people met untimely ends in ways that could have balanced their karma, the soul decided that more balancing was required. Thus the energy of those three individuals was blended into one lifetime—that of my present lifetime as Lauren, in order to repay and balance the karmic energy necessitated by the soul. Thus Lauren would experience abandonment, sexual abuse, physical harm, poor health, and relationship difficulties. However, she was given skills, talents, and abilities, as well as the Elders' assistance, in order to achieve spiritual equilibrium and further evolution.

CHAPTER 4

LAUREN'S STORY

I found it easier to write this litany in a third person perspective.
I am the child/adult Lauren to whom I refer below.

1947—A daughter was born to two people who didn't want to be, and were not prepared to be, parents. They had been recently reunited after five years of World War II. The woman did not want to be a woman, a wife, or mother, but had a man's job in an advertising agency until her husband returned, a man who had been in close company with prostitutes in France for years until WW II ended. The child felt hated and reviled, ignored to death, and was sexually and emotionally abused, neglected and abandoned. Perhaps they didn't hate her personally but rather what she represented. There was no safe person around to protect and nurture her.

When the child's mother was five years old, she had watched her own oldest sister Irene, 17 years old, die in front of her, bleeding to death all over the house, of tuberculosis. The woman's parents, only brother, and sister-in-law had all died in one year sometime before the child's birth. It was a terrible shock and a blow. The mother's father was a raging alcoholic, trained the mother to be a man, and was often cruel to her right up to the end of his life. At some point the mother experienced sexual molestation. She was damaged, neglected, and abused in her own right.

The father of the girl was the youngest of nine children. The child's grandfather died when the father was 18 months old. There was no time, energy, or money to devote to the fatherless child. He would always be searching for love. The father was damaged, neglected, and abandoned in his own right.

His wife was years older than he—a perfect mother surrogate. The mother would look the other way when he was having affairs, including with their daughter, I suspect so that he wouldn't leave her. They both were needy and had been brought up without love. They had no love to share with their first child and had no idea what to do with each other. Many people referred to the father as a handsome, charming "wolf."

1948—The first time the father fondled and fingered the daughter was while she sat on his lap while he had an erection. She was 18 months old. A pedophile often begins sexual abuse at a time that represents a critical period in his early life—in this case 18 months. Three quarters of all sexual predators are male; from large families; neglected; with no close ties to friends, relatives or his wife; a loner; isolating himself; with poor communication skills. Sometimes a predator has been abused as a child.

The sexual abuse from the father continued to escalate for 3½ years, leading to oral and perhaps other kinds of sex. The man would creep into his daughter's room at night or wait until his wife was gone. The daughter was terrified and lonely. There was no one to protect her, except dozens of stuffed animals on her bed to keep unwanted intruders away. Based on years of research by experts, being neglected and abandoned, coupled with sexual and emotional abuse, leads to all kinds of physical, emotional, mental, social, and relationship problems and insatiable love hunger for a child. Meanwhile the mother was emotionally and physically absent, telling the little child to not feel anything, to deny the child's feelings, and to tell the child that emotions were bad, often punishing or abandoning the child for feeling or crying. This kind of behavior is crazy making. No loving, hugging, or cuddling, or rocking, or soothing of any kind. So the child's feelings went underground and because there was no safe place to express herself and be loved, she began to wither from neglect and abandonment. In the 1950's research came out about babies in orphanages who died from lack of physical touch. Only through lies and deception can incest, sexual and emotional abuse, neglect, and abandonment exist and thrive in the dank abyss of the dysfunctional family. And then the pattern spreads out like a fan.

The child's personality split to an 18 month old toddler by the name of Lambie Pie, who wanted desperately to escape or die.

In addition to the father's abuse of her at night or when the mother was absent, he never spoke to the child or had any contact with her in any way at other times, day or night. The child looked "forward" to being abused, as there was no other form of contact with either mother or father.

"...since the daughter herself is emotionally needy, the contact may be gratifying, at least at first. It may later put her in a totally untenable position with each parent." —*Healing the Incest Wound*, Christine A. Courtois

Being "ignored to death" is a feeling as terrible as the abuse itself. Pete Walker, author of *Complex PTSD, From Surviving To Thriving*, calls that the abandonment mélange.

The child had one surviving solitary memory that came in the form of a fantasy or fairy tale:

> The 4-year-old child is in bed with blankets pulled up around her ears. The room is very cold. The windows are frosted over and it has been snowing outside. There is a spotlight shining on her, the room, and her bed. She is surrounded by many stuffed animals, to protect her from any intruder, as there is no room for anyone else, and just barely enough for her. Four blocks down the street from the apartment complex a "wolf" gets off the train at the local train station. He is jaunty, hand-

some, standing upright and carrying a cane. He strolls the four blocks to the apartment complex. He enters the main door. He climbs the stairs to the second floor. He opens the door to the apartment and appears at the door to the child's room. At that point the child forces herself to fall asleep.

No one knows how much or how often or in what way the father incested the child. However, a memory appeared in therapy. The mother had gone shopping. The father took his 4-year-old daughter to bed and proceeded to have his way with her. The mother suddenly returned home and found her husband with their daughter, naked and intimately together in bed. The daughter remembers the look of horror, anger, and hatred on the mother's face towards her daughter, now seen as a rival.

When the child was 12 she was 5'8" tall and weighed 97 pounds. When she was 20 and married her first husband, she weighed 105 pounds. The medical term is called failure to thrive. Children die of that condition. It commonly is brought about by incest, neglect, emotional and other abuse.

The girl child lost her memory to protect herself. She had a recurring dream that a wolf was chasing her and was about to leap at her throat, fangs bared, when she would awaken. She was afraid all the time. She often hid in the closet to be safe. She apologized if she hurt herself or got sick. Clearly she realized early in her development that people were not safe or helpful, and she felt uncomfortable around them.

1950—Enter Uncle D. Because the child had been sexually trained from early on, it was not unusual that another pedophile would begin to abuse her. The child does not remember all of what Uncle D did to her. He was an alcoholic. He dressed up and played Santa Claus every

Christmas, while the child was seated on his erection, being held tightly and fondled, smelling his drunken breath, while all the adults were oblivious to the abuse going on in front of them.

1951—Just before Christmas the child was sent to Uncle D's house to spend the night. Uncle D got drunk and entered the bedroom where the child was sleeping, only to awaken to his adult body writhing on top of her. Being trained to not call out or make a commotion, the child lay still. She stared at the ceiling, dissociating from the abuse. The following morning the mother came to claim the child. On the drive back home, the child was in torment from the night before. There were deep drifts of snow. The mother drove slowly. The child was bundled in a snowsuit, holding a large phallic candy cane that Uncle D had given her. She made a decision to die. She opened the car door and let herself fall out. She was unhurt physically but cried hysterically. The mother thought it was because the candy cane had been broken into many pieces.

Like the candy cane, the child's personality split again into 4-year-old named Nornie Pie. She was always crying and in grief.

Many decades later Uncle D died. His widow sent the girl's mother a cassette tape, reproduced from an original reel-to-reel tape. On it the small girl was heard saying, "I love you, Uncle D. This is Nornie Pie." The widow told the mother that Uncle D played that cassette tape *every day* until he died.

1952—The father and mother slept on a sofa bed in the living room. Next to the sofa bed was a decorated Christmas tree with lights and tinsel. The mother had gone shopping. The father was in his pajamas, with his erect penis bulging out of the front flap. The child was forced to go down sexually on her father, he holding her neck tightly, she gagging and choking as she did.

1952—Because the child had been sexually trained from early on, it was not unusual that another pedophile would begin to abuse her. Enter the building superintendent. One day the girl was heading down the front stairs to go outside to play. The superintendent, drunken, unshaven, reeking of cigarettes and alcohol, grabbed the girl and took her into a nearby utility closet. There he had her perform oral sex on him.

1952—Because the child had been sexually trained from early on, it was not unusual that another pedophile would begin to abuse her. Enter two teenage boys. The girl was sitting outside in the front yard of the apartment complex, hidden in a clump of bushes that made her feel safe. Somehow the boys spotted her and took her to a black car nearby. One thing the child remembered was the metal belt buckle of one of the boys pushing coldly against her forehead while she performed fellatio on him. The child made a decision that being outside wasn't safe either, which helped to create agoraphobia and social phobias.

1952—The child asked Aunt E if she could live with her and Uncle E. Aunt Edna's house was safe and the woman was kind and loving. The aunt refused, not understanding what the child wanted.

1952—The girl turned five. There was no safe place. No person was safe. No one would save her from torment, abandonment, cruelty, and sexual abuse. The family was staying at their lake cottage. The child went into the bathroom and got a bottle of iodine from the medicine cabinet. There was a skull and crossbones on the label, which the mother had shown her, and warned the child to be very careful. The child uncorked the bottle and drank the liquid until she passed out.

Some days later the child awoke from her coma on the sofa in the living room, with a terrible burning in her throat, and finding it difficult to swallow or breathe. The family doctor had been called to attend her, driving 87 miles each way. For the first and only time Aunt E mailed her cute postcards every day for two weeks. Was the aunt feeling guilty or wondering what had happened? This is not known.

The child's personality split again, this time to a 5-year-old by the name of Dorothy the Destroyer, who was angry and full of rage. Dorothy dressed all in black and carried a hatchet.

The iodine incident was never discussed or spoken about in the family. When the child became an older adult, she confided the story to her cousin. He said he had heard about the poison incident from his parents but he assumed falsely it was an accident.

There are no further memories of the father or Uncle D sexually abusing the girl ever again. Was it because of the poison and the suicide attempt? Were the adults now watching the girl carefully?

1955—A second daughter was born to the family. Apparently the father didn't abuse her. The young girl took care of her little sister, protected her, and loved her, acting as a mother to her for many years. However, the second daughter was terrified of Santa Claus, often hiding under the bed if the name of Santa was mentioned and she was also afraid of clowns.

1955–1967—The girl was called "shy." She found it practically impossible to make friends. She spent lunches eating by herself. She spent recesses by herself. She walked home by herself. In college she smoked cigarettes by herself on the back stairs between classes, afraid to be around classmates or students walking the campus. Otherwise, she felt too visible and vulnerable.

1956–1961—9-years-old to 13-years-old—was forced to go to square-dancing classes every Saturday which she hated and feared. Terrified of the people. Unable to be sociable, but pretended. She felt that she didn't belong anywhere. The mother often scolded her for not being able to fit in. At 13 she met P at the classes. He was the only boy who asked the girl to dance. She finally felt loved and loved P in return. After a short time P decided he wanted to be with another girl instead. She was three years older, and had breasts. The group went to Colorado for a square-dancing convention. The girl was supposed to be partners with P, but because of the break-up, she had to dance with the ugliest, most moronic boy of the group. She had to watch P with the new girl-friend all the time in Colorado and at classes, causing a pain in her solar plexus and heart area.

The girl's family moved to a suburb. Aunt E called to tell the girl that P had gone swimming, hit his head on a rock, and drowned.

The girl and the mother went to the wake. P's mother was 8 months pregnant. The new girlfriend took center stage and everyone was sympathetic towards her. The younger girl cried, but no one noticed.

The girl's personality splintered again—a 12-year-old called the Protector, who was invisible and never spoke but carried a club. The girl's memory of the past 12 years had been erased, not to re-emerge until she was 35, when the memories came in bits and pieces and she had to organize them like a jigsaw puzzle, until, after years of therapy, the history became clear.

1960-1965 High school—the girl didn't make any friends, but one girl made friends with her. Her name was E. The mother hated E and did everything in her power to drive her away. She called E a big fat Jew, ugly slob, loud mouth kike, etc. She encouraged the girl to stop being friends. But E was the girl's only friend. Just before the girl turned 18 she had an appendectomy. A week later the mother arranged for three girls from high school to come to a birthday party for the girl. The mother did *not* invite E.

The girl loved to act, which was the only place where she could allow her emotions to be free, while she had genuine talent and passionate desire to act. She was in plays in elementary school, high school, and college. Her father and mother came to her first play, but never again. They demeaned and belittled her performance and her desire to act. In her senior year the girl won awards for best actress, best director, and best drama student. Her drama teacher told her she had the unusual ability to make acting her career.

1965–1967 College—the girl still had difficulties making friends. A handsome 19-year-old B was sent by his father in Chicago to work for the girl's father. B had been involved with an older woman with kids and his father wanted to stop the liaison. Because B had no friends, he went to the girl's house often. He took her on drives in his car. He cried about his lost love. The girl fell in love with him. B was drafted and needed to return to his home state. On his last day, he brought the girl over to his apartment and wanted to have sex. The terrified girl didn't do so, thinking she was a virgin. She didn't remember her abuse at that time. When B returned home, he married the woman with two kids and was able to stay out of Vietnam. The girl never heard from him again.

The girl dated an older Italian boy, who was in pre-med at the college. She wasn't particularly interested in him but was lonely. She thought she was a virgin so they didn't have sex.

1966–67 College—the girl decided that the only way a boy would be interested in her was to have sex with him. This was a conscious decision, but also one that had many unconscious origins and terrible repercussions. The first try was a boy she met briefly. They had sex, short and unfulfilling for the girl. The boy commented: "I thought you said you were a virgin," indicating she was not. She got pregnant that first time. She never saw the boy again. She made plans to give the child away for adoption when the time came.

The girl attracted a boy in her acting class. He wanted her to give him hand jobs and she did so repeatedly, sometimes even in public under blankets. She was well-trained from childhood to be a prostitute. She broke up with him when she got too nauseous and ashamed to continue.

The girl started dressing in an alluring manner. She attracted a boy. He asked her to drive them to a party at friend's house. Her parents had bought her a car so she could go to college. She drove the two of them there, but the house was dark, and no cars were parked outside. She had a bad feeling but ignored it as she was taught to do. They went into the house. The boy was already drunk. He raped her. She got away and drove home quickly. Once home the girl threw away her clothing, and never told a soul about the rape for years.

A boy at one of the girl's classes asked her out. He took her to a bar and proceeded to get drunk. The girl drank 7-Up. Then he drove them to a nearby motel and rented a room. The girl was passive, as she had been taught to be from toddlerhood. She acquiesced. He was sexually ferocious with her. She miscarried. Blood was all over the bed, as if someone had been murdered there. The boy took her home, dropped her off at the driveway, and drove away quickly.

She bled intermittently for some months because of the miscarriage. The girl started bleeding heavily in a college class. She went home and lay down on her sister's bed. The house was empty. She began hemorrhaging and felt herself float out of her body. Maybe she was dying. The mother came home, found her and took her to the emergency room. A doctor put her on hormones to stop the bleeding.

The girl's personality splintered again. Her name was Catherine, 17-years-old. She would lure men to her, then reject them in order to hurt them as she had been hurt.

Two boys fought over the girl sometime later. The girl wanted revenge, not realizing that vengeance came from very early in her life but all memories of that were suppressed.

The girl went to a Halloween party and met A. He was smitten with her. She was unbearably lonely and dated him. On one of their first dates she brought him home for dinner to her parents' house but it was instant hate. The parents then gave her an ultimatum. "You have to break up with him now." The girl tried very hard not to see A, but she had no one else in her life. Her only friend E lived in Los Angeles and went to college.

Also the girl's mother told her she would have to change majors in college the next semester. She could no longer be a Theatre Major, which had been the girl's dream since she was 7, but had to go into Business instead. If she didn't conform, they would stop paying her tuition. E came home for the weekend from college. Her parents were absent on a trip. She invited the girl to spend the weekend at her family home. E invited her boyfriend. The girl invited A. The girl and A couldn't have sex because the girl was afraid she would start bleeding again. So A slept on top of the blankets and the girl inside the covers.

When E's mother came home, she found a diary entry in E's journal that discussed the weekend. She told E she would also tell the girl's mother, but only after the semester ended. Both E and the girl were terrified. They moved out together into an apartment. They had little money but they figured they would each get a job.

Soon after, the girl, E, and A were invited to go see the girl's parents. When they got there, the parents harangued, harassed, insulted, and impugned all three of them. The father called Ellen a whore and a streetwalker. A – "a dirty greaser." The three teens left in a hurry; angry, hurt, and feeling emotionally violated. A week later E moved out of their apartment to be with her fiancé.

The girl had no more money and no job. The mother called the girl and told her that she could move back home again, but she would have to give up A. The girl talked to A. He asked her to marry him. She was unsure. He got furious and hit the wall with his fist, making a hole. The girl moved back in with the parents, but told them she was

going to marry A. The parents yelled, complained, and lectured the
girl every day. The more they did that, the more the girl wanted to run
away. They would point to the younger sister who was crying and say,
"See what you're doing to her!"

The mother tried many ploys to get the girl to change her mind:

You can go live with your favorite aunt; (a lie)

We'll enroll you in the University of the Seven Seas; (a lie)

We'll buy you a new wardrobe; (a lie)

You are doing drugs; (the girl never did drugs)

The doctor called and said you need to have surgery; (the doctor never called and the girl didn't need surgery)

All your friends called and say you need to have surgery; (the
girl checked, but no friends had called)

I'll send you to a counselor (now which was a good idea, especially because the girl thought she was losing her mind. She
went to a psychologist, talked to him for a while. The girl told
him she was afraid of her father. The psychologist talked to the
mother at the end of that first session and explained that the
therapy would be easy. "Other girls have had that same problem." There was no way yet for the therapist to know about
the extensive sexual and emotional abuse and neglect.)

The girl got ready the next week to go to the 2nd therapy session.
The mother stopped her and casually asked, "Where are you going?"
"I'm going to the psychologist for my next meeting."

"Oh, no, you're not," replied the mother. "I talked to the psychologist and we both agreed that you are a hopeless case. We cancelled
your therapy."

The girl never called the therapist to confirm, but there is a strong likelihood that the mother never consulted with the psychologist. Perhaps the mother was afraid of what would be discovered in sessions.

The girl couldn't take any more mistreatment. She talked to A and they decided to go to Las Vegas to get married. The girl asked the mother for her birth certificate.

The mother replied, "Here it is. But don't come back to this house ever again. You are disowned and disinherited. You cannot take the car. Nor your bedroom furniture. And if it doesn't work out, you cannot come back. You've made your bed. Now you sleep in it."

The girl left with just her clothes. She and A went to Las Vegas but the girl had a bad feeling on the trip. They had a small wedding party in their new apartment. Her parents were invited but never showed up.

Six months later a different Aunt talked to the girl. The Aunt encouraged her to make up with the mother. The girl agreed. When the girl confronted the mother about being disowned and disinherited, the mother replied, "I never said anything like that!" It wasn't the first time the mother lied.

The rest of her adult life is a replay of the beginning. A was cruel, abusive, neglectful, an alcoholic, and addicted to sex. A's father was a raging alcoholic, who owned a seedy topless bar, and fooled around with the dancers. A's mother was codependent. A was abused and abandoned in his own right.

By the time she was married to A for six weeks, she knew she had made a terrible mistake.

She told A that she wanted to try out for plays in a local community theatre, where her former drama teacher now directed plays.

A replied: "I will break both of your legs if you do."

She was sick, anxious, and depressed all the time. When she gave birth to a daughter two years later, she sent out birth announcements to family, friends, and relatives. None of them knew she was married and called the mother to find out what was going on. The mother had-n't told any of them that the girl has been married two years before.

The parents refused to have A come into their home, including holidays, birthdays, or anniversaries. Five years later when a son was born, the girl put her foot down. "If he's not welcome, I'm not com-ing." She should have done that years earlier.

The mistake she would play over and over again: looking for love but instead finding her parents disguised as partners, with neglect, abandonment, sexual abuse, as well as emotional and sometimes phys-ical abuse.

At 27, immediately after she had given birth to a son, her body collapsed. She was in bed for a year and took that time off work. She became suicidal, depressed, and anxious. Her alarmed supervisor from work arranged for her to go to therapy with a psychologist who took her pro bono—free. It was the first time in her life ANYONE listened to her. She has continued to go to therapy more or less continuously for 40+ years of counselors as she discovered and uncovered secrets, lies, and the hidden world inside her. Begged for relief. Longed to have someone listen and care. To somehow heal the pain and memories.

She went through a string of relationships but was always looking to be saved from her torment and loneliness, to find love and caring. Her physical body had been sick for most of that time and her sexuality disappeared for years at a time. A beat her up when she told him she wanted a divorce.

T, her next husband, molested her daughter and his own daughter. He was an alcoholic and sex addict as well as a pedophile, abandoned in his childhood. She left him.

She started intense therapy in her 30's, as she slowly remembered and re-membered the past. In therapy she regressed to an infant, some-times a child, for the 18 months the psychiatrist treated her. She got hysterical seeing Christmas lights. "Don't make me do Christmas!" she cried and hid in a closet. She called her parents for support but her father hung up on her.

At 46, she moved in with P. She went on permanent social security disability: "Psychosomatic disorder of unknown origin."

Every time she went to her parents' house, she felt like she was losing her mind as she walked through the front door. She was relieved when her mother was killed by a bus and her father died of cancer. At least she wouldn't have to pretend she loved them anymore or to be around them, which was torture.

She cried hysterically at her mother's funeral, when she realized that she would NEVER have a good mother. All her hopes for that eventuality had vanished with the bus.

Two weeks after her mother died, her father hired a "housekeeper" although she had never been seen keeping house. The father gave the woman his new Pontiac and $35,000 when the "housekeeper" left a year later. The father was a sick man mentally, emotionally, and then got cancer.

After pretending and being a "good girl" at her father's memorial, she called the minister who officiated, who had referred to the father as a good man, a good husband, and good father. She couldn't stand the lie and talked to him for four hours. The minister told her he also had been incested and it was a relief to find someone to tell the truth about her father and to be understood so deeply. The minister commiserated with her torment of "pretending" through the memorial service.

She continued to get flashbacks, both physical and emotional. Before P died she found Judith Herman's essay on the internet about COMPLEX PTSD. Finally she could understand what was happening with her. She has worked intensely on herself for last three years using Pete Walker's book, *Complex PTSD: From Surviving to Thriving*.

When her sister told her that she "wrecked the family," she felt deeply hurt. Trust is a huge issue with her as with all people with complex PTSD. The family wrecked her when she was little and helpless and she had to heal herself of the massive wounds. She's practiced forgiveness and surrender—not for any of the perpetrators, but for herself, for peace. With LH, she wrote *Forgiveness Equals Fortune*.

Ever since P died in 2013, she's been in crisis. She had financial support and stability with him. Her income dropped to $700. Then she couldn't afford to live in her house and rented it out. Her dear friend H died a few months after P did. PD asked her to move to Santa Fe with him, but unfortunately he also had complex PTSD (incest and abandonment issues) and they clashed terribly. After a month PD left her. She had three suitcases, no car, no furniture, and no household goods. Not being good with people and having agoraphobia, panic attacks, anxiety, depression, anger, and mistrust, plus not much money, she was challenged to live in a new city and state and start all over yet again.

She had to start from scratch when she married A.

She had to start over again after D broke her toe and thumb. She went to a battered woman's shelter, then D got a court order that she had "abandoned" the house and she couldn't go back to their rental, nor could she remove her possessions. She had to declare bankruptcy because all their loans were in her name.

When she finally pieced the memories together of Uncle D, she talked to her parents. Her father never sat down but paced the floor, agitated and enraged. "How dare you speak of my friend D like that? Get out!" Her mother sat and cried, never speaking.

A year or so later when the memories of her father's abuse of her got clear, she decided not to say anything more to them. She didn't want to be mistreated all over again. Her mother came over very early one morning and asked, "Is it true about Uncle D?"

"Yes, Mom, it is. But that's not the worst part."

She looked at the girl funny.

"The worst part is dad did it, too."

The mother blanched. Her only response was "Who have you told?"

"Everyone."

The day that her mother died, the spirit came to the girl that night, as many newly-deceased people do because the girl can see them and hear them, which is comforting to them. The mother's spirit only said one thing (not I love you or something like that) but a question: "Is it true about your dad?"

"Yes, mom, it is."

The spirit disappeared.

The woman had a relationship with J for over three years. But as with the others, she experienced abandonment, emotional and psychological abuse, and physical abuse. J's father was a raging alcoholic, so J was also damaged. His favorite sayings were: "I'm going to do what I want to do, when I want to do it." "You can't tell me what to do." "I'm going to say whatever I want." J. acted like a narcissist and had characteristics of a sociopath.

J. lectured, insulted, harassed, harangued, and belittled her and many other people. His lease at the apartment complex where he lived was not renewed, because of how he treated the manager, the maintenance man, and the company who owned the complex, and also did several illegal things there. J. had done that kind of behavior for most of his life, with the IRS (lost his business and home), with nursing school (got kicked out), with several of his doctors (kicked out of their offices), and removed J. from the bank after he lectured and insulted tellers and the manager, who then closed his bank account, among others.

J took the matter of his apartment to court to fight having to move, which then went to trial. The girl/woman had already left J months before and testified against him in court about his abusive behavior to her and others. Her testimony was painful but important. She felt as though she was standing up in court against her mother, father, Uncle D., A., T., D., PD., and other perpetrators as well as J.

According to many recent books on incest, girls who are sexually incested as children are *lucky* if they are not: in a mental institution; chronically ill; in jail or prison; a drug addict; an alcoholic; a prostitute; or dead.

Karma

As you can see, this is a karmic story with various damaged individuals interacting with one another, looking for love and trying to learn and evolve. I have no blame, only hope that we humans on this planet can heal ourselves, and bring peace and love to our relationships.

Several footnotes about the parents: Most people who die come to visit me in spirit form soon after death. The Father did not. After some weeks I went psychically "looking" for him. I found him in a place I can only describe as purgatory. I don't "believe" in purgatory, so it was interesting to get that notion. I was "told" the father was sleeping in a spiritual medical facility, working off karma from his former lifetime. My son who is also psychic told me he got the same impression; the Father was sleeping and resting in a purgatorial place. Not long after, when the Father was reborn as my sister's second son, he was extremely shy, with terrible social phobia, even hiding away when he saw me. His looks were not like in his previous life when he was handsome and charming, but he was instead rather homely, quite obese, and anti-social. His life was taken up with computers, the internet, and internet games. The reincarnational person has quite a quick temper, as did the Father.

The Mother was reborn as my sister's first son. The Mother always wanted to be a man and so she got her wish. The Mother was highly intelligent, studied on her own, loved to travel, and was interested in all things Japanese, including being friends with a Japanese neighbor.

My nephew also was interested to the point of even learning the Japanese language. The reincarnation saw her/him in a long educational stay in Hungary, and recently attaining a Masters' Degree in psychology.

Catherine

This book includes a novelette (see Appendix 1), which is a recounting of Catherine's life events and decisions, circa 1400 in France. I adore France especially in the Loire Valley and Paris which I visited several times in 1996 and 1997. I explored Nancy, France near the Moselle River and the surrounding area, to get a sense of where Catherine lived. The area felt extremely familiar and I experienced *deja vu* on numerous occasions.

I didn't remember Catherine's life chronologically. Rather, memories from various stages of her life surfaced on their own, beginning when I was five years old; she has "been" with me since then. I've been expunging her from my life, performing a life-long spiritual exorcism. Often I retrieved the most detailed memories by being around a person who had known Catherine personally.

In the course of Catherine's tale as it unfolds in Appendix 1, you will find that she acts in many wicked and thoughtless ways to people in her life and suffers consequences. However, you may feel she didn't deserve horrendous punishment to repay those deeds.

I've lived with memories of Catherine since I was five. I'm quite psychic, one of the gifts I have been given in this life. Part of that gift is I have comprehensive recall of past lives both mine and others. I remember 102 of my lifetimes in vivid detail. As Lauren (in this lifetime) I have known individuals from when I was Catherine, who have showed up in my current life. Sometimes these people had similar personalities and interests from the past life.

Often the common denominator between each of the men I met in this life were difficulties in relating — intense, odd feelings and actions that couldn't be explained in any logical way. Often men acted towards me as if I was a highly erotic woman, even a courtesan or prostitute, regardless of my age (starting at 18 months!), circumstances, or appearance. As I grew older, I could easily spot men who had known me as Catherine because they each treated me in an uncomfortable, aggressive, sexualized way. Some of them described their actions and relationships with Catherine to me that dovetailed with what I had previously remembered.

Throughout decades I experienced truly awful events and relationships that, for the most part, had a direct connection to Catherine. In fact, Catherine is me, or I was her in a past life. As I grew to adulthood, memories of past lives matured and expanded. In my early 20's I posited a theory that my difficult life as Lauren was karmic repayment, atonement, and making amends for those deeds and for mistreatment of people that I as Catherine perpetrated.

However, I was not and am not a victim. I chose the life of Lauren as a learning experience in just the same way I chose to be Catherine, the Empress, and Philippe in earlier times, to learn unusual lessons. I believe that as souls we come to learn different modes of behavior, while living in various locales and time periods, races, sexes, economic and social status, all of which have unique curricula by which our souls learn spiritual lessons. There are no good or bad people, just people living out their lives within the framework of their cosmic creations.

Catherine was abandoned by her father and reviled by most of the people in the small village she and her mother lived in. My own complex PTSD has a lot to do with emotional abandonment as well as difficulty making and keeping friends.

Catherine's behavior towards others was sexual and amoral. She wasn't immoral; she simply had her own code of behavior. Much of Catherine's amends have come through the working out of sexual karma as me—Lauren. Although today women with sexual adventures and multiple partners are more commonplace, in 1402 Catherine's behavior was shocking, as it was during the early part of my life before our culture changed in the '60s and '70s. So you may not be as upset reading about Catherine's exploits as earlier generations might have.

Pluto

While working on this manuscript, I studied *Healing Pluto Problems* by the respected astrologer and therapist Donna Cunningham. Ms. Cunningham got her M.S.W. from Columbia University, and spent 17 years counseling abused women and children, alcoholics, and other troubled people. Her book discusses personality and character profiles for people who have been victimized who coincidentally have difficult and significant Pluto aspects in their birth charts and transits.

Pluto and its ruler Scorpio involve power in the guise of sex. I thus realized that Catherine's, the Empress, and Philippe's traits don't have to do with sex or sensuality as such, but are frankly about *power*, its misuse in overpowering others as well as its opposite—powerlessness. The traditional astrological concepts for Pluto and Scorpio are birth, death, sex, and transformation. According to Cunningham's analysis, my birth chart is quite "Plutonian," so my chart and my life reflect the importance to heal Pluto/power/sexual missteps from the prior lifetime as Catherine. To make matters worse, from early 2012 – November 2018 I had four major Pluto transits, which activated even more Plutonian issues, while I had near-constant flashbacks to both my early life as Lauren, as well as flashbacks to my three problematic past lives.

I am learning to transform and transmute sex and power into unconditional love and cosmic balance, while learning to live in spiritual consciousness. The entire story of Catherine in Appendix 1 is true as far as I remember. My life history as Lauren is also my own recollection. Much of my childhood up until age 12 was a blank until my early 30's because of complex post-traumatic stress disorder. I have pieced together my past through forty years of counseling and therapy; many consciousness workshops and classes; 100 sessions of rebirthing (now known as conscious breathing); 22 hypnosis sessions; hundreds of sessions of bodywork; astrology; as well as spontaneous recall and spiritual epiphanies. Like a detective, I have taken hundreds of various memories—jigsaw puzzle pieces—and created a coherent narrative for myself.

I include a treatise of my molestation and incest, neglect and childhood abuse to understand how early actions affect adults by replaying their early traumas. I intimately understand complex PTSD, depression, anxiety, and phobias—problems caused by abusive and neglectful behavior from others, starting with my parents, who were playing out their pieces of my/our karmic healing.

A wise spiritual teacher once asked me: "Do you want to be a spiritual warrior?"

"Yes," I replied.

He continued. "The greatest warrior goes to the most difficult boot camp available."

Memories are emblazoned in my mind and soul. They've repeated for decades. I forgive, find gratitude, compassion, and surrender. And still I remember—in 3-D, stereophonic, high-definition details. Do I mean Lauren? Or Catherine? The answer is yes to both. They are here connected to my soul, probably into infinity and recorded in the Akashic Records. Their memories help me remember the most important aspects of human life, the frailties and the complexities, so that I may treasure these in my soul. To understand and forgive are lessons for my growth and evolution. So that I can write about them; share them with you. To tell you—and myself—*there is no one to blame.* We are all equal players on this stage; wise, fragile, thoughtless, and strong. We are human.

I met most of the important players of Catherine's life during this lifetime as Lauren, and I usually recognized them as such. I had major relationships with some of them. Since I realized what was taking place—that I was attempting to balance Catherine's past karma in present time —I strove to create a balance, to become friends or deepen friendship with each person, to release them with unconditional love, to forgive and be grateful for each of them, and to forgive myself as well—both in this life and as Catherine. And to bless them. If I didn't take the spiritual route of healing, I would only make myself more miserable.

Partly I attribute my ongoing recovery of both Catherine and myself to my working 12-step programs with the help of my loving higher power, including ACA, Alanon, Co-Dependents Anonymous, and Survivors of Incest Anonymous. I'm enormously grateful for each of these spiritual programs and what they offer to suffering humanity and to me—of release and healing.

In some small way I hope my book can be a learning tool about the challenging after-effects that plague millions of individuals worldwide. I've attempted to write my/Catherine's story for more than thirty years, having gone through three complete manuscripts as novels, but discarding each version. Recently I realized that a non-fictional accounting would be most powerful—especially for me.

You can read the true story/full-length novelette in Appendix 1: *Catherine*

My hope is that through sharing my saga with you, you may find fellowship, respite, comfort, serenity, and forgiveness for your own story. We are spiritual beings in human clothing and can rest in that knowledge, gently consigning our wills and our lives into the care of a loving higher power.

CHAPTER 5

Complex PTSD Including Sexual Abuse and Incest

[This chapter focuses primarily on girls and women, although boys and men have complex PTSD as well, with problems similar to their female counterparts. Mic Hunter in Appendix 6, Stages of Recovery, addresses males in particular.]

"Complex post-traumatic stress disorder (C-PTSD) is a psychological injury that results from protracted exposure to prolonged social and/or interpersonal traumas in the context of either captivity or entrapment (i.e. the lack of a viable escape route for the victim) that results in the lack or loss of control, helplessness, and deformations of identity and sense of self. Forms of trauma associated with C-PTSD include sexual abuse [especially child sexual abuse/incest], physical abuse, emotional abuse, domestic violence, abandonment, neglect or torture—all repeated traumas in which there is an actual or perceived inability for the victim to escape. Trauma and flashbacks can be repeated on behavioral, emotional, physiologic, and neuroendocrinologic levels [chronic fatigue, fibromyalgia, deregulated hypothalamus]" —*Google.com*

Traumatologist Dr. John Briere, Ph.D., Associate Professor of Psychiatry and Psychology, Keck School of Medicine, University of Southern California, states that the Diagnostic and Statistical Manual of Mental Disorders (DSM) could be reduced to the size of a small pamphlet if all the symptoms of complex PTSD were grouped together, instead of separate diagnoses.

"C-PTSD symptoms can include prolonged feelings of terror, worthlessness, helplessness, and deformation of one's identity and sense of self. Researchers concluded that C-PTSD is distinct from, but similar to, PTSD with the main distinction being that it distorts a person's core identity, and involves significant emotional dysregulation. It was first described in 1992 by Judith Herman in her book *Trauma & Recovery.*

The diagnosis of PTSD was originally developed for adults who had suffered from a single event trauma, such as rape, or a traumatic experience during a war. However, the situation for many children is quite different. Children can suffer chronic trauma such as maltreatment, family violence, and a disruption in attachment to their primary caregiver. In many cases, it is the child's caregiver who caused the trauma. A child's developmental stages may be significantly disrupted or damaged, which can lead to their symptoms.

The term developmental trauma disorder (DTD) has also been suggested. This developmental form of trauma places children at risk for developing psychiatric and medical disorders. Bessel van der Kolk explains DTD as numerous encounters with interpersonal trauma such as physical assault, sexual assault, violence, or death. It can also be characterized by subjective events like betrayal, defeat or shame.

Repeated traumatization during childhood leads to symptoms that differ from those described for PTSD. Cook and others describe symptoms and behavioral characteristics in seven domains:

Attachment—problems with relationship boundaries, lack of trust, social isolation, difficulty perceiving and responding to others' emotional states

Biology—sensory-motor developmental dysfunction, sensory-integration difficulties, somatization, and increased medical problems

Affect or emotional regulation—poor affect regulation, difficulty identifying and expressing emotions and internal states, and difficulties communicating needs, wants, and wishes

Dissociation—amnesia, depersonalization, discrete states of consciousness with discrete memories, affect, and functioning, and impaired memory for state-based events

Behavioral control—problems with impulse control, aggression, pathological self-soothing, and sleep problems

Cognition—difficulty regulating attention, problems with a variety of "executive functions" such as planning, judgment, initiation, use of materials, and self-monitoring, difficulty processing new information, difficulty focusing and completing tasks, poor object constancy, problems with cause-effect thinking, and language developmental problems such as a gap between receptive and expressive communication abilities.

Self-concept—fragmented and disconnected autobiographical narrative, disturbed body image, low self-esteem, excessive shame, and negative internal working models of self.

Adults

Adults with C-PTSD have sometimes experienced prolonged

interpersonal traumatization beginning in childhood, rather than, or as well as, in adulthood. These early injuries interrupt the development of a robust sense of self and of others. Because physical and emotional pain or neglect was often inflicted by attachment figures such as caregivers or older siblings, these individuals may develop a sense that they are fundamentally flawed and that others cannot be relied upon. This can become a pervasive way of relating to others in adult life, described as insecure attachment. This symptom is neither included in the diagnosis of dissociative disorder nor in that of PTSD in the current DSM-5 (2013). Individuals with Complex PTSD also demonstrate lasting personality disturbances with a significant risk of re-victimization.

Six clusters of symptoms have been suggested for diagnosis of C-PTSD:

1. alterations in regulation of affect and impulses;
2. alterations in attention or consciousness;
3. alterations in self-perception;
4. alterations in relations with others;
5. somatization [physical manifestations];
6. alterations in systems of meaning.

Experiences in these areas may include:

Changes in emotional regulation, including experiences such as persistent dysphoria, chronic suicidal preoccupation, self-injury, explosive or extremely inhibited anger (may alternate), and compulsive or extremely inhibited sexuality (may alternate).

Variations in consciousness, such as amnesia or improved recall for traumatic events, episodes of dissociation, depersonalization/de-realization, and reliving experiences (either in the form of intrusive PTSD symptoms or in ruminative preoccupation).

Changes in self-perception, such as a sense of helplessness or paralysis of initiative, shame, guilt and self-blame, a sense of defilement or stigma, and a sense of being completely different from other human beings (may include a sense of specialness, utter aloneness, a belief that no other person can understand, or a feeling of nonhuman identity).

Varied changes in perception of the perpetrators, such as a preoccupation with the relationship with a perpetrator (including a preoccupation with revenge), an unrealistic attribution of total power to a perpetrator (though the individual's assessment may be more realistic than the clinician's), idealization or paradoxical gratitude, a sense of a special of supernatural relationship with a perpetrator, and acceptance of a perpetrator's belief system or rationalizations.

Alterations in relations with others, such as isolation and withdrawal, disruption in intimate relationships, a repeated search for a rescuer (may alternate with isolation and withdrawal), persistent distrust, and repeated failures of self-protection.

Changes in systems of meaning, such as a loss of sustaining faith and a sense of hopelessness and despair." — *Complex PTSD, Wikipedia*

Incest

Incest is described as sexual activity ranging from fondling, kissing, petting, stroking, and digital insertion, to oral, anal, and vaginal sex. Often the incest begins as a small gesture, which increases to more intense and intrusive behavior over time. The incest is perpetrated by someone known to and trusted by a child—such as parent, step-parent, grandparent, uncle, cousin, sibling, and this definition includes others such as priests, scout leaders, church members, neighbors, and child care persons.

Parker and Parker (1986) documented additional antecedents of father-daughter incest. They found that inadequate bonding of the father with his own parents and lack of early physical contact and involvement with his child were the two best predictors of incest. Referring back to Chapter 4 of *Catherine, Karma, and Complex PTSD*, recall the description of the father. He was dependent on the mother for comfort lacking in his childhood and had no one else close in his life, friendless, isolated, with little ability or desire to communicate.

Incest can begin as early as infancy. "Dr. Michael Durfee of the L.A. Department of Health Services reported in 1982 that more sexual abuse was reported on 2-year-olds than any other age group." *Secret Survivors*, E. Sue Blume

Incest with Lauren's father began at 18 months old. "According to the dominant mother/dependent father variant this may be more common in the development of incest with the preschool child than in the development of incest with the preadolescent or adolescent."
— Waterman (1986), Chapter 3 *Healing the Incest Wound*, Christine A. Courtois. Reprinted by permission by Christine Courtois.

The mother's lack of nurturing can open the door to incest and other destructive behaviors within the family. In Chapter 4 of *Catherine, Karma and Complex PTSD* recall the description of the mother's failure to nurture and her dislike of even being a mother, coupled with her lack of parenting by her father (my alcoholic grandfather).

"Baumrind (1973), Maccoby, and Martin (1983) found that the manner in which a mother anticipated parenthood and mothered her child was related to the manner in which she experienced the parenting she received as a child." —*Socialization in the Context of the Family*, Maccoby and Martin

Incest is thought to continue through generations of girls. In my own family incest has afflicted my mother, my sister, me, my daughter and possibly my granddaughter. Cooper and Cormier (1982) documented several patterns of intergenerational transmission of incest. In incestuous families, it is not unusual for both parents to have been emotionally deprived and/or sexually and/or physically abused during their childhoods. A mother with an unresolved history of incest with her own father (and possibly with another relative as well) may be unable to prevent an incestuous relationship between her husband and daughter.

When my daughter was 4 years old she was sexually abused by her babysitter's husband, along with two other little girls at the childcare center. Was she already abandoned, in need of comfort and love and attention, because I was physically and psychologically ill? I have made amends and asked for forgiveness from my daughter, although I have not yet fully healed my guilt.

The mothers of the other two little girls came to me and we discussed what we were seeing in our daughters. I immediately went to the babysitter and reported the abuse of these three little girls. The babysitter was horrified. Her husband was subsequently arrested and was found guilty in court. He had to go to therapy and other programs. He was defrocked from his position of Deacon in the local Mormon Church. He had to stay far away from the children that his wife was caring for. I removed my daughter from that childcare center and found another.

My daughter was then sexually abused at age 11 by her stepfather, T., who was my second husband. I left my second husband immediately. Several years later I heard about Gloria Allred, attorney in Los Angeles who specializes in sexual abuse, and attempted to make an appointment to sue my ex-husband. I was unable to get our day in court, due to the statute of limitations of 2 years for oral sex towards a child had run out.

I believe my granddaughter was molested at four years old while staying at her paternal grandmother's house. Although the girl had been toilet trained for several years, she started wetting the bed, having violent nightmares, couldn't tolerate nighttime, especially seeing the moon, and became quite anxious. I have my suspicions of who the perpetrator might be. My granddaughter is now 33 years old. She and I have discussed at length the possibility of sexual abuse including the perpetrator.

> "...Incest is a manifestation of family dysfunction which is supported by intergenerational family process. The family functions in such a way that its reality is distorted, the distortion treated as the reality. Although incest occurs, it is largely denied and unacknowledged by all family members. This disconfirmation allows for its continuance while communicating to the victim that it is something that is not to be discussed. Victims are placed in a double bind made all the more intolerable because it cannot be escaped and cannot be discussed. In order to contend with the paradox inherent in the bind, they transform their reality and ultimately to suit the family rules and injunctions."

> —*Healing the Incest Wound*, Christine A. Courtois. Reprinted by permission by Christine Courtois.

"The [incestuous] family develops a series of messages or rules for members to follow to protect the family...The most predominant of these messages are:

> Don't feel. Keep your feelings in check. Do not show your feelings, especially anger.

> Don't show weakness. Be in control at all times. Do not ask for help.

> Deny what is really happening. Disbelieve your own senses/perceptions. Lie to yourself and to others.

> Don't trust yourself or anyone else. No one is trustworthy.

> Keep the secret. If you tell you will not be believed and it will not get help.

> Be ashamed of yourself. You are to blame for everything."

> — *Healing the Incest Wound,* Christine A. Courtois
> Reprinted by permission by Christine Courtois.

My sister initially said to me in 2013: "You wrecked the family." Since then she has altered her opinion when she came to understand my early traumas.

"Girls are more likely to experience incest than boys (1 out of 4), although boys are not far behind (1 out of 5), mostly perpetrated by men." — Judith Herman, *Father/Daughter Incest*

My theory that this occurs because of the power dynamic of men with a sense of entitlement and ownership of females and children, as well as the model of manhood and fatherhood, going back thousands of years.

Often we see that a victim is represented as the offending party, thus belittled and shamed, and generally disbelieved. In November, 2018, politician Steve Pierce running for governor in the State of New Mexico allegedly stated that "women should submit..." He was defeated by a Hispanic woman, Michelle Lujan-Grisham.

America remembers the recent battle to confirm the Supreme Court Justice Brett Kavanaugh over sworn testimony by Dr. Christine Blasey Ford of Kavanaugh's sexual misconduct.

> "The Kavanaugh story dragged on, with an apparent strain on many survivors that the Harvey Weinstein and Bill Cosby allegations did not inspire—and it will continue to do so as he takes his seat on the Supreme Court. Experts say that all that has happened could have lasting effects on the psychology of many victims of sexual assault." —Oct. 11, 2018, *Time Magazine*.

This scenario is similar to that of Anita Hill testifying against upcoming Supreme Court Justice Clarence Thomas' confirmation in 1992.

> Even "President Donald Trump... directly mocked Dr. Christine Blasey Ford's testimony before the Senate Judiciary Committee by casting doubt on her testimony during a campaign rally." —Wed. Oct. 3, 2018, CNN

However, the tide may be turning. Many women who were running for congressional and gubernatorial offices for the first time in November 2018 were elected. My hope is that planetary dynamics and consciousness are shifting, while men and women are becoming equal in all ways.

I submitted an essay to an anthology proctored by Rev. Karen Tate and including essays from many powerful, articulate women and men entitled *Awaken the Feminine,* now available on Amazon 11/20/2018. (You can read my essay in Chapter 9 of that book "How to Reboot Humanity.") I believe feminine energy is awakening. Perhaps my experiences recorded in this book highlighting abuses as well as healing and forgiveness are not in vain.

Estimates in most research shows that 1 out of every 4 girls [1 out of every 5 boys] are sexually abused, usually by someone they trust, like a father, stepfather, uncle, grandfather, priest, or neighbor. Sexual abuse is one of the most damaging types of abuse imaginable, and often takes an entire lifetime of on-going psychological treatment to heal. Trust and self-esteem are extensively harmed while sexual and relationship problems last for decades, sometimes to the point of the victim becoming a recluse. Shame, recurring abuse, uncontrollable anger, difficulties in parenting, along with unstable lives and relationships become major themes.

> "With complex PTSD there is a danger that the abused person will be re-traumatized and victimized by other people. The younger the age at onset [of trauma], the more likely that the child will be multiply molested either within or outside of the family." — Walsh (1986a) *Healing the Incest Wound*, Christine A. Courtois. Reprinted by permission by Christine Courtois.

> "While not all sexually abused females become prostitutes, 60% – 90% of all prostitutes have experienced sexual abuse and incest as children…The estimated age of entry into child prostitution is 12 years old, while girls as young as 9 years old *http://www.rapeis.org/activism/prostitution/prostitution-facts.html*

"Yet becoming a prostitute is not the only way that sexually abused girls grow into an adult life of despair. Statistics show that generally a sexually abused girl continues to be victimized throughout the rest of her life. Partners, boyfriends, lovers, and husbands often take the place of the original abusers, treating the woman inappropriately, cruelly using domestic violence, emotional and sexual insensitivity, and acting as if she is his own private whore. Because of very early training which includes changes in hormones, glands, and brain function, the girl feels powerless to change her circumstances, often leaving one abuser only to end up with another...Parent-child incest has the greatest potential for harm because it involves the betrayal of the parent's role as nurturer and protector of the immature child. The child's development is compromised in a number of significant ways when a parent meets his/her own needs through sexual contact with the child. Furthermore, the child's accessibility and dependency allow parent-child incest to continue over long periods of time and contribute to the child's entrapment and powerlessness."

— *Healing the Incest Wound*, Christine A. Courtois.
Reprinted by permission by Christine Courtois.

Refer to Chapter 4 of *Catherine, Karma, and Complex PTSD*, which describes my on-going traumas through various relationships.

Father/Stepfather-Daughter Incest

"Incest between father and daughter has been the most documented type because of its prevalence, its violation of the taboo against sex between parent and child, and its potential for wreaking havoc in the nuclear family. The father's traditional family role of provider and protector is grossly betrayed when he perpetrates incest. Instead of protecting, he violates. Instead of nurturing, he uses. Family roles are violated and generational boundaries are blurred. The parents' relationship is triangulated, resulting in conflicted roles. The mother loses her status and authority in the family and becomes a rival of her daughter. The daughter is removed from her role as a child as she is made her father's lover.

The symbiotic father came from a non-nurturing family and so was emotionally deprived as a child. He has strong unmet needs for closeness and affection, which he has learned to satisfy in sexual ways since he does not know how to establish a close relationship in a nonphysical or nonsexual way. Symbiotic incestuous fathers have been organized into four subtypes: [introverted, rationalizing, tyrannical, and alcoholic].

The symbiotic introvert is the prototype of the isolated, distant incestuous father. Even if he appears outgoing, this man is unable to reach out to others and to be genuinely close. He may appear strong, competent, and capable of intimacy, but beneath this façade he is starved for affection and craves someone to nurture and comfort him. From the outside, this father appears to be the "good husband and father." He typically spends his nonworking hours with his family and has few, if any, outside social or professional contacts or sources of support. He may feel highly stressed by his work and family responsibilities and cope by withdrawing and expecting solace and safety from his family. In part, his withdrawal, isolation, mistrust of anyone outside the family, and inability to ask for or seek help are explained by depression. [Lauren's father appeared to be very depressed and certainly coldly aloof.] Sexual estrangement, which is usually part of this withdrawal, leaves

the father without his main method of achieving closeness. In this context, he turns to his daughter, whom he may view as 'belonging' to him, substituting her for his wife."
    — *Healing the Incest Wound*, Christine A. Courtois.
    Reprinted by permission by Christine Courtois.

For the purposes of my book, I don't describe rationalizing, tyrannical, and alcoholic incestuous fathers.

At 82 my mother died suddenly in an automobile accident. After talking with the mortician and discussing the funeral arrangements, my father left the room. The mortician turned to my sister and me and said: "This is the coldest man I have ever met in all my decades of undertaking." Wow! Someone had noticed what I had experienced all along!

The inner critic

"Unrelenting criticism, especially when it is ground in with parental rage and scorn, is so injurious that it *changes the structure of the child's brain*…Incessant repetitions result in the construction of thick neural pathways of self-hate and self-disgust…With ongoing parental reinforcement, these neural pathways expand into a large complex network that becomes an Inner Critic, that dominates mental activity. [*Moreover the receptor sites in the brain for receiving love and caring from others often lay dormant and undeveloped.* Being on-goingly assaulted with critical words systematically destroys innate self-esteem and replaces it with a prevailing consciousness of toxic self-criticism.]" — *Complex PTSD, From Surviving to Thriving*, Pete Walker

(See Appendix 7 of *Catherine, Karma, and Complex PTSD* for

1) "Solutions for Fighting the Inner Critic" and 2) Appendix 8 "Voice Fighting.")

What is an emotional flashback?

"One of the most difficult features of [complex] PTSD is extreme susceptibility to painful emotional flashbacks. Emotional flashbacks are sudden and often prolonged regressions ('amygdala hijackings') to the frightening circumstances of childhood. They are typically experienced as intense and confusing episodes of fear and/or despair—or as sorrowful and/or enraged reactions to this fear and despair. Emotional flashbacks are especially painful because the inner critic typically overlays them with toxic shame, inhibiting the individual from seeking comfort and support, isolating him in an overwhelming and humiliating sense of defectiveness.

Because most emotional flashbacks do not have a visual or memory component to them, the triggered individual rarely realizes that she is re-experiencing a traumatic time from childhood. Psychoeducation is therefore a fundamental first step in the process of helping clients understand and manage their flashbacks. Most of my clients experience noticeable relief when I explain [complex] PTSD to them. The diagnosis seems to reverberate deeply with their intuitive understanding of their suffering. When they understand that their sense of overwhelm initially arose as an instinctual response to truly traumatic circumstances, they begin to shed the awful belief that they are crazy, hopelessly oversensitive, and/or incurably defective.

Flashbacks strand clients in the feelings of danger, helplessness and hopelessness of their original abandonment, when there was no safe parental figure to go to for comfort and support. Hence, Complex PTSD is now accurately being identified by many as an attachment disorder. Flashback management therefore needs to be taught in the context of a safe relationship. A client needs to feel safe enough with the therapist to describe their humiliating experiences of a flashback, so that the therapist can help him respond more constructively to his overwhelm in the moment. Without help in the moment, the client typically remains lost in the flashback and has no recourse but to once again fruitlessly reenact his own particular array of primitive, self-injuring defenses to what feel like unmanageable feelings."

—*Reprinted with permission by* petewalker.com

(see Chapter 9 of *Catherine, Karma, and Complex PTSD* for "Healing — 13 steps to dealing with an emotional flashback.")

Abandonment

Although not as well known, abandonment is a serious form of abuse leading to complex PTSD.

"Traumatic emotional neglect occurs when a child does not have a single caretaker to whom she can turn in times of need or danger...Emotional neglect makes children feel worthless, unlovable, and excruciatingly empty...The emotional hunger that comes from parental abandonment often morphs over time into an insatiable appetite for substances and/or addictive processes [including destructive relationships; desperate for love]. Healing from PTSD is a long, gradual process because recovering our developmentally arrested instincts of full self-expression requires practicing new self-championing behaviors that trigger flashbacks to times when we were punished or abandoned for acting in our own self-interest. Without such understanding, her crucial, unmet needs for safe and comforting, human connection will continue to cause her an enormous amount of unnecessary suffering." [Our recovery efforts are impeded until we understand how much of our suffering constellates around early emotional abandonment—around the great emptiness that springs from the dearth of parental loving interest and engagement, and around the harrowing experience of being small and powerless while growing up in a world where there is no-one who's got your back.]

— Pgs. 93-94 *Complex PTSD, From Surviving to Thriving*, reprinted with permission by Pete Walker

The Abandonment Mélange

"The Abandonment Depression is the complex painful childhood experience that is reconstituted in an emotional flashback. It is a return to the sense of overwhelm, hopelessness and helplessness that afflicts the abused and /or emotionally abandoned child. At the core of the abandonment depression is the abandonment mélange – the terrible emotional mix of fear and shame [and grief] that coalesces around the deathlike feelings of depression that afflict an abandoned child. Surrounding the abandonment mélange of the flashback are perfectionistic and endangerment cognitions and visualizations of the toxic inner and outer critic…and at the surface is the self-destructive enactments of the fight, flight, freeze or fawn responses. [Addictions are early adaptations that are attempts to soothe and distract from the mental and emotional pain of complex PTSD.] —*Reprinted with permission by* petewalker.com

Triggers

"A trigger is an external or internal stimulus that activates us into an emotional flashback. This often occurs on a subliminal level outside the boundaries of normal consciousness, and is why recognizing flashbacks is both difficult but crucially important. External triggers are people, places, things, events, facial expressions, styles of communication, etc., that remind us of our original abuse or abandonment in a way that launches us into reliving the painful feelings of those times; e.g., revisiting your parents or childhood home, seeing someone who resembles your childhood abuser, experiencing the anniversary of an especially traumatic event, or hearing someone use a parent's shaming turn of phrase. The individual needs to understand that emotional flashbacks are direct messages from her child-self about how seriously her parents hurt and injured her."

"In a typical flashback, an individual is recapitulated into the original experience of abandonment. Fear is immediately triggered and soon produces shameful feelings of self-hate. This self-hate is a self-rejection that mimics parental rejection and that is equivalent to self-abandonment. Self-abandonment in turn deepens the abandonment depression and creates an even more fearful state, which in turn generates even more shame about the fear, which triggers increasingly depressing self-abandonment. This process then becomes a self-perpetuating, perpetual motion cycle that can spiral around and around in a despairingly painful descent that at its worst culminates in feelings of panic and suicidal ideation. During particularly extreme flashbacks, more than a few of my clients have uttered things that sound like this: 'Life is so hopelessly depressing, I might as well be dead. Take me now God, why don't you!"

"Most notable of these [triggers] are other people, especially unknown people or people even vaguely reminiscent of the parents. Over time, the critic comes to assume that other people are dangerous and automatically triggers the fight/flight/freeze/fawn response whenever a stranger or unproven other comes into view. This process becomes the social phobia that is frequently a symptom of complex PTSD." — *reprinted with permission by* petewalker.com

Responses to triggering

Defenses triggered by emotional flashbacks are:

"…fight, flight, freeze, or fawn responses. These misfirings then cause dysfunctional warding off of feelings in four different ways:

fighting or over-asserting one's self with others in narcissistic and entitled ways such as misusing power or promoting excessive self-interest;

fleeing obsessive-compulsively into activities such as workaholism, sex and love addiction, or substance abuse – (uppers);

freezing in numbing, dissociative ways such as sleeping excessively, over-fantasizing, or tuning out with TV or medications (downers);

fawning in self-abandoning and obsequious codependent relating." —*Reprinted with permission by* petewalker.com

Complex PTSD is not simply emotional or mental dysregulation but can be accompanied by multiple physical symptoms as well. In 1994 I was diagnosed with "psychosomatic disorder of unknown origin," for which I was granted permanent Social Security disability. Complex PTSD was unknown at that time. I also have a laundry list of other complaints beyond or including complex PTSD, including MTHFR (a genetic disorder activated by stress now referred to as epigenetics), Tietze syndrome (severe chest pain of the intercostal muscles), multiple chemical sensitivities, and adrenal exhaustion.

Following is a list of physical and neurological symptoms that I and many other victims of complex PTSD suffer.

Chronic Fatigue Syndrome (also known as Myalgic Encephalomyelitis) and Fibromyalgia

Sensitivity to Noise, Light, or Emotions

Sleep Issues

Poor Coordination

Feeling Worse with Stress and exercise

Extreme Mental Fatigue and brain fog; cognitive dysfunction; inflammation of the brain

Extreme Physical Fatigue, not made better with rest

Lightheaded or Dizzy

Problems with Concentration

Feeling Unwell After Being Active

Pain

Housebound or bedridden

Disruptive biological process involving the central nervous system, immune system, energy metabolism and stress system

As you can see, complex PTSD is a distressing reaction to abuse and abandonment, which can impact one's life in various and destructive ways.

CHAPTER 6

COMPLEX PTSD— LAUREN, CATHERINE, the EMPRESS, and PHILIPPE

There are fascinating correlations between me and my three past lives as Catherine, the Empress of Titania, and Philippe. All of us had major shocks in our early childhood. All of us were abandoned, despised, turned away, betrayed, injured psychologically, as well as verbally and emotionally abused. Catherine and the Empress were considered suitable for infanticide. All of us had sexual dysfunction in one form or other as a result of our victimization. Fortunately, as Lauren, I did not become a criminal, while the other three lived criminal lives, all dying violently at an early age.

Were these three people evil? Did Catherine (see Appendix 1) indeed carry the "mark of the devil" on her face? Why did those in authority want to kill Catherine and the Empress? Why were all three of them cast out of their societies? Was it part of the soul's plan?

I have spent decades practicing forgiveness for their crimes. It wasn't until I realized three years ago that Catherine, the Empress, and Philippe suffered from complex PTSD, and then forgiveness was complete. Those people didn't set out initially to hurt others but were lashing out as a hurt animal might, continuing to act out their early traumas, as survivors of Complex PTSD often do.

Putting Philippe's story aside for the moment, let's look at eroticism today. Our society of females (at least in the USA and perhaps the entire western world) are sexualized in books, magazines, advertisements, television shows, and movies. Young girls go into beauty pageants, made up and dressed to look like provocative adult women. Super Girl and Wonder Woman are scantily dressed, wear revealing, erotic costumes, are shown with big breasts, small waists, and lots of bare skin. Movies, ads, and TV shows show women as either undesirable (unattractive, dressed conservatively, wearing glasses) or highly desirable, with highly attractive faces and bodies, showing off breasts, buttocks, and legs in tight fitting clothes, often wearing extreme and fashionable high heels. Very seldom are men shown in erotic ways.

Men, including our current President, make ongoing jokes in public and private about women, employing sexual innuendo or outright sexual insults. Women and girls are "made to be laid." Rape, incest, and domestic violence are often assumed to be the "fault" of women, who dressed provocatively or in other ways "asked for it."

Philippe, on the other hand, perpetrated his sexuality on women—mostly as a necrophiliac—primarily dead women.

Why are men given permission to express their sexual desires on often innocent girls (1 out of every 4 girls are victims of incest), women and children (1 out of every 5 boys are molested)?

This is found even as far back as the Old Testament of the Bible (Genesis 19:30-38) with the story of Lot, whose two daughters supposedly plied him with alcohol in order to seduce him into sexual intercourse. According to scripture, the daughters pitied their widowed father, who would be deprived of future sexual intercourse and heirs; therefore, they decided to seduce him in order to preserve the family line. This incest account demonstrates the use of rationalizations, all of which attribute responsibility and blame for incestuous behavior to the victims. Given the effect of alcohol on sexual performance, one must wonder whether Lot was more involved in the seduction than scripture suggests. Such a story supports the rationalization of victim responsibility and also lends implicit support to the idea that there are occasions when incest is allowed.

> "In the book of Leviticus (18:6-18), the Bible cites numerous sexual relations that are prohibited. Many of these relationships, such as marriage between father and daughter or mother and son, can only be termed incestuous. Nowhere in these injunctions is there an exception allowing participation in such relationships. Yet throughout the Bible one finds references to violations of the edict. One such reference (2 Samuel 13:1-39) tells the story of Amnon and Tamar. According to scripture, Amnon fell in love with his half-sister Tamar. Knowing that such a liaison was prohibited he feigned illness in order to have her come to his aid. He then raped her. After the rape, his love supposedly turned to hate and he thus ordered that she be cast out. Tamar was branded as a sinner, and thereafter lived in exile in a brother's house while Amnon continued to live the life of a prince. Again this clearly reflects a double standard regarding sexual behavior. Women are seen as evil seductresses who tempt unsuspecting men into their rape. The alternative explanation that men are the initiators and perpetrators of sexual victimization has not been the dominant belief." — *Healing the Incest Wound*, Christine A. Courtois. Reprinted by permission by Christine Courtois.

Where does the blame rest? Is blame the appropriate action to take? No, I don't think so, even considering my history and observing the current milieu. Perhaps I'm part of generations who are working towards changing the status quo, altering the consciousness of men and women towards equality and respect.

CHAPTER 7

ASTROLOGY AND COMPLEX PTSD

Could it be there is no blame—at least not on our three-dimensional phase of planet Earth? Could it be that the origins of complex PTSD are cosmic in nature? In other words, a soul chooses a lifetime of challenges from the beginning of life in order to evolve spiritually.

Perhaps that is too strong a statement for you to digest. That would mean there is no one to blame. Not any other individual, parent, lover, or friend. Not one's self nor God. Not health or accidents. That in fact the trials are positive in nature, which includes free will before inception (when a soul choses parents and her entire life), and can be found in one's astrological birth chart. Therefore, a soul choosings one's life and the astrology chart is a reflection of that.

For modern day astrologers the perspective is *not* that planets directly have an effect on us. Rather they illuminate and reflect trends from a "higher" level (as above, so below) as we humans experience on a "lower" earth level. As such, as an astrologer, I can gauge what is happening in my (or others) life, where a tendency will most likely show up, and for how long. I call the birth chart and all the ramifications, transits, progressed charts, as well as chart comparisons to other people, a "personal cosmic blueprint" for one's life.

As a practicing professional astrologer for more than 46 years, I continue to discover in myself and my clients indications of "karmic" choices in our birth charts and transits.

One of the strongest indicators of challenging choices has to do with the planet Pluto, even though it has been scientifically demoted.

Although small, Pluto delivers a powerful punch to people connected
with it. Pluto is far away from the sun thus making a huge orbit. Pluto
takes 248 years to journey through the entire solar system! The moon
takes 28–29 days while the sun takes 365¼ days. Therefore, the effects
of Pluto can linger for a lifetime in the birth chart. Furthermore, while
considering transits (Pluto in its current movement making impacts
on other planets in one's birth chart), it generally takes about five years
to go through a complete transit cycle of Pluto.

Pluto and its moons are the most unusual in our entire solar system, the details of which I have researched in awe and appreciation
for several years.

> "Pluto, the dwarf planet that was once considered the ninth
> planet, has a growing entourage of satellites. The tiny world
> has five moons of varying sizes in orbit around it that tumble
> and dance in a strange and chaotic pattern…'The way I would
> describe this system is not just chaos, but pandemonium,'
> Mark Showalter, a co-investigator on the New Horizons mis-
> sion, said at a press conference last November….Pluto's entire
> moon system is thought to have formed by a collision between
> Pluto and a similar-size body early in the history of the solar
> system. The collision threw out material that coalesced into
> the family of satellites orbiting Pluto…New Horizons found
> that the moons were surprisingly chaotic. 'Hydra is the fastest-
> rotating, spinning once every 10 hours during its 38-day orbit
> of Pluto, or 89 times every orbit. If Hydra were spinning much
> faster, material would fly off its surface due to the centrifugal
> force,' Showalter said in a statement from NASA. The other
> three moons rotate between 6 to 10 times during their orbit,
> which is still surprisingly fast. In addition to that, Nix is tilted
> on its axis by 132 degrees and rotating backward." – ————
> —*https://www.space.com/16535-plutos-moons.html*

Pluto's effects have to do primarily with birth, death, power, sex, and transformation. Pluto effects are not subtle, but probing and stimulating a person to the depths of her being for long periods of time. Pluto in ancient mythology was considered the god of the underworld, an apt title for such a forceful influence. Pluto was first recognized by astronomer Percival Lowell although it took another 10 years to scientifically confirm his findings. On March 13, 1930—the anniversary of Lowell's birth and of William Hershel's discovery of Uranus—the discovery of Pluto was publicly announced. In 1945 the atom was split, commencing the nuclear age. Pluto is astrologically considered the "ruler" of atomic power and volcanic activity, also potent forces.

What is a Plutonian?

"Plutonians are those people with a strong Pluto, Scorpio and/or 8th house tendencies who have difficult childhoods that feature losses, betrayals, or abuses of power."
—*http://www.neptunecafe.com/donnaC1.html*

"If we do indeed choose our charts and our parents, as reincarnational studies suggest, then perhaps Plutonians select such rough [life] circumstances to impel them in the direction of helping people. "— *pg. 45*, Healing Pluto Problems, Donna Cunningham

A Plutonian may need time to heal without others around, without having to deal with other people, especially those who may not understand or even exacerbate the process of deep, intense and painful transformation.

I have Pluto conjunct Midheaven, which is considered to be an attribute of a researcher. I spend a great deal of time alone, often in contemplation. Dr. Marie Curie, the discoverer of plutonium (Pluto is the ruler of plutonium as well), had Pluto conjunct her Midheaven. A Plutonian is a natural psychologist. My own education includes a B.S. in Transpersonal Psychology. I've been a spiritual and astrological counselor for over 40 years, as well as a published author of transformational information, poetry, and novels.

Healing Pluto Problems is astonishingly accurate and concise about all things Plutonian, since Ms. Cunningham wrote the book especially for me and other Plutonians. I could quote many pages from it that are congruent with the rest of *Catherine, Karma, and Complex PTSD*. Donna Cunningham was a psychologist and prominent astrologer. Her insights reflect her dual background in astrology and psychotherapy. She received a Master's Degree in social work from Columbia University and had 40 years' experience working with people.

> "… one of the reasons Plutonians became secretive is that people around them as they grew up lied [Mother and incest] about how they were feeling and also tried to stop Plutonians from expressing their own emotions." —*pg. 192,* Healing Pluto Problems, *Donna Cunningham*

Would you be considered a Plutonian?

How strong is your Pluto, the 8th house and the sign Scorpio? [See Appendix 3 for worksheet to determine how strong is your Pluto.]

I scored 51 points on this test, which makes me a strong Plutonian.

Pluto transits are another way to trigger karmic lessons and losses.

Being alone, being a recluse, and isolated during a Pluto transit is common, often therapeutic.

I've gone through 4 grueling Pluto transits—2012–2018. I encountered: death of my partner of 21 years; death of my best friend of

37 years; loss of friends and family, as well as major financial losses. I rented out my home, sold all my possessions and moved to Santa Fe to be with a new lover. After one month I was abandoned by that lover and had no car, furniture, or household goods, only three suitcases to my name. I had endless demanding crises and needed to stand up for myself over and over again. I broke up with yet one more dysfunctional, karmic love relationship during that period. I labored ceaselessly working on my childhood and other issues and cried an ocean of tears. It seemed as though time, relationships, and karma had been compressed, while my life exploded like a nuclear bomb with plenty of fallout. Now that those Pluto transits are completing, I'm finishing this book, working with clients again, and I'm more at peace. There is life after Pluto!

Another karmic feature is that of Saturn in strong aspect to Pluto.

> "Pluto and Saturn are the planetary titans. Pluto represents power and Saturn denotes authority, so people with the combination prominent [Saturn conjunct Pluto; Saturn square Pluto; Saturn opposition Pluto] wrestle with how authority is used, both in their lives and in the world at large. They're mistrustful of the powers that be, often with good reason, for many have been targeted by authority figures, starting with their parents…When Pluto and Saturn combine and are strongly featured, a tough childhood is far more likely. Many of my clients who had this combination were faced with physical, sexual, or emotional abuse or *sometimes all three*." — *Donna Cunningham,*
> http://www.neptunecafe.com/donnaC2.html

I have Pluto and Saturn conjunct in my chart, thus Ms. Cunningham's descriptions are all too familiar.

To read more on Saturn/Pluto descriptions, you can go to these links:

http://www.neptunecafe.com/donnaC1.html
http://www.neptunecafe.com/donnaC2.html

On January 20, 2020 Saturn will connect by exact degree to Pluto. Astrologers are speculating as to the outcome of that connection, both for the children born at that time, as well as the entire planet and its welfare.

Chart comparisons

Another use of astrology is to determine interactions between individuals, most particularly between a child and parent, by using comparisons between their two charts. If there are highly challenging interactions, it can indicate abandonment, neglect, familial difficulties, or even abuse.

The chart comparisons between my mother and me—and my father and me—are extremely problematic. Yet comparisons between my sister's chart and each of our parents are both relatively easy! My sister hadn't experienced childhood difficulties with our parents and has little comprehension of what I tell her about mine.

Thus it can be seen that astrological influences can and do indicate problems in life, in some cases identical to complex PTSD. Restating my thesis: the soul has picked these problems while the Cosmic Engineer confirms those challenges through astrology. There is no one to blame. These are simply tribulations to reconcile and work through.

CHAPTER 8

WHAT IS AN EMPATH AND A HIGHLY SENSITIVE PERSON (HSP)? WHAT IS AN INFJ? WHAT IS A CONDUIT?

I'm a card-carrying member in all these categories. Hence, I'm an extremely sensitive and psychic person, able to pick up a lot of information about myself and others, and emotionally/ physically react to it. Are you? If so, these descriptions may help to understanding yourself. Here are some descriptions of these categories.

What is an empath and what is a highly sensitive person?

"Empaths share … traits of what Dr. Elaine Aron has called 'Highly Sensitive People'…low threshold for stimulation; the need for alone time; sensitivity to light, sound, and smell; and …aversion to large groups. It also takes [HSPs] longer to wind down after a busy day, since their ability to transition from high stimulation to being quiet is slower. [HSPs] are typically introverts, while empaths can be introverts or extroverts … Empaths share [HSPs'] love of nature and quiet environments, …desire to help others, and … a rich inner life.

…Empaths take the experience of the highly sensitive person much further: … [Sensing] subtle energy and actually absorbing it from other people and different environments into our own bodies. Highly sensitive people don't typically do that.

This capacity allows us to experience the energy around us, including emotions and physical sensations, in extremely deep ways. And so we energetically internalize the feelings and pain of others —and often have trouble distinguishing someone else's discomfort from our own. Also, some empaths have profound spiritual and intuitive experiences—with animals, nature, or their inner guides—[unlike] highly sensitive people.

Being a [HSP] and an empath are not mutually exclusive: One can be both, and many [HSPs] are also empaths. ... In terms of an empathic spectrum, empaths are on the far end; highly sensitive people are ...further in; people with strong empathy who are not HSPs or empaths are in the middle; and ...[those with] 'empath-deficient disorders' are at the far opposite end." — *Reprinted by permission from Dr. Judith Orloff*, https://drjudithorloff.com

What is an INFJ?

INFJ is one of 16 personality types as found in the Myers-Briggs personality inventory. "The purpose of the Myers-Briggs Type Indicator® (MBTI®) personality inventory is to make the theory of psychological types described by C. G. Jung understandable and useful in people's lives. The essence of the theory is that much seemingly random variation in the behavior is actually quite orderly and consistent, being due to basic differences in the ways individuals prefer to use their perception and judgment." —*Myersbriggs.org*

Why is it important to know your type? It can help you to understand yourself and possibly lead to further healing.

What is your personality type? Here's a free test to determine: *https://www.16personalities.com/free-personality-test*

Lauren's personality—INFJ

"What is an INFJ?

"Exact percentages vary but the INFJ, the rarest of the personality types, is said to account for 1-2% of the overall population, females slightly more often than males. The INFJ has been called "The Mystic," "The Counselor," and "Empath." They are described as original, gentle, caring, and highly intuitive. The quality of extrasensory perception, or ESP, is often attributed to them. People who have known INFJs for years continue to be surprised when yet another layer of their complex personality is revealed. As a result of their inferior sensing function, they can be stubborn and obsess about an inconsequential detail, usually when they are under stress. Their ability to see the big picture can be affected during these times. INFJs are deeply concerned about their relations with individuals as well as the state of humanity at large. They are, in fact, sometimes mistaken for extroverts because they are so genuinely interested in people— a product of the auxiliary feeling function they most readily show to the world (Introverts show their auxiliary function, or the function that supports the dominant function, to the world first). Still, INFJs are true introverts, who can only be emotionally intimate with a chosen few from among their long-term friends, family, or mate. Yet, INFJs will suddenly withdraw into themselves, sometimes shutting out those closest to them. This apparent about face is necessary, providing both time to rebuild their energy and a filter to prevent the emotional overload that can happen as they deeply experience other individuals. This is perhaps the most confusing aspect of the enigmatic INFJ character to outsiders particularly if experience with this type has been limited. I have three INFJ's in my life, my brother, my daughter, and my best friend and I can attest to the fact that they are like Russian nesting dolls, when one doll is exposed, another one lies inside.

The INFJ has a curious mix of psychological preferences that both serve them well but also create almost constant dynamic tension. The first of these is the tendency to desire closure and timeliness battling with an even stronger preference to keep generating more options and perspectives (N vs. J). This can lead to a feeling of being confused or disorganized because even as an INFJ is trying to complete something on time, new ideas keep appearing which try to displace that which has already been decided. One of my earliest recollections of this in my daughter was when she shouted, "Mom! Help me stop this video in my head!" An INFJ may begin a project or a paper and find themselves operating under a time crunch not because they are disorganized, but because they have yet to call a truce between their imaginative mind and their need for closure. Hence, an INFJ may report a preference for "P" or perceiving characterized by working best under pressure, keeping an open schedule, and allowing events to unfold when in fact this behavior is not preferred but is a byproduct of the battle between an internal brainstorm and the need for closure. The upside to these opposing forces is that the INFJ, having an awareness of what is happening, can consciously turn off the debate, and enjoy a rare combination of creative thinking and follow through. An INFJ wants both!

Another interesting nuance of this personality type is the feeling preference combined with introversion. As feelers, INFJ's are focused on people: listening to them, encouraging their growth, and honoring their unique qualities. Many

INFJ's are counselors, ministers, and teachers. They are often in the forefront of significant movements to change the world. Famous INFJ's include Eleanor Roosevelt, Martin Luther King Jr., and Nelson Mandela. They are often actors and comedians such as Adam Sandler, Carrie Fischer,, and Jamie Foxx. A preference for introversion merely means that the individual has to retreat into the mind at some point, to recharge energy. Introverts, particularly those who have a people-oriented feeling preference (INFP, INFJ), can and do extravert well but when the battery has been drained, such individuals may abruptly withdraw from the scene. The jewel in this dynamic though is that, as introverts, these individuals also tend to be observers and can therefore experience people at a deeper level, identify the ironies in life and, combined with their rich imaginations, dream of a more ideal world than the one that exists today. As far as verifying type, I versus F dynamic might result in a reported preference for extraversion. Another possibility is that the richness of their feeling experiences may feel overwhelming at times so they rely on thinking to manage their thoughts and emotions. Hence a "T" preference may be reported. This complexity can lead to confusion on the part of the INFJ during the type verification process

A logical question at this point might be, "Why is it so important to know one's type? An INFJ might mistype as an INFP, INTP, ENFJ, or INTJ. The brief answer to that is when type is known, one can better understand cognitive strengths and make choices that will make use of an individual's greatest gifts. Type identification can also uncover blind spots and illuminate reoccurring sources of frustration in work/school situations, communication, relationships, and identification of

overall life purpose. For general information on the value of psychological typing please see my link at:
http://annholm.wpengine.com/myers-briggs-type-indicator-mtbi-is-psychological-type-the-key-to-uncovering-your-potential/.

There is also an excellent website for all things INFJ at
http://www.infj.org/public/infjcharacter.html

One of the characteristics often attributed to INFJ's is ESP. Sometimes they seem to sense "something in the air."

INFJ's are also prolific writers such as Dostoyevsky and JK Rowling."
—*http://www.annholm.net/2009/08/the-mysterious-infj.*
Article reprinted with permission of Ann Holm http://www.annholm.net

What is a Conduit?

"Out of 7 billion people, there are approximately 5 million human beings on this planet right now who are Conduits. There is one Conduit for every 144,000 people—men, women, children, babies, old people, disabled people, dying people, those in comas—in every corner of the globe. When a human being dies or is born, there is an instant restructuring, so that every person remains shielded and serviced by a Conduit.

My Council of Elders first explained about Conduits in 1995 and told me that I was a Conduit. I believed them, yet was skeptical at the same time. I needed, wanted proof. So far I have discovered no proof. Except what I experience in my own body.

I'll start with some definitions of the meaning of conduit: *Merriam Webster's Collegiate Dictionary:*

A natural or artificial channel through which something is conveyed;
fountain;

a pipe, tube, or tile for protecting electric wires or cables;
a means of transmitting or distributing (such as payments or
information).

The Elders extended their explanation into two further classifications.

A Conduit is a transformer (converter) and a transponder (a 'radar' set which is tuned to a specific signal).

> *To Conduct: Act of leading from a position of command; escort; guide.*
>
> *To act as a medium. To show the way.*
> *Conductor: capable of transmitting a form of energy.*

Specifically what the Elders explain is that each Conduit receives inharmonious physical, mental, and/or emotional energy from their own group of 144,000 individuals, then subsequently cleanses, filters, and neutralizes that energy.

The energy next goes deep into the earth's crystalline iron core, where it is transformed into positive energy, ultimately returning to the surface of the planet, to be utilized by earths' inhabitants. Why not just send positive energy instead? They haven't explained that to me.

The means of cleansing, filtering, and neutralizing must be done through a physical body. A Conduit requires a three-dimensional body and looks like any other human being. The job of Conduit cannot be done by Ascended Masters, Angels, or ET's—only by ordinary, earthly human beings alive today.

A Conduit agrees to perform this job, and signs the contract, before conception. The job lasts continuously from birth until the last moment of life. A Conduit is a vitally important job for this planet.

Without Conduits, I'm told, the earth would implode with negativity. You know how much negativity currently exists, even with the ongoing help of Conduits. Imagine what existence would be like without Conduits.

From what I understand, those 144,000 individuals can change when the need arises, such as an individual or group being more stressed at any given time. So my group of 144,000 can be different from day to day. Yet if there is a global crisis such as 9/11 all the people are very upset, which I can feel. Sometimes I may wake up in the morning and know some problem is afoot, just by how I feel…(such as the day after the election of Donald Trump as well as when the USA started bombing Iraq; mass shootings; hurricanes; tornados; and earthquakes).

Furthermore, as I have contemplated my job I believe I am hooked up with people in my own time zone, which at the time of this writing is Mountain Time in the USA. This idea is based on the fact that often late at night I feel less energy coming through to me to deal with. Also I can tell what day of the week it is—Sundays are generally quieter—and holidays. Christmas is more restful than Fourth of July.

Speaking from my own experience, the job of Conduit is difficult, taxing, painful, emotionally and physically draining. I often feel what the consciousness of the planet is experiencing. I chose to be a Conduit because I have an immense love of our planet, all the people, plants, and animals that exist upon it, and wanted to make a tangible difference. I often regret my agreement because, quite frankly, it makes me sick. I've been sick my entire life, and the problems are only getting more intense. You're probably saying to yourself right now: "She must be an idiot to have taken on this job." I would agree with you. I don't think I realized just HOW difficult and painful it would be to do this job. After all, I agreed to it while still in the spirit realm, without a body or emotions. At the moment of my birth, unpleasant sensations flooded through me and have been doing so ever since. Why am I sick? I think I'm sick so I can remain quiet and conduct energy more efficiently.

So being a Conduit does NOT make me feel special and I don't feel egotistical. (Here! You do it!)

With the culmination of the Mayan calendar of evolution in 2012, the energy is increasing exponentially, daily.

The Elders tell me my job will get harder. During the Occupy Movements, protests, and events happening globally. I was sicker than usual and felt really, really ANGRY! And hostile, and irritable, and cranky, and ranting. There was nothing going on in my personal life. I must have been absorbing anger from the planet (and my 144,000 dear people). I woke up like this!

So I need to relax, do whatever I can to be at peace. The Elders tell me to do whatever makes me feel good in the moment, generally quiet activity—playing games and surfing the internet. Watching movies. Sleeping. I don't have to pay attention. The energy runs through my body 24/7, without having to consciously pay attention. I don't have to know, nor do I consciously know, how to cleanse and filter. That happens automatically. Thank goodness, or I might make a mess of it!

For those of you who are NOT Conduits, let me tell you some secrets about your feelings.

It isn't necessarily your negativity—rather it's your withholding of or denying your emotions— that are difficult for me to process. So feel your feelings all the way to the end. You'll know when you've hit the end, because suddenly you won't be feeling that feeling any more. It could take moments, days, or longer to get to the end, but persist. The next worst thing is when you don't let go of the emotion you are feeling. Relax and let the feeling run through you, without stopping it or holding on, as if it is water. Feelings and emotions are just vibratory energy, although they seem very real.

And the third worst thing is when you inflict your emotions on others—particularly anger, hate, and vengeance, which are the building blocks of conflict of all kinds (internal, familial, and global); war; disease; and sometimes earth changes. You can process your emotions within yourself without abusing others. If need be, go for a walk in the woods (or a drive your car to a deserted mall) and scream. Hit a pillow. Cry. See a counselor. Talk to a trusted friend. Practice gratitude, forgiveness, surrender. Whatever it takes.

But … aren't negative emotions bad? Nope. In fact, emotions are what we are here to learn about and evolve *through* on this planet.

Negative behavior: What you do to another goes out into the universe like a sledgehammer (like greediness and other negative behavior). What you do to yourself also goes out into the universe. Remember that—when you are treating yourself or someone else badly.

Negative thoughts, too, have consequences. Just ask me, and the other Conduits, and we'll tell you! So when you have a negative thought, all you have to do is briefly notice it, then let it go. The thought isn't real. It will disappear. If it doesn't leave, you can always read "From Suffering to Bliss in Two Easy Parts" [Chapter 6 from my book *Cosmic Grandma Wisdom*] and apply the necessary actions to your thoughts.

The next time you suppress, hold onto, inflict your emotions on others, or behave or think negatively, remember me and the other five million Conduits trying to make your life better. We will do our jobs anyway. But we could use a little help from you. Thanks!

One more thing—because of the changes that are happening to human beings at this point in evolution, we are ALL beginning to experience each other's emotions, behavior, and thoughts. You will experience those as your own, if you haven't already. We are all connected as one and are beginning to wake up to that connection. Negativity hurts us all.

For those of you who ARE Conduits, the universe appreciates you and your work. I know this job can be thankless sometimes. I know you can feel inundated by stuff that isn't even yours. But keep up the good work. I believe we are coming to the end of the need for our job. Perhaps also the Conduit goes both ways. Maybe we conduct energy, knowledge and wisdom to and from others. So we receive as well as give. I like that idea!"

—Excerpt from *Cosmic Grandma Wisdom* © 2017

(From an article originally published on *Galdepress.com* 5/1/2012)

Now that you know what a Conduit is, here is more information I've processed recently.

According to my Elders, disharmonious energy has been ramping up steadily since 2012.

I'm told since 2017 to early 2019 at least five conduits have committed suicide, because they couldn't tolerate the increasingly difficult energy. The energy is hard to differentiate; the feelings seem like they belong to us conduits, and it can feel like we are losing our "minds" when the energy intensifies.

That means 720,000 (144,000 x 5) people have to be divided up among the remaining conduits.

A group of unidentified beings recently came to visit me. They told me they are providing me (and I presume other conduits as well) with extra moral support, due in part to the loss of conduits who were overwhelmed and killed themselves.

If we adult conduits are having difficulties, I have no idea how new conduits in the form of babies and children could tolerate the intense energy. Are there new conduits being born at this time?

CHAPTER 9

HEALING

Although, as I have explored earlier in this book, there may be cosmic reasons for suffering, one must still deal with the pain and "fallout" from karma, past lives, complex PTSD, being hyper-sensitive, physically ill, and other problems.

I encourage you to seek help if you are suffering. The path to recovery includes tenacity, determination, patience, willingness, along with trying whatever methods you can locate, what you resonate with, and what you can afford. My book *Alternative for Everyone, A Guide to Non-Traditional Health Care* is a good source to determine what is available.

COMPLEX PTSD

Recuperation from complex PTSD is often complex and long term. Generally a complex PTSD survivor has experienced decades of problems regarding work, health, and relationships. Thus the survivor is disabled and often cannot afford the costs of long-term therapy. Generally most therapists do not take Medicare or Medicaid, which can leave the survivor bereft of healing. Therefore I am including a number of low-cost (or free) healing modalities to effect your own recovery.

Divine Timing in healing Pluto and other problems — a personal story

My already painful healing journey went into overdrive in 2012 when Pluto began transiting my Mercury, Sun, Mars and Moon. I practice astrology from the perspective of reflection—as above, so below. So for me the planets mirror the tendencies and timing of a particular challenging period in which I find myself. In this instance Pluto represents death, rebirth, sex, power, and transformation. Thus I was able to ascertain when Pluto influences would begin, what areas of my life would be implicated, and most importantly, when they would end!

Pluto indicated divine scheduling, time for me to travel on a hero-ine's journey through the underworld. I slogged through the muck of hell, abandoning everyone and everything. I hid in my apartment. The outside world felt threatening. I suffered emotional flashbacks and peo-ple would often trigger them. Old terrors reared their nasty heads. Now in November 2018, as those Pluto transits are ending, I feel as though I'm beginning a whole new life, washed clean of old wounds and proclivities. All the hidden junk in my "closet" has been brought out, examined, and discarded.

Part of the Pluto influence relates to power—to stand up and take one's power back. Although it was upsetting to stand up to more than two dozen people during those six years, including judges, publishers, doctors, hospitals, counselors, neighbors, friends, lovers, insurance companies, Medicare, and many situations from the period September 2012 – November, 2018, I believe that this practice, including letter writing, saying no, as well as avoiding certain people, has created an increased ability in me and my self-respect to fully take care of myself. I discovered I was what Pete Walker calls a "fawn" type, which essen-tially means to be a co-dependent. I struggled to overcome and repair the underlying wounds from abuse, shame, depression, anxiety, dissociative disorder, abandonment mélange, sexual innuendo by different men, and horrendous emotional flashbacks. I turned away from others in order to renovate myself, mostly in isolation. The Hermit in the Tarot deck is a card I drew often. Out of my seclusion came reparations to the soul.

SURRENDER is a simple yet powerful tool
"Made a decision to turn our will and our lives over to the care of a higher power as we understood that higher power." —Step 3, all 12-step programs

My "John Travolta surrender dance"

Here god.   Here god.   Stayin' alive. Stayin' alive.

(April 2017—My Higher Power told me that that if I stood up for myself, while surrendering my pending lawsuit to that higher power, I would be taken care of. It guaranteed I would receive the entire amount of my legal judgment, although not from the person who owed me, but someone else entirely. Which is precisely what happened.)

"FORGIVENESS is the major problem
that we are here to heal on earth."
Eckhardt Tolle, Nov. 17, 2018

Forgiveness is a potent form of healing used for millennia. How does one go about forgiving?
—*From the back cover of* Forgiveness equals Fortune, *2nd edition, 2017*
Liah Holtzman; Lauren O. Thyme

> "Never before has forgiving been so appealing, practical and user-friendly. Never before has the relationship between forgiveness and abundance been so clearly demonstrated. Never before has the healing power of forgiveness been so accessible. Reading the *Forgiveness Equals Fortune* book is a life-changing experience! You will discover: how to forgive yourself and others; how to ask for forgiveness; how to understand emotions; how to find compassion; how to see other perspectives; how to clear blocks to money; how to receive good fortune. Based on Liah Holtzman's successful Forgiveness equals Fortune method, this workbook is filled with valuable exercises designed to empower life, relationships, work and abundance. Liah's approach to forgiveness is simple and clear, fun to read and easy to put into practice. Her matter-of-fact, witty wisdom will gently lead you through the process of clearing negative thoughts, emotions and patterns in your life. Immerse yourself in an adventure of forgiving as Liah and Lauren show you how and why forgiveness does equal fortune."

GRATITUDE

"Gratitude unlocks the fullness of life. It turns what we have into enough, and more. It turns denial into acceptance, chaos to order, confusion to clarity. It can turn a meal into a feast, a house into a home, a stranger into a friend. Gratitude makes sense of our past, brings peace for today and creates a vision for tomorrow." — *Co-dependent No More* by Melody Beattie

---

TRUTH CAN DISPEL DENIAL and CUT THROUGH BARRIERS TO RECOVERY

Excerpts from Cosmic Grandma Wisdom © *2017, Lauren O. Thyme:*

"**Lauren's Law #18**—Tell the truth ... as fast as you can. This may not mean immediately. Sometimes appropriate timing is involved. Truth opens up all kinds of avenues that may not have been open before.

Lauren's Law #19 —There is no such thing as a lie, not even a "little white lie." This includes telling outright falsehoods as well as failing to tell the truth. Lies cannot and do not exist. Everyone is psychic. Everyone intuits another's emotions and intentions and behaves according to that intuition, even if the intuition is unconscious. Attempting to lie (or failing to tell the truth) creates problems for everyone including oneself. Many of today's world problems are based on subterfuge.

HEALING MODALITIES; BOOKS; WORKBOOKS; AND WEBSITES (see Appendix 4)

STAGES OF RECOVERY (see Appendix 5)

In Appendix 6 you can study the Stages of Recovery of sexual abuse by both Judith Herman and Mic Hunter (reprinted with permission by Dr. Jim Hopper *www.JimHopper.com*).

FIGHTING THE INNER CRITIC (see Appendix 6)

VOICE FIGHTING (see Appendix 7)

---

13 STEPS FOR MANAGING AN EMOTIONAL FLASHBACK (See Appendix 10)

HOW TO REBOOT YOURSELF USING SACRED FEMININE CONSCIOUSNESS - SACRED HEALING (see Appendix 11)

WHAT ARE THE SIGNS I'M RECOVERING?

For some people, the condition of complex PTSD poses lifelong challenges. The general rule of thumb is when symptoms are: 1) less often; 2) less intense; 3) lasts a shorter amount of time.

Reprinted with permission by petewalker.com:

"Effective recovery work leads to an ongoing gradual reduction of emotional flashbacks. Over time we become more and more proficient at managing them and alleviating unnecessary states of activation; this in turn results in flashbacks occurring less often, less enduringly, and less intensely.

"Another key sign of recovering is that the critic begins to shrink and lose its dominance of the psyche. As it shrinks, the user-friendly ego has room to grow and to develop the kind of mindfulness that more readily recognizes when the critic has taken over, which in turn allows us to more readily dis-identify form or fight against its perfectionistic and drasticizing processes.

"Another sign of recovering occurs as a gradual increase in our ability to relax—to resist overreacting from a triggered position, i.e., from an inappropriate fight, flight, freeze or fawn response… Moreover, there is an increase in our ability to use our fight, flight, freeze and fawn instincts in healthy non-self-destructive ways, so that we only fight back when under real attack, only flee when odds are insurmountable, only freeze when we need to go into acute observer mode, only fawn when it is appropriate to be self-sacrificing. Another way of describing this is that we have good balance between the polar opposites of fight and flight, i.e., we can vacillate healthily between asserting our own needs and compromisingly acquiescing to the needs of others. Moreover we can balance the polar opposites of flight and freeze, which in their moderate manifestations looks like a balance between doing and being, between sympathetic and parasympathetic nervous system arousal, between left and right brain processing.

"Advanced recovery correlates with letting go the salvation fantasy that we will never have another flashback, and moving into an attitude of accepting the inevitability of a modicum of flashbacks. This attitude then allows us to easily recognize and quickly respond to them from a position of self-compassion, self-soothing, and self-protection."

I wish you *bon voyage* on your healing journey!

CHAPTER 10

CONCLUSION

"A penny for your thoughts." I found a dime on the ground yesterday. Inflation…

As I was working on Chapter 5 (Complex PTSD) I had the sudden realization that perhaps my current Lauren life is not simply my karmic healing of Catherine, the Empress, and Philippe. Maybe I have been gifted with an awareness of the danger of negativity in whatever form it may take and to describe that danger to an audience—you and myself. In other words, I'm a messenger with positive information, personally benefited by it, in order to recover and discover myself and pass it on. I'm here to shine a light on the problems of our world—on personalities, and bodies, as well as worldwide suffering, fear, anger, hatred, war, and planetary degradation—to share that all can be healed.

For years I believed I was suffering to pay back karma, to correct past wrongs. I was mistaken. The Elders have told me for decades that my karma is completed. I confess I didn't believe them. How could I? Now I do believe what they say. Catherine, Philippe, and the Empress of Titania can rest in peace and so can I.

The Elders have endlessly explained that I'm "finishing" my sojourn on earth. That means there can't be any loose ends to attract me back here, no relationships, no unfinished explorations or incomplete business, nothing. I have to finish everything and detach.

I forgot I'm also a "Plutonian," intensely committed to personal transformation and to be of service. From past experience, I seem to hold a sign reminding all those with whom I come in contact:

"Be Aware. Transformation just ahead."

Perhaps my feeling everything profoundly through horrendous experiences was my excuse to trick me into plumbing the depths to find myself, to write this book, to share thoughts, feelings, and experiences. As a friend of mine from a 12-step group commented, "To be an undercover agent for God."

There are seven billion of us on earth with seven billion differing opinions, beliefs, religions, and lifestyles. Who is right? Who is wrong? Perhaps it doesn't matter. Maybe we are all right. Individual thoughts, beliefs, emotions, and actions that are considered to be the ONLY RIGHT PATH may be causes of unhappiness, dissension, and fractiousness on our planet. However, there is no one to blame. Problems are illusions so we can fathom deeper, spiritual meanings. All of us souls on this beautiful planet—we're all in this together—are learning, growing, and evolving in unison, one day at a time.

Not only that, but an awareness is growing about the damage that child abuse, neglect, and abandonment creates in individuals, which then is passed on as dysfunction to families, communities, nations, and the world. Have we become a world of Adult Children? Is that why violence, shootings, wars, tension, mistrust, suspicion, blame, and fear are rampant? Is that why extremists are popping up, to shout, shoot, and terrorize? To think in terms of THEM and US creates separation. To survive and thrive in the highest spiritual and religious traditions, all of us can join hands in unity and shift consciousness, one person at a time. One person does make a difference. YOU make a difference.

There is a tipping point of a small percentage of people that can cause positive change. According to Gregg Braden, *The Divine Matrix,* "It takes just 8,621 people living peace on Earth to shift our culture."

To those of you who think that actions are more appropriate to survivors of terrorist attacks or war than "our thoughts and prayers are with you," let me share something with you. In my 71 years of experience, it is when I'm focusing on a higher level of consciousness that has the greatest impact and has created the most miracles in my life. Dr. David R. Hawkins in his book *Power vs. Force* repeats the same information from years of diligent research with over 100,000 participants. The highest level on the Power vs. Force chart is enlightenment, registering 700–1000 points. Peace is 600, while shame, anger, and guilt have been shown to be quite low, from a mere 20–100 points. Thus to be at peace (540 points) or to practice forgiveness (350 points) has immense power to shift our world to harmony and healing.

Serenity shows up at 540 points. "God, grant me the serenity to accept (350 points) the things I cannot change. Courage (200 points) to change the things I can. And wisdom (would that be enlightenment at 1,000 points?) to know the difference."

In April 2017 in succinct response to a prayer, Jesus Christ appeared in my bedroom. "Just love. Just love. Just love."

Step 3 of all 12-step programs: "Made a decision to turn our will and our lives over to the care of god as we understand god."

*"It's only by giving yourself up to a higher power
that you can find yourself."* —*The Elders, 10/8/2018*

If I can forgive unforgivable people and situations and bless them, so can you.

If I can heal and recover, so can you.

The Seed

A Gardener decided to plant a seed, which had an elongated shape, with white and brown stripes along its body.

The Gardener dug a small hole in the rich earth with her fingertip and gently placed the seed in it. Then she covered the hole with earth.

The seed felt the large foot firmly tramping the ground above it, packing it down.

The seed lay in the dark, moist, cool soil. Wondering what would become of itself.

Time passed. Stillness. Darkness. No companions lay in the ground with it. Silence. Emptiness. The earth grew cooler still, even cold. Sometimes water seeped in from above. Often the seed could feel microscopic aerobic bacteria all around. Worms wriggled past, leaving their rich castings behind. Time felt endless, without day or night to differentiate.

The seed felt its body expanding, ready to burst with the moisture and the denizens surrounding it.

One day the seed detected life from within itself. A living filament broke through its shell, squirming its way towards the surface, seeking light. The shell broke apart, its job finished, falling to the side. All that was left was the kernel of the seed and its living tendril searching above itself.

One day in a tremendous burst of growth the tendril broke free of the soil and could be seen from above. It seemed puny at first, but gathering strength moment by moment, it was growing at a phenomenal rate. Growing higher and stronger. Within days a "plant" could be seen, green leaves growing out of the main stalk.

Within some time the entire plant was over five feet tall, with green leaves and branches. A head began to form at the top and soon a flower began to expand and open. The shape was round while yellow petals formed around it, opening to the sun.

The center grew abundant new seeds that each could be planted in soil when mature, just like its parent seed had been.

The seed had reached fulfillment and was content.

With love and blessings

Lauren O. Thyme   November 10, 2018

ACKNOWLEDGMENTS AND GRATITUDE

To my dear sister-friend, Sue Stein, for helping me format and edit in her inimitable Virgo-esque style. Without her I wouldn't have most of my books available online. For all her invaluable support and wit— and always being there, I bless her. She is a jewel in the crown of editing. With deepest and sincere gratitude and love.

I acknowledge the following for being instrumental in my life, my healing, my evolution, and thus this book. Thank you! Blessings and love to:

The Elders	Karen Tate
Dr. Kwiker	Paul 1
Dr. Edelhofer	Paul 2
Pete Walker	Devon
Judith Herman	Tom
Bessel Van Der Kolk, M.D.	Al
Christine Courtois	Mark
E. Sue Blume	Pat
Dr. Jim Potter	Bob
Dr. Judith Orloff	Teresa Arguellos
Myers-Briggs	Ellen Hope
Dr. Sue Morter	Diane Dowden
Liah Holtzman	Hudlene Harney
Sareya Orion	Chuck #1
Steph Lucas	Chuck #2
Donna Sandoval	Mother
Rebecca Lehman	Father
Vivianne Pulido-Price	Uncle Dodie

Sister, Daughter, Granddaughter
Grandson
12-step groups—ACA;
ALANON; CO-DEPEN-
DENTS ANONYMOUS;
SURVIVORS OF INCEST
ANONYMOUS
Edgar Cayce
Sekhmet
Hathor
Astrology
the planet Pluto
John
Peter
The Minister #1
The Minister #2
Rev. Duchess
Frannie
Valerie
Barb
Barbara
France
California
Egypt
Lemuria
Atlantis
Hudson Lake, Indiana
Santa Fe, New Mexico
Prime Time Acres, Washington

Aunt Evie
Aunt Edna
Deb Mizell
Beverly
Dana
Vandya
Crystal and Greg Kubas
Kay Navrat
Joy
Akn Shn Ahu
Richard
Dalene
Lauren Rose
Lindy
Jean
Phyllis
Amy
Ilya
Anita
Silvianne
Peter Paddon
Center for Spiritual Living
Marilyn Hager
May Salisbury
James Holmes
Lynne Ebel
Salomae Hill
Dr. Linda Hill

And many others. The Universe and I know who you are and bless you!

INTRODUCTION TO APPENDIX 1, CATHERINE

Catherine, Karma, and Complex PTSD is a non-fiction book. Although Appendix 1 reads like fiction, it is a non-fiction novelette of my most difficult past life as Catherine, for which I have been working out karma in my current lifetime. I waited many lifetimes before dealing with Catherine as Lauren. Appendix 1 is the detailed, entire true story of Catherine who died in 1402 AD in France.

I began remembering my past life as Catherine when I was 15 years old. Soon after that I began meeting various people from Catherine's life, people with whom I was intended to heal past relationships.

At 23 a friend gave me a crystal ball as a gift. Not knowing what to do with a crystal ball, decades before Google and the Internet, I stared at it and was instantly transported to 1402, experiencing Catherine's entire death event as written in this Appendix. Afterwards I quickly returned the crystal ball to my friend although the experience confirmed my remembrances as Catherine.

During 57 years I met and recognized many of the people from Catherine's life some of whom, in this current lifetime, I had various forms of relationships. These relationships often bore an uncanny emotional resemblance to the past life of Catherine.

I have met and recognized these individuals from my life as Catherine in my present life. (I follow their name or identity with a description of my relationship with them in this lifetime):

Magistrate Baron Du Font—the man I had a short relationship with had been a prison guard, then a parole officer, and was at the time

I knew him going to law school to become a lawyer. He dreamt of speaking French to me, with vivid descriptions of my long dark hair and blue eyes, and called me Catherine, at which point I disclosed our past to him.

Catherine's mother Antoinette – a friend of mine for a short duration

The pig farmer – a neighbor from my apartment complex

Colonel Pouissent – a man whom I employed at my farm.

Two soldiers -- both men in this life had attained black belts in various martial arts and also collected, studied, and practiced using weapons, including swords. They each remembered me consciously as Catherine.

Cardinal Malplaquet was a lover in my lifetime; an extremely troubled, long-term relationship. At the end of our time together, the man abandoned me and stranded me without a car, furniture, or household items.

Fialdini – a married man who flirted with me behind his wife's back.

Rene - my last relationship, with a man who was movie-star handsome and quite strong physically.

I had other brief experiences with others, particularly men, several of whom fought over me. I can easily discern when I meet a man I knew from Catherine's life. They treat me as if I am still Catherine, sexy, amoral, desirable, and difficult for them to leave me alone. They flirt outrageously and act inappropriately, even if they are married or in a committed relationship.

Thus Appendix 1 is historical, personal ,and karmic truth written like fiction.

APPENDIX 1: CATHERINE

Part 1

I didn't channel Catherine's life. I remember it, much as you can remember what happened yesterday or last week. However, it took many years of bits and scraps of memory to emerge to put together the whole memory from the beginning to the end of her life. I've included it here in this book to encourage you to understand beyond the boundaries of a single lifetime. My life as Catherine has been exceedingly and negatively impactful to my current lifetime, while remembering the details has stimulated my healing.

I had written *Catherine* in 1987 then decided to do research to make sure I had details correct. In 1402 in France the Inquisition was in force, including burning of witches, heretics, or anyone declared to be an evil influence. At that time in France, only Barons were allowed to be magistrates.

CATHERINE

"The village center looked surreal in the swirling morning mist. The sun had just risen, and it glowed dirty yellow in the haze. Many people were impatiently gathered, expectant and excited.

Straw, dry underbrush, small branches and twigs had been piled high around the stakes buried deep in the ground, awaiting the six human offerings.

The mob watched breathlessly, their eyes glittering with blood lust and revenge, awaiting the violent spectacle. "Kill the witches!" they howled.

Crowded close together, waiting for the executions, stood ragged men and emaciated women with scraggly gray hair. A mother with a bawling infant in her arms brushed away a yelping dog snapping at her skirt.

Noble men and women held fine linen handkerchiefs to their mouths to shut out the stench. Their elegant velvet clothes became soiled in the dusty town square, as they rubbed elbows with the unruly crowd.

Craning their necks to get a better view were actors, craftsmen, friars in threadbare robes, and soldiers, bristling with weapons beneath their leather doublets.

"What are their crimes?" a peasant woman whined to one of the soldiers, pulling her raggedy shawl closer around her bony shoulders.

"They have spoken diabolical curses against the name of God, stolen the Holy Sacrament from churches, and willfully committed many unspeakable acts of murder and violence." The officer drew himself up with arrogance, standing guard at such an important event.

The woman shuddered with abhorrence, being so close to the

loathsome witches, yet exhilarated at the coming execution. She pulled her rough woolen shawl even tighter around her, seeking warmth from the chilly morning air. She shoved a beggar in front of her. "Move out of my way, old man. I can't see."

Acrid smoke blew through the once-thriving town of Lebec. Homes of plague victims were burning, along with their possessions. Wagons loaded with plague victims' bodies could be heard creaking down the dusty road to the cemetery, where the dead were hurriedly buried in mass graves. Survivors huddled in whatever shelters they could find. Orphaned children wept.

The residents of Lebec muttered among themselves. "The infection is a curse, the evil eye. The Priests must cast out this evil from among us. We must be rid of wickedness."

The crowd began yelling again. "Burn the witches!"

A priest stood on the platform, murmuring, periodically crossing himself, pleading with the Almighty. "Father, purge evil from Lebec this holy day, All Hallow's Eve. Cleanse these six witches of their putrid possession by the Prince of Darkness, so that we may live without fear of pestilence." The holy man solemnly crossed himself.

The gathered crowd of residents, beggars, vagrants, and travelers imitated his gestures.

"Pater noster qui es in coelis, sanctificetur nomen tuum..."

The mob bent their heads while he intoned the litany.

"...*et no nos indicas in tentationemv sed libera nos a malo...*" His voice became quieter while the words flowed over the crowd like a healing balm. "...Amen." Once finished with his prayer, he sprinkled holy water over the wooden stakes, mouthing words, beseeching God to save his flock from further sin and disaster by offering up six people and their satanic ways as sacrifice.

Boys jostled each other impatiently, their voices rising in anticipation of the trial by fire. A fight broke out among two of the young men.

Just then, Lebec's highest official, the Magistrate, stood up. His long black robes swirled around him in the freshening wind. A hush fell over the throng. His rich, deep voice intoned, "By the Most Holy Scripture and the Penal Code instituted by his Majesty the King, Charles VI, in the year of grace 1402, do state and ordain that the most heinous, abominable, and dreadful sin of witchcraft and sorcery be punished with the harshest and most fearful penalty as may be inflicted on man, by burning to death, serving as a public example of their sins and vices of an infamous and vile nature."

After the resonant voice fell silent, the tenseness of the crowd gave way to a stir of excitement. The executive justice seized his staff, symbolizing his sovereign office and raised it above his head, to signify the start of the execution.

The head executioner, his coarse, black hood hiding his identity, motioned to his assistants. "Bring the men here," he commanded.

Two men accused of witchcraft were unceremoniously herded from the wooden cart that had brought them to the town square. They were then tied to the wheel; the cruel instrument wrested the life out of their already broken and tortured bodies. The executioners tied the two lifeless men to the stakes.

Three women were quickly strangled, also in preparation for the healing fire, and were fastened to the funeral poles. All five witches were now beyond the fiery horror still to come. Except one.

The remaining witch was brought forward. The solitary young woman had watched the executioner and his assistants in their horrible duties. She strained against the restraints from her captors. A rag covered her mouth, preventing her from spewing profanities.

Her guards roughly bound her to the last stake, tightening the ropes until her skin whitened. Because of her crimes, too hideous to comprehend, she was to die the slow way, by burning, death a torturous process for her. She struggled to free herself from the constricting cords. One round, firm breast burst free from beneath the ragged gown.

One man gasped, mentally caressing the voluptuous body beneath the torn, faded dress. "A beautiful woman. She must have been enchanting." In the midst of his daydream, he guiltily looked around, hoping no one had guessed his profane fantasy.

He was not alone in his lewd thoughts. The sorceress' savage beauty radiated from the wooden platform in spite of her starved and tortured appearance, causing many a man to lick his lips and surreptitiously finger his private parts.

Some women began to throw rocks and stones at her. The pitiless missiles tore redly through the witch's thin robe, piercing the delicate white flesh. They shrieked their judgments and shook their fists, cursing the evil that she brought to their beloved town. "Death to the Sorceress!" they chanted.

The accused woman's frantic thoughts fought against the appalling reality around her. "Why do they hate me? What have I done to them?" Vainly she struggled to free herself.

The hooded executioner lit his oily torch and thrust it rapidly into the piles of wood and straw around each dead body. Flames crackled up and darted to catch twigs and branches. The crowd watched the execution with rapture and yowled its approval.

As the masked executioner approached her in agonizing slowness, the witch strained to escape the flame. *Oh, no!* she thought, unable to cry out, hysterically looking around her. *Someone save me from the fire! Please!!*

The executioner held the smoking flare to the dry, bleached wood at her feet, which burst into flame. His hood fell back, exposing his grinning face.

She tried to scream but couldn't...

CATHERINE

Part 2

On the rough straw bed lay a woman, obviously in misery. Another large, older woman with red hands stood over her, attending a childbirth.

This is not going well, thought the standing woman quietly, drenched in sweat. *She has been laboring too many hours, since day before yesterday, and doesn't seem to be progressing properly.*

The laboring woman's face had a sickening pallor to it; the efforts she was making drained her usually rosy complexion to a haggard ashen white. "Thank you, Blanche, for being here. I know everyone else refused to help me."

"Think nothing of it, dearie. After all, this is a great occasion, the birth of your first child..." The older woman pushed away sparse strands of grey hair stuck to her perspiring face. To herself she continued out of earshot, "...even if it is a bastard."

Another violent contraction began. The laboring woman's belly rose up high and hard as her body labored to move the baby out. She screamed and writhed about on the bed, trying to avoid the pain. "Oh, help me!"

"Come on, now, Antoinette, you need to push a little harder."

But the mother lay exhausted on her straw mattress. "I can't. I just can't!" When the long and dreadful contraction finally ended, the young woman lay panting from her exertion, her face shiny from the intense effort.

"She's too old, having her first baby at twenty-five." Blanche muttered to herself. The midwife murmured again, "This is a bad one," as she again examined the mother's bloody vaginal cavity with her thick fingers, prompting more cries of anguish.

Antoinette's womanly figure was ample and plump, yet attractive. Her sweat-soaked blonde hair was loose around her neck, spread out on the pillow-less bed. Although contorted with pain, her narrow face was unusually pretty, almost beautiful, the features clear and regular. Her blue eyes had an almond shape to them, hinting of a foreign influence. Her lips were large and sensuously bright pink, almost too pink to be natural.

Blanche sponged the sweat from Antoinette's face.

Antoinette moaned as another contraction started. "Please. Help me. It hurts so much." She quickly bit her large lower lip, in a vain attempt to keep from crying out.

The midwife, in accordance with local superstition, slid her special birthing knife under Antoinette's straw mattress. "This will help cut the pain."

The laboring woman reached up and grabbed hold of the midwife's dress. Her knuckles were white. "Is my baby going to die?"

"No, no, of course not," the midwife hastened to assure her, prying off the hands clinging to her in desperation. But she turned away so Antoinette could not see her pained, frightened expression. Blanche knew that babies died often, and mothers, also. She crossed herself.

In the distance thunder pealed, then the sound of falling rain filled the old shack. Lightning flickered through the window opening covered with a ragged cloth.

Behind her Blanche heard gasping and she turned around swiftly. Antoinette's body was hunched up, her face red with exertion. Her old dress had slid up around her thighs. She had her feet flat on the old mattress, knees bent, and was straining with all her might, bearing down with a tremendous effort. Between Antoinette's legs blood spurted and the top of the baby's head could be seen emerging from the birth canal.

Blanche quickly bent down to help the laboring woman deliver her child. "Hold your breath and push down hard," she told her with authority.

Antoinette did as she was told. Monica could hear an awful ripping noise as the baby's head tore through flesh and emerged between Antoinette's legs.

The midwife gently took hold of the child's head and turned it slightly and the baby's body was propelled the rest of the way out of the birth canal as the mother once again bore down.

Antoinette fell back on her bed, eyes shut. Her breathing became more normal as did the color in her face.

As Blanche turned the newborn child over and placed her on Antoinette's stomach, she froze. A white membrane covered the baby's face. The midwife stared in terror at this Diabolical Sign. She quickly made the sign of the Cross, then leaned over and whispered into the ear of the exhausted mother. "This child is evil. She has the Mark of the Devil on her face. She must be put to death immediately!"

"No!" exclaimed Antoinette, pulling her daughter to her. The umbilical cord still connected them and was pulsing with the life force from the mother. She quickly tore the white spider-web film from her baby's face with her trembling fingers. "She is my child! Get out!" And she clutched the baby girl desperately to her chest.

The midwife backed out of the doorway in terror and ran down the narrow street as though Satan himself was after her, splashing through puddles quickly forming from the storm.

Antoinette remembered the midwife's knife still under her mattress. She reached underneath, her fingers searching for the sharp instrument. Clutching the baby to her chest, she eased over onto her side, laying the baby down on the soft mattress covering, while she brought the blade out and laid it on the dirty floor. She sat up, then ripped off a piece of her skirt and tied the umbilical cord tightly with it, several inches from the baby's belly. Then she took the blade and cut the cord off cleanly. She, too, had some training in birthing—and other things. The baby began to breathe normally and turned pink, but surprisingly, didn't cry.

The mother lay back as several more strong contractions took hold and the afterbirth was expelled from her uterus. She examined it, content that it was intact.

Antoinette relaxed on her straw mattress, holding her newborn infant. She put her baby daughter to her breast to suckle, humming softly to calm her. The infant sucked for a moment, but was still trembling from the birth experience. "It's alright now, my darling. I won't let anyone harm you."

The child's trembling subsided.

"What tiny fingers you have, my dearest one." She stroked the small fingers gently with her own, marveling at the tiny fingernails. "You're so perfect, not like any other newborn I've ever seen. You are beautiful and rosy, with thick black hair like your father." Icy blue unblinking eyes returned Antoinette's gaze, as though she could already see. She kissed the staring child softly on the cheek, mouth, and forehead.

She lay the baby down and the child began to squall for the first time. "I'll be right back," she promised. On legs that shook violently when she stood, Antoinette hobbled across the small dim room to the alcove where her jars of herbs, remedies, and poultices were kept. Blood was dripping down her legs.

"This is normal bleeding," Antoinette, spoke out loud, reassuring herself

She got out a bottle of amber-colored liquid. She brought the rim to her lips and drank some quickly, trying not to choke. The burning liquid brought warmth to her belly and she felt a little stronger. She found some rags and a cord. She tied the cord around her waist and fastened the cloths front and back so that they would absorb the blood that continued to run down her thighs and legs. Then she returned to the bed and, with her fingers, spread a few drops of the thick, yellowish liquid on Catherine's lips. The infant licked it off, watching her mother with the wide staring blue eyes.

She returned the bottle to the alcove, this time a little steadier on her feet. She found a small jar of purplish colored ointment and brought it back to the bed. As the child watched intently, Antoinette smeared the oily purple unguent on the stump of the cord. She smiled to her dearest child. "I shall name you Catherine, after a Druid Queen," she declared to her wide-eyed child.

"You're very quiet for a newborn," Antoinette told her softly. Her breasts were swelling with the rich new milk. A few drops leaked out.

Antoinette lay down beside her beautiful child, less than an hour old, and positioned herself so that her daughter could nurse. As Catherine worked her mother's nipple with her small, soft lips, sucking out the precious, life-sustaining colostrum, Antoinette could feel small rippling contractions pulsing within her womb as it began to return to its former shape and size.

She stroked her precious child's head, shoulders, and arms as the tiny girl fed. The baby hungrily sucked and the mother lovingly stroked the black hair on the tiny head. "I love you, my daughter," Antoinette whispered tenderly. "You are beautiful and intelligent, too, I can tell. You are special and I will cherish you all the days of my life."

Glancing out the open doorway, she continued in a louder voice, "Because you are part of me, I will defend you like a mother wolf with fang and claw. I will shield you against all others. I will protect you with my last dying breath."

After a while, the baby relaxed its grip on the nipple, and the tiny eyes grew heavy. Very gently Antoinette raised the child up, while supporting the wobbly head with her hand. She lightly patted and stroked the tiny back. After a few minutes, her fingers had massaged all the gas out of Catherine's stomach.

Then Antoinette washed her off, gently wiping away the thick, white coating of vernix that had protected the baby in the womb, and saved it in a clay container for its healing and magical properties. Finally she arranged some absorbent rags around the baby's bottom for when she would wet herself, wrapped the child in a soft cloth and laid her down on the bed.

"I'm hungry." She got up and found a hardened crust of bread, which she chewed on until it satisfied her. "When I wake up tomorrow, I will be stronger. Then I will make a remedy for myself, and thoroughly clean everything." Lying down, she put her arm around her baby daughter protectively and the exhausted mother slept.

CATHERINE

Part 3

Antoinette's baby had grown into a lovely child. Catherine's black glossy hair grew long in wavy ringlets down her back to her waist. Her startlingly clear blue, intelligent eyes intensely inspected everything. She had her mother's high cheekbones, which were colored pink, as was her full childish mouth. Catherine was exquisitely beautiful; the combination of dark hair and blue eyes brought stares wherever she went. Catherine's mother, on the other hand, was visibly aging and gray strands streaked her hair. She had never been quite the same since Catherine's difficult birth.

Antoinette was an accomplished herbalist and searched most days for healing plants, roots, berries, and flowers in the thick forest, the swampy bogs, and in the sunny glades to restock her herbs. She always took her daughter with her, to teach Catherine about the various plants.

Her mother talked to her like she was an adult. Even though Catherine was only five years old, Catherine spoke and acted like a child many years older. Antoinette smiled at her precocious child, listening to her repeat the instructions on how to use the healing herbs in her childish lisp.

Many medicinal plants grew in abundance. Antoinette knew most of them by name and all by sight and use, while Catherine was learning fast. The thatched hut they shared was cool, which helped keep the remedies, poultices, and ointments in a stable condition. Herbs could be dried without over-heating, thus avoiding losing the valuable medicinal qualities.

"Some plants can be deadly. However, correctly prepared, those same harmful stalks and roots can save lives, cure illness and diminish pain," she instructed Catherine. "And don't ever put anything into your mouth unless I tell you it is safe. And never, never leave my sight. I don't want anything to happen to you." Antoinette was still afraid the people of Quimont believed the old midwife's story about her child's birth and might hurt Catherine. "There are gypsies that might steal you," she lied.

"All right, Mother," replied the child. "But I wish you weren't so afraid. Nothing can happen to me," Catherine spoke arrogantly.

"Dig the roots here, like this."

The child pursed her lips, concentrating mightily, trying to follow her mother's actions with the plant and its roots.

Her mother watched Catherine as she worked. "You will be a tall woman. Already you are taller than most of the children around Quimont. Your limbs are sound and straight, and you're very healthy, and quite strong...for a girl." She smiled fondly at her daughter.

That spring day had turned exceptionally warm and rivulets of perspiration rolled down their faces. Antoinette and her daughter rested in a clearing, on a green hummock, surrounded by graceful daisies waving in the breeze.

They had removed stockings and shoes and delighted in the feeling of rich green grass on bare feet. The grass tickled Catherine and she giggled. "I will never wear shoes again," she pronounced.

Antoinette sighed at her impetuous statement. "When the snow is on the ground, you will change your mind."

But Catherine shrugged her shoulders impatiently. Then she wrinkled up her forehead a little. She cleared her throat and began to speak. "Mother, who is it that you sneak out to visit very late at night?" Catherine asked hesitantly, "when I pretend to be asleep?"

Antoinette was caught by surprise at Catherine's seemingly innocent, but direct question. Antoinette looked away and hesitated. She took a long, slow breath to sort out her tumultuous thoughts and choose her words carefully. "He is my—protector. Perhaps someday he will be yours as well." She let out her breath and watched Catherine's young face to see how she reacted to this news.

Catherine pouted. "I don't need a protector. I don't need anyone!" she said with a flounce and tossed her head proudly. "I just want to know who you visit, and what he wants with you."

Antoinette again carefully picked her words. "Don't be worried, little one. Are you afraid I will leave you? You are my precious, sweet child. You are my treasure, more than life to me. I would never abandon you!" She hugged Catherine to her fiercely.

Catherine could feel her mother breathing deeply. Her heartbeat was rapid and pounded strongly with emotion.

"You are special. You are precious beyond gold, beyond jewels, beyond value. Never, never, will I leave you. And I will protect you even until my death, if need be!" Antoinette spoke with great intensity of feeling.

Catherine felt suffocated and began wiggling out of her grasp.

Her mother released her tight hold on Catherine, held her at arms' length and looked deeply into her child's eyes.

Her daughter stared back without blinking at the searching gaze. What Catherine saw was love, adoration, and sincerity and she softened. Looking off into the distance, and with a feigned, nonchalant air, Catherine asked her mother an even more important question. "Is it true that the Devil was once your lover and that I am the Devil's daughter?"

Rage surged through Antoinette's belly. "Who has told you these malicious lies?" She grabbed hold of Catherine's shoulders and looked angrily at her. Sparks seemed to fly from her eyes. "Tell me!"

Catherine had never seen her mother look so angry before. She squirmed out of the woman's powerful grasp. "Sometimes the children in the village shout those things at me. They say it is why they are not allowed to play with me," replied Catherine casually. "Is it true, Mother?"

"Hush now. I don't want you to pay any heed to them. They only want to hurt me—and you. They are jealous because of your beauty and power, and because..." Antoinette had said more than she wanted to. Her cheeks flushed bright red, but Catherine couldn't tell if it was anger or embarrassment. "Just stay away from those children, and their stories!" She got up and picked up the bags full of plants. She hefted them onto her back and began walking in the direction of their home.

Catherine ran to keep up with her. "But who is my father then?" she demanded.

Antoinette kept walking, avoiding her questions.

"Mother..."

"No," replied Antoinette over her shoulder, but not stopping. "We will speak no further of this."

Catherine followed behind, more slowly now. She was annoyed at not being able to get the truth out of her mother, yet curious. She began to wonder about the stories.

CATHERINE

Part 4

On the porch of the graceful manor house of an enormous estate stood a tall, strong-looking man. The lines of the Baron Jean duFont's still-youthful face proclaimed the nobility and power of his position.

He spoke to himself. "Planting time again. My hands itch to feel the soil, and plant the tiny seeds that grow into food. What a miracle." He had an insatiable wonder of growing things that he inherited from his long-dead mother. "Whenever I look at the roses blooming in spring, I feel close to her." Jean's mother had died following a miscarriage, shortly after his fifth birthday.

He ran his fingers through his thick shock of glossy black hair. It matched his bold brown eyes, which saw life clearly and vividly.

Jean dimly remembered his mother's silky, blonde hair and eyes so light blue, they were almost transparent. But her intense love of growing things, especially flowers, was vivid in his mind.

The elder duFont, Jean's father, had grieved for the beautiful, delicate lady for twenty years. "Keep her room the same," he told the servants. "You may clean, but do not disturb anything in it." There was an air of expectancy in that room, as though Madame DuFont would suddenly come to life one day and reside in her room once again.

When he was twenty-five, Jean's father had died, leaving his entire estate and office to his only child. "I will become the most trusted and valuable of all the Magistrates in the King's realm," Jean vowed emphatically.

At age thirty-three, duFont's position as Lord Magistrate, handed down through many generations, was an impressive combination of lawyer, sheriff, and judge. He was the last of an illustrious family. He had remained unmarried, without an heir, thus his noble office and family name would die with him.

When he was younger, Jean had been engaged to a quiet girl from a nearby village, a Viscount's daughter. "Her dowry is respectable and her personality passable," he was advised. However, a fever swept darkly through her village and she quickly died, as did the rest of her family. Her family's estate had been burned to the ground to rid itself of the pestilence.

Jean withdrew into himself after the tragedy. It was not grief, but a superstitious attitude that kept him from becoming betrothed again. "I am bad luck to women; first my mother and now my fiancé."

He had listened to the men in the fields talk. "Witches are powerful; when a man offends a local witch in some way, she puts a curse on him."

Jean was sure he had drawn the disfavor of some witch in the area and consulted a necromancer.

"You are indeed cursed," the old crone had advised him, after studying the entrails of a dead chicken. "It is a powerful curse that has you enveloped in a jealous bubble. Whoever the witch is, she does not want you to be with any other woman." She shrugged. "A curse too powerful for me to change. With time, though, it may disappear. Be patient and watch carefully."

Jean was afraid to be openly involved with any woman after that, although there were rumors that a lowly commoner had won his heart and that he rode to her side in the dead of night.

"Who do you think he could be seeing? Is it someone from our village?" The gossips' tongues wagged day and night. But no one had actually seen him in his midnight forays.

Jean thought of those rumors as he stood on the porch, in front of his precious library that glorious spring day. "It is amazing what idle minds can think up to create excitement in their lives." He looked past the steps, to the lush, well-kept lawn and the rock wall beyond. Fruit trees were budding and flowers were blooming.

From his vantage point, he could see the comings and goings of Quimont on the main road in front of his manor house. The roads were bumpy and perilous, deeply rutted from the spring rains. Dust was thrown up from big wagons driven by serfs, who brought produce to trade or sell for their masters. He could see an occasional musician walking past or, if the talented man had a rich patron, on horseback. Vagrants and tramps, sometimes whole families, plodded past, enormous packs of their possessions strapped to their backs.

"It is very warm and dry for March. I can almost smell the dust from here." He smiled to himself at his fancifulness. It was at least five hundred feet from the porch to the main road.

The sun was exceptionally bright, making him blink with the glare. He returned to his library, beside the massive wooden table. Sitting down on the stiff wooden chair, he opened his book again.

"No one has such a library as I," he said proudly. Some books were bound in pigskin, the more valuable ones in calf's leather, and all had been laboriously hand-written. He had spent many happy hours thumbing through his priceless volumes.

Jean could hear the cows bawling towards the back of the house. "Milking time. The afternoon is getting late and I'm thirsty." He rang a bell for his manservant, Pierre.

"Yes, My Lord," said the servant, when he appeared at the door. "What do you wish?"

"I'd like some of the wine we made last fall, Pierre. I have a thirst to match this warm dusty day. And maybe some rolls or cakes to go with them."

"Yes, my Lord." Pierre bowed and went to fetch Jean's modest snack.

The servant fetched a bottle of wine out of the cellar and removed the cork. It smelled delectable, light and fruity. *Perhaps Master would like some cheese as well. The Baron did not mention guests for dinner today. Possibly cook knows,* Pierre thought. He hurried to the pantry to talk to the plump old woman who had cooked for the duFont family since she was a young girl.

Pierre had been with Jean's family since his own birth. His parents had both been servants there, meeting when younger, marrying and having children within that house. A fever, which took the lives of both parents and his only sister, had also stricken Pierre.

As Pierre got duFont's food together, he thought fondly of his years in the duFont house. *I practically grew up with Jean, though he is several years older than me. We played together as children, until Jean reached 13 and adulthood.* Pierre remembered his pride at being named as Jean's personal manservant, which suited both young men immensely. The short man served Jean well, was discreet, and had a fervent affection for his strong and brilliant master. *With my own family dead, I owe absolute fealty, even my life to Baron DuFont,* Pierre thought.

Jean read out loud to himself, a habit he had gotten into while young, having been alone a great deal. He also did it for the sheer enjoyment of hearing his own voice.

Pierre smiled as he heard the magnificent voice reverberate down the hall. "I have your supper, Monsieur," he said deferentially, stepping into the open doorway.

The Baron's eyes widened at the delicious meal that Pierre had helped to put together. "Thank you, Pierre," he replied fondly. The servant put the tray down on the ancient wooden table. DuFont put aside his book and sampled the wine. "It is perfect," he added, and Pierre left him to his solitary meal.

Jean enjoyed his own company. Sometimes he invited guests to dinner, but he bored easily. Most people could not match his intellect or his inquiring mind. He was gone from Quimont a good deal, traveling extensively, when called to various trials and the notorious Auto-Da-Fe, as the Inquisition was then known.

DuFont leaned back in his chair, savoring the smells and tastes of his delectable, although simple, dinner.

His meal was suddenly disturbed by a commotion outside his window.

Pierre poked his head in. "There are some people who need to see you most urgently, Master."

Jean went outside.

A small crowd had gathered at his front door.

A woman ran up to him, her face contorted with grief, rage, and terror. Had she not been in such extreme distress, she would have curtsied at seeing duFont. She began without the formalities. "My boy, my son..."

"Yes, Madame. What is it?"

"He was found floating in the Moselle this morning."

"Ah, an unfortunate accident. My utmost condolences."

"No, Monsieur, you do not understand. He only disappeared yesterday, except that, when he was found, his body was blackened and swollen. His mouth open as if in a scream of terror." She crossed herself. "It is the work of a witch. I demand that you find the one who has done this evil deed."

The others murmured in assent.

"I assure you, there is nothing to fear. It must be the work of gypsies, before they left town yesterday. Or perhaps a freak accident of nature." The Baron gave her several silver coins. "I hope this will take care of the funeral arrangements."

The woman collapsed then, while several of her friends held her up. "Thank you, Monsieur, you are very kind," and she was half-carried off the Baronial estate.

After they had gone, within the refuge of his library Jean was plagued with doubts of his own into the wee hours of the night.

Mothers watched over their children for many days and worried if any wandered off or were gone too long. They hung special amulets on their children, to protect the young ones from Maloick, the Evil Eye.

The same day the child had been found drowned, Antoinette was looking through her potions and bottles. "Something is missing," she puzzled to herself. I really can't remember which one. I guess I'm getting old and forgetful."

Little Catherine stood in the open doorway, staring out at the village, her mouth set grimly, humming to herself, fists clenched at her side. "No one better say bad things about us ever again!"

CATHERINE

Part 5

"Where has the time gone?" Antoinette asked. "It seems like only yesterday that I gave birth to you." She looked closely at her daughter. "The years have passed quickly and I have not been aware of the changes in you. You are becoming a woman."

At twelve, Catherine was fairly tall, much taller than her mother, and her muscular arms and legs belied a soft, rounded feminine body. Her breasts were already large, heavy spheres, while her waist was still a narrow girl's waist. Her hips, though, were substantial and the lower half of her torso was as voluptuous and fleshy as the upper.

A little worry caught at Antoinette's heart. "I must talk with you. With your looks, I am sure that you will find a good husband to take care of you. If you don't chase one away with your arrogance and coolness, that is." She cleared her throat, hesitating, afraid of her daughter's anger. "You know, it is important for a man to think he is smarter than a woman," she said to Catherine while they worked.

"Hmmm?" replied Catherine, not paying attention.

"When a man is interested in you, you must not act cleverer than he is, or you might lose him."

"Then he would indeed be a fool and I would be a greater fool if he would want me to be stupid!" responded Catherine hotly. "I want a man who knows who and what I am. I won't pretend! Not for a man, not for anyone." She continued concocting the rheumatism poultice she was working on.

Antoinette sighed at her headstrong daughter's words. "Someday you may regret your stubbornness," she said. Then Antoinette noticed that her daughter was not preparing the recipe correctly for the remedy. "No, my love, not so much of that particular root."

"I've been doing it this way for months," replied Catherine, "and we have been asked for more of this remedy than ever before." She continued on, her teeth clamped shut, faint red streaks of annoyance flooding her face.

Antoinette appraised her daughter" expression. For the first time she noticed a hard set to the jaw beneath the pretty pink cheeks.

"I didn't know you had changed the formula," said Antoinette softly, looking intently at her child.

"Well, I have."

"Show me how you have changed it, my darling."

"It's better than ever. And this is not the only one I've changed either!" retorted Catherine defensively.

"Hush now. Don't be upset. I'm not scolding you. I want to see how you did it."

Catherine continued working, showing her, without saying another word.

"I don't understand you," murmured the mother, more to herself than for Catherine's sake.

But Catherine had heard her. She turned, a half-smile on her face. "You never will. But don't worry about it. There are things I don" understand about you either."" Her eyes grew bright. "Such as I don't understand why you sneak out to see your lover in the dark forest in the middle of the night. Why do you invite more gossip and trouble? Why can't we just go to his house, openly?" She stamped her foot, wanting to control her mother.

"It would not be proper," said Antoinette, looking away quickly.

"Well, I don't want you to do that anymore. Let us go to his house and be respectable, as you are always talking about."

"Very well," Antoinette sighed. She felt prickles of fear and apprehension crawl down her neck and her spine. She shook herself to remove the anxious feeling. "I will talk to him of this."

"Good," replied Catherine and she turned to complete the remedy she was working on.

Some days later, true to her word, Antoinette spoke to her lover, while they lay beneath the old trees. He was immensely happy, much to her confusion.

"You don't know how thrilled this makes me," the Baron said. "I have not liked our little charade either. I've been waiting for a long time." DuFont thought uneasily about the old seeress' words, of the curse. To his lover he said only, "Our affair needed to be private for certain reasons. Now I think we can be openly happy together." He firmly held Antoinette to him, kissing her.

Antoinette hugged him tightly with gratitude, while shivers of joy mixed with fear ran down her back, and a knot clenched her stomach.

CATHERINE

Part 6

Catherine stood in Monsieur DuFont's garden watching a couple of blue jays bathing in a puddle, chirping and splashing. She looked around at the beautiful flowers bursting into bloom around the manor house.

"This garden is the pride of my family. Do you like it?" asked duFont, coming up behind Catherine as she observed the noisy birds.

She jumped slightly, not hearing his step. "I like looking at all the flowers and smelling them, too," she replied, her bare toes digging into the soft, powdery earth. "In fact, I like everything here," replied Catherine, said meaningfully, and slowly turned to face him, her icy blue eyes meeting his brown ones.

As their eyes met, Jean felt warmth spread through his body, beginning at his groin and moving up. "Long ago my mother planted these flowers. Because of the lush, sandy soil deposited by the Moselle and the manure from our farm animals, we have the most wonderful garden in the whole area." He made a wide gesture with his arm.

"Mm. Exquisite," she murmured, not taking her eyes off him.

The warmth spread into his face, and brought a hot flush to his cheeks. "You seem to be much older than twelve."

The girl coolly appraised the older man, her mother's protector, with eyes that seemed to search deep within him. She smiled a slow, inviting smile, which lit up her whole face. "I especially love the roses," as she brushed aside his comment.

"They were my mother's favorite as well," he said, a slight tug at his heart at the fond memory. "I'm told she nearly drove my father wild searching for new and different varieties to plant here." He laughed slightly but Catherine didn't join in.

She continued to appraise him again with a searching, intense look that made him extremely uncomfortable.

"Your mother is preparing dinner, which should be done shortly." With that he quickly turned and walked back into his house.

Fragrant aromas wafted through the warm kitchen. Antoinette was cooking fish, freshly caught from the river. The smell of pungent and sweet herbs and spices, onion and garlic, drifted up from the heavy iron pot. His lover was bent over, tasting a little of the sauce with a pewter spoon.

DuFont walked over to her, pushed Antoinette's long hair aside, and begin to lightly kiss the back of her neck. She set the spoon down, turned, put her arms around her lover and, standing on tip-toe, kissed him sweetly. She sighed a deep sigh of contentment and lay her cheek against his massive chest.

"You were right. This is perfect."

A cold breeze blew over them. In the doorway stood Catherine, smiling at the two of them, her head tilted to one side.

"How long have you been standing there?" Antoinette went over and put her arm around her daughter. "I'm glad that you two have finally met. This is the happiest day of my life." She gave Catherine a little squeeze. Neither Catherine nor duFont said a word.

Antoinette shrugged it off. "It is common to feel a little shy with someone you just meet," she told her daughter. "The two most important people in my life will learn to like each other. I'm sure of that. Sit down," she told duFont and Catherine. "Let's eat."

They ate informally in the Baron's huge kitchen. Antoinette served up the savory fish, pouring a stew of vegetables on top of it. A loaf of fresh crusty bread was on the table along with a bottle of red wine.

"This is last year's harvest." He poured a glass for himself and Antoinette and a small amount for Catherine. As he poured the fragrant red wine into the young woman's glass, he glanced at her, and for a brief instant, their eyes locked. He quickly looked away, but not before something had passed between them.

The silence continued. Antoinette began to feel a little nervous and fidgeted. She looked at Jean, but his face was in shadow. "Don't you like dinner?" she asked her handsome lover.

"Hmm? What? Oh, yes, my darling, it is without a doubt the most delicious meal I have ever tasted." He leaned over and briefly kissed her full lips.

Antoinette was satisfied, pleased with his response. She sampled her own plate. "It is the best I ever cooked." Then she noticed that Catherine was picking at her food. "What's the matter my sweet?" she asked her.

"I'm not hungry, Mother. I think I will go for a walk instead. Do not wait up for me."

Antoinette was used to Catherine's sudden disappearances. "Of course, my dearest. I will save some dinner for you on a plate in case you get hungry later. We will be staying the night here, but in the morning we must return home. Monsieur DuFont has to travel far to preside over a sorcery trial. We can come back to visit again when he returns." She looked inquiringly at the Baron, who nodded. "Come and kiss your Mother good-night."

Catherine dutifully presented her cheek to Antoinette and allowed herself to be kissed, all the while looking at duFont.

Violet pools darkened in Catherine's eyes. She walked over and boldly kissed Jean on the mouth. "Good night, Monsieur," said Catherine casually. "Have pleasant dreams."

DuFont blushed. He tried to ignore the warm, tingly feelings that erupted in his low belly. *This is embarrassing, especially with Antoinette sitting so close,* he thought.

It was late when Catherine returned from her walk. Pierre, the manservant, lit her way upstairs to the bedroom that she would occupy that night. As she entered the bedroom, a sweet fragrance greeted her. A huge bouquet of fragrant red roses, with many blooms on each stem, was displayed on a small table by the window. Catherine ran over to the flowers, stroking the soft petals with her fingers.

"The Master instructed me to put these in this room," the servant replied sullenly, in answer to her silent question. "This used to be Madame's room."

She breathed deeply in sudden happiness. "Thank you, Pierre. You may go now," she spoke haughtily, acting as if she had been wealthy and pampered all her life.

The servant bowed dourly, insulting her with his dark look, and left, closing the door.

In the library, Jean and Antoinette were finishing the bottle of wine.

Antoinette got up and went to her lover's side. "Isn't Catherine as wonderful as I told you? I love both of you so much and hope you will get along. Thank you for being so kind to us."

"It is my pleasure, dearest."

Antoinette brushed some of the hair out of his eyes so she could kiss his forehead, and was instantly alarmed. "My sweet, you are burning up! Are you ill? Let me put some cooling ointment on your forehead."

Jean felt a sickening tug just below his navel, knowing the reason for his fever. "No, no," he protested. "I'm fine. I am not sick. I am anticipating the coming trial. Why don't you go upstairs and get some sleep. I need to pack for my trip."

"Can't Pierre do that?" she was puzzled.

"I like to do some things myself," he answered curtly. 'I may be up all night," he warned her. "I have many papers to put in order."

"Very well." Antoinette kissed him again on the top of his head, very gently and lovingly, but with concern. "Will you say good-bye to me before you leave?"

"Yes. I warn you, though, I will be leaving very early."

Antoinette felt him pull away slightly. Then she left to go upstairs to her room, puzzling over his sudden strange mood.

Catherine lay awake in the beautiful room. The roses' perfumed aroma permeated the room. A candle burned brightly in a pewter holder on a stand beside her bed. "Baron Jean duFont is a very wealthy man."

She lay on the enormous goose down bed, having taken off her clothing. She slid her legs back and forth under the sheets, feeling their silkiness.

"I could lie on this forever," and Catherine heaved a deep sigh of contentment. She heard the doorknob turn a little. Then very slowly and quietly the door opened.

DuFont stood in the doorway.

She looked up at him, not at all surprised. "I have been waiting for you," she whispered huskily. "Come in and close the door." Catherine had turned on her side to face him when he came in. A tendril of her black hair had fallen over her eye, giving her a sultry quality. She chewed on her lower lip.

As if in a dream, Jean stepped into the room, then closed and quietly bolted the door. *Her lips are full and red, like Antoinette's,* he thought. His face was flushed. He ran his fingers through his thick black hair. Several drops of red wine stood out on his white linen shirt.

Catherine let the sheet slide off from her bare shoulder.

The throbbing in his body intensified. "This was my mother's room, when she was alive," duFont said in a raspy voice. "Everything is the way she left it, even her clothes." He trailed off, not knowing what else to say.

"Come closer."

He opened his mouth but no words came out. He licked his dry lips. All the while he could not take his eyes off the lithe figure under the sheet.

Catherine took a strand of her lustrous hair and began to tease her mouth with it, still staring intently at the feverish man.

DuFont's voice growled. "I can't believe I've come here. I tried to stay away. My God, I did try. I don't know what I'm thinking of, with my precious Antoinette just down the hall. And you, her daughter!" His voice broke, and he leaned back against the door for support. His pounding heart hammered in his ears.

Catherine lay on the bed, watching her mother's paramour. "You are upset, but you have come to me, haven't you?" Power poured out of her body and wound itself around duFont like a snake. "Come over to me."

Jean duFont felt the pull. He took several staggering steps towards her, resisting mightily. Standing in the middle of his mother's bedroom, struggling with himself, Jean cursed his weakness. "Why am I drawn to you, a mere child?" He stumbled jerkily to the bed and dropped silently to his knees. With a hand that trembled violently, he reached up and gently touched her face.

"Your skin is so soft," he said, caressing the texture of her cheek. "Like the finest cloth, smooth as rose petals." His fingers couldn't stop themselves.

Catherine took his hand and playfully nibbled the fleshy end of his fingers. She could feel the snake wind tighter and pull him closer.

Hot bursts of pleasure exploded inside his body. "I must be mad," he moaned. He was paralyzed, unable to leave her side.

He looked into Catherine's face, partially in shadow. "You are under my protection and I must not harm you," he said as if in a carefully prepared speech.

"I know you will be gentle with me," replied Catherine, talking low into his ear. She reached out her hand and smoothed his shirt, her hand lingering on his chest. An icy-hot chill raced through his body.

"That wasn't what I meant. I'm trying to..." but Catherine stopped his words with her soft reddened lips brushing his mouth. She lifted the cool sheets of the dead woman's bed, beckoning.

Jean pulled off his clothes, dropping them in a pile on the floor, then crawled in beside her.

The snake pulled taut as duFont slid in beside Catherine, his old world lost forever. He disappeared into a delicious, timeless ecstasy. "I could touch and kiss you forever." His body alternately shivered and burned. Hours later he fell into an exhausted sleep.

Pink rays of morning were seeping into Madame DuFont's room. Catherine was sitting on the side of the bed, stroking Jean's cheek, forehead, and lips with a rose, caressing his face with its flowery fingers, careful with the thorns. A few drops of water had slid off the petals, arousing him.

"You are a magnificent lover." He leaned over to kiss her, but she moved away from his touch.

"It is already dawn. You had better go before Antoinette discovers you are here." She went to the door, unlocked and opened it quietly.

Jean gathered up his clothes and Catherine pushed him out of the room closing the door behind him. He heard the bolt slide shut. He stood in the hall, a confused look on his face, shivering with the chill of early morning. He had been dismissed.

When mother and daughter returned home that day, Antoinette was jubilant. "I think you made an impression on Jean," she said to Catherine. "He couldn't stop looking at you last night." She blushed. "How would you feel about my marrying him, darling? Then you could have pretty clothes. We could live in his beautiful house, and we'd never be hungry or cold ever again." She waited for a reply from Catherine, who was standing in stony silence.

Catherine clenched her teeth together. "I don't want to talk about it."

"Of course, my sweet daughter. Let's think about it for a while."

"All right." replied Catherine, chewing on a jagged fingernail, her teeth clenched, not looking at her Mother. She gazed around at the ugly mud walls of the shack they lived in, and yearned for the elegance and comfort of the duFont mansion.

CATHERINE

Part 7

Jean duFont fled from Quimont after the night he had spent with Catherine. In his infrequent, brief letters to Antoinette, he told her that he had "been detained on a long trial, then had gone to the High Country for a cure, as my health was poorly."

During Jean's long absence, his fiancé suffered acute loneliness, and worried about his well-being. "I wish he would return home. I could heal him." She spent more and more time working with her remedies and passing time in the countryside gathering her precious herbs and flowers, waiting for the day when he would return back to her.

Catherine was spending more and more time away from home. Sometimes she would be gone for days at a time. The willful girl had created her own secret, separate life. Her mother couldn't control her daughter anymore.

Then one day a note arrived for Antoinette:

"My Dearest Antoinette,
    I'm sorry. Oh, so dreadfully sorry. I am tied to something, a powerful force. I can't help myself. I need you to talk to you, explain what has happened to me.
    I'll be home in in a week or two. Tell Pierre I expect you."

The crude letter had obviously been crumpled, then made smooth again, sealed with wax, and posted to her.

Writing the letter had been anguishing for the Baron. Guilt and emotional pain etched themselves deep into duFont's conscience. *An-*

toinette, he thought, I cannot ever be with you again! Your devil daughter has enchanted me. I, who am respected and powerful, a Magistrate of his Majesty the King. Pushed into my cold hall like a serving boy, left there to tremble with still unfulfilled desire. And he pounded on his temples with clenched fists, trying to force the girl out of his memory. But parts of his body remembered all too well.

Jean had taken a long rest in the mountains, hoping that the soothing waters would heal him. Every day he had walked alone, bringing a fresh red rose to the water's edge with him. He would caress his lips and cheeks with its velvety petals until it fell apart. Sometimes the thorns would draw blood from his fingers, but he never noticed.

"Damn you," he hissed. "Let me forget your touch, your taste, and those jeweled blue eyes. Leave me in peace." But Catherine was buried deep within him.

At dusk he would invariably return to the inn and drink great quantities of wine until he lost consciousness.

Time passed. Slowly, but ever more surely, the serpent began to pull him back to Quimont.

He left his miserable room and walked downstairs. He handed Antoinette's wrinkled letter to the innkeeper. "Post this for me."

He returned to his chamber and drank himself into a stupor. In a few days, when he felt strong enough to travel, Jean gathered up his possessions, walked downstairs to the coach, and settled in for the long trip home. He had been gone three years.

Antoinette paced back and forth in the Baron's library, talking to Jean's chair as though he was seated there. "I fear for you, my darling. I know that you are in trouble." Her healing heart reached out to him. "Dearest, let me help you." She talked out loud, as if he could hear her.

As she waited the long, lonely hours in the huge manor house, she began to feel anger. "You never told me you would be gone so long. I've been lonely, missed being with you, missed your touch, your calming deep voice, your reassuring love." She gathered her shawl close around her, the autumn wind blowing in under the cracks of the door.

She sat down in his chair clasping her hands, looking at the backs of them. "I am getting old." Antoinette felt a sickening feeling in her stomach. "Maybe he has tired of me. Where would we go? How would we live? He protected me for so many years, I am afraid to imagine what would become of Catherine and me if...." She pushed those thoughts away. "No, I am making up stories. There is a sound reason for his absence. And he's asked me to be here to meet with him and tell me all about it. We can make plans for our wedding." She smiled to herself and leaned back in the chair. But her stomach churned and her heat pounded rapidly.

Antoinette napped in the chair. Shortly before dusk she heard the large outer door open and close. "Jean!" She could hear the brown leaves scrabble across the wooden floors from the strong breeze. Dread held her fast in the chair.

"My Lord, the lady waits for you in the library."

"Thank you, Pierre." Jean's voice sounded very tired.

Antoinette held her breath as his footsteps creaked across the wooden floor. They seemed to walk reluctantly towards her.

Jean slumped into the room.

Antoinette jumped to her feet. Even in the dark, she couldn't believe what she saw. He had changed. Age lines had cut deep into his face. He looked unkempt and ill. But the worst part were his eyes, for they were streaked with red, and had a haunted look to them, with deep dark circles around them.

"My dear," she exclaimed as she ran over to her, touched his cheek, his forehead. He smelled of old, stale wine, sweat, and travel. "This is not the Jean I remember. You feel cold to me." She looked into his eyes, hoping to find something. But it was not there. She flung her arms around him, but he was a pillar of stone.

DuFont gently pulled her arms off him. "Antoinette. Please sit down." Then he turned away. He stared into the dying embers in the fireplace.

"You must tell me..." began Antoinette, but Jean held up his hand for silence.

"This is not easy for me," he murmured. "If you have any love for me, or pity even, pray let me find my words. I have tried for so long to tell you. Ached to tell you," but he couldn't finish.

In the dim light, Antoinette saw tears well in his eyes and run down his cheeks. He angrily wiped them away.

She couldn't breathe with anxiety.

Still staring into the smoldering embers, duFont continued. "Something has happened...to me. I cannot rationally explain. Something which must keep me from you...for a long time...perhaps forever."

"Oh, no!" With a cry, Antoinette started to get up.

He motioned her to sit down again and she slowly sank back into her chair.

He swallowed hard, a lump in his throat, talking to her with his back to her. "I will always love you. And I will make sure that you will always be cared for, protected, even after I die."

She gasped. "What?"

He turned to face her. "No, I'm not dying, although I must surely look like it." He laughed a low, humorless laugh. "I have contracted a kind of sickness. This sickness is...incurable, I'm afraid. I've gone to the Baths for a cure, but nothing will heal me. It is my soul which is sick." He hung his head and clenched his hands together. Outside the wind had picked up and was rattling the dead leaves on the trees.

He looked up at her with pain-filled eyes, misery showing in every inch of his being. "Please go now, and try to forgive me."

Antoinette sat stiffly in her chair. The look on her face was total confusion, mixed with her own pain. "I love you and forgive you for whatever is troubling you. Just don't send me away. You know that I am good at healing. Let me do something. Please."

Jean slowly shook his head back and forth, denying her words. "I am beyond your remedies. This sickness would kill you, too, if you stayed with me."

"I'm willing to..."

"No!" Jean strode over to her. He took both her hands in his and stood her up to face him. "I command you to stay to away. Only, remember, no matter what you hear about Jean duFont, know that he did love you once." He released her hands and went to the doorway.

"Pierre, make sure this good lady gets home safely. A storm is on its way. I can smell it in the wind." He pushed a large velvet bag into Antoinette's hands. The gold coins inside made a clinking noise as he handed it to her. "You will never want for anything, so long as I am alive."

Then he put her cloak around her shoulders, squeezing them a little as he did, and guided her to the front door, where Pierre was standing, waiting for her. Then he turned and went into his cold library.

Antoinette was too stunned to cry out. Numbly she walked to the wagon and got in.

DuFont watched through the library window as the wagon rolled past the stand of leafless birch trees near the end of the property. He could see the wind blowing Antoinette's cloak wildly, as she sat humbly in the wagon.

Jean ran up the stairs to his dead mother's room after Antoinette had disappeared from view.

***

Catherine kissed duFont lightly, then rolled off his bed. She began putting her clothes on.

"Where are you going, my little seductress?" he asked somewhat surprised. "I've only just arrived."

"I'm going home, of course."

He sat up in bed. "Why? You can live here now."

"But what about Mother?"

DuFont turned a bright shade of red. He didn't want to be reminded of Antoinette.

"It would be wise to keep her from knowing about me, about us, as long as possible. Don't you think so?"

"Yes, yes," mumbled the Baron, turning his head to the wall.

Catherine came around the bed to see his expression, and kissed him on the tip of his nose.

He grabbed her. "Don't stay away too long. I go mad with wanting you."

She pulled her shoulder away from his insistent hands.

A horrible thought entered his mind. "You are not with anyone else, are you?" He reached out, but she was quicker and eluded his grasp.

Catherine took a step backwards from him, the playful look on her face turning to dark fury. She glowered at him.

The nobleman felt his heart sinking.

Then her look softened. The anger disappeared and she smiled a teasing smile. "Would you mind if that were true?" and she laughed a merry laugh.

"I couldn't stand it," said her lover, morosely.

"Well, don't worry yourself for one minute about that, my darling. Now you be a good boy until I get back."

"When will that be?" called duFont behind her.

But Catherine merely stopped at the door of the bedroom to blow him a kiss and in an instant was gone.

Jean lay back against his pillows. "She is maddening, a fever in my soul. I can never get enough of her." He closed his eyes wearily, putting his arm over his eyes as though to ward off a blow

CATHERINE

Part 8

Catherine sat in her corner of her mother's cabin, sulking.

Antoinette spoke again. "No daughter of mine is going to join that lewd gang of actors, gypsies and acrobats. You know what they say about the women who join them?" Antoinette put her hands on her hips. "I absolutely refuse to let yourself be compromised like that."

Red streaks tinged Catherine's cheeks. She opened her mouth to speak, but thought better of it, and quickly closed it again. She took several deep breaths to regain control. She closed her eyes for a moment. Then she opened them, stood up and faced her mother. Quietly she said, "I'm fifteen now. I am old enough to do as I want."

Antoinette replied, "You're a woman now, that's true. But women are not allowed to do what they want. You'll understand that when you're older."

But Catherine just flung her head back, and pouted some more. "Michel is going to teach me things." The memory of the swarthy, curly-haired actor flitted through her mind. She pulled on a strand of her hair and tickled her lips with it.

Antoinette had lost control of her daughter and she wasn't sure what to do about it. "I have let you get your way before. But now you must understand that joining a traveling acting troupe is a poor idea. She changed the subject. "Supper is ready, my darling. Let's eat before it cools off."

Catherine shook her head. "No, you eat without me. I'm going to take a little walk down by the river."

Later that evening, after Antoinette had fallen asleep, Catherine tip-toed around their one-room cottage. She collected her clothes. She found a few coins that she tied into the corner of her shawl. With one last look around, Catherine departed her family home.

"Michel," she whispered to herself. She hurried through the night to meet him.

***

Months went by. Late one night Catherine pounded on duFont's bolted front door. Perspiration dripped down her sides from running. Even though it was midnight, the air was very hot. "I wish a cool breeze would blow in from the Moselle," and she wiped her sweaty forehead.

The memory of the fight was fresh in her mind. "Michel was strong but the other man was faster. The sharp blade went in under Michel's ribs and then he lay bleeding on the ground." Catherine had stared at the fallen body, like a puppet with its strings cut, and at the widening pool of blood around him. "The fool. He didn't have to fight over me. They could have shared me. Now neither can have me." Catherine straightened her shoulders. She pulled her shawl tight around her, clutching at the material, wiping her eyes with a corner. "He made me laugh. And he adored me. But not anymore."

The old crone, Therese, from the troupe had encouraged Catherine. "I think you better leave before the authorities get here. With all the talk that's going on, there's no telling what might happen to you."

"You're trying to help but I hate being scolded." Catherine gathered up her few belongings from Michel's wagon. It had been only six months since she left her Mother, but she had learned a great deal."

Michel was older, smart and quick. Not only had he taught her to act, but her lover discovered Catherine had a natural flair for dancing. She liked the wild gypsy tunes, but her favorite was slow and sensuous music. She could draw men's attention by her undulating movements, looking directly into their faces with her hypnotic eyes.

Performing was not all that Michel taught me. In the moonlight she smiled, remembering how Michel instructed her how to bump into prosperous gentlemen, innocently brushing an arm with her breast or pressing her pelvis against a leg to distract. Then, with a quick flick of her fingers, lightly removing his valuables. With a deep breath, drawing attention away from her hands, she would murmur, "So sorry. Please excuse my clumsiness."

Usually the gentleman would stop for a moment, hoping she would be clumsy again, this time a little longer. She laughed. *They knew what I was doing, but didn't mind losing a little money in exchange for my touch.*

Catherine shook her head at the folly of men. *Michel was a wonderful teacher, but now he's dead, lying in a pool of blood in a dusty street.*

The front door opened suddenly. It was Pierre, Jean's manservant. He peered into the darkness, and, seeing who it was, scowled at her.

Catherine ducked inside, under his arm, and took off her cloak. She handed him the bundle of her belongings.

"Master has gone to bed," he informed her grumpily. He disliked being awakened almost as much as he hated Catherine. He instinctively knew she would bring trouble to the household.

"That's fine, Pierre. I'll find his room," and she ran up the stairs before he could object.

DuFont's bedroom door was ajar. The light from a single candle flickering and inviting. She looked in.

He was staring into the silvered mirror at his dressing table, his chin propped on his hands. He glanced up at her like a man awakening from a long and unpleasant dream. "Catherine! My sweet!" He jumped up and ran over to her. He touched her face, her bare shoulder. He ran his hand through her long, damp hair. He bent over her and kissed her long and lovingly on the mouth. A sweet scent reminiscent of oranges rose from her body. He held her desperately and so tightly that Catherine began to squirm.

"I was afraid I would never see you again," Jean whispered in her ear. "Your mother wrote and told me you had run away. Where have you been?"

"I joined a traveling acting troupe," said Catherine, defiance glittering in her eyes.

Jean gasped. "Those thieves and scoundrels have a bad reputation. You have been with them?"

"The villagers love us," she said defensively. "And it's fun." Catherine walked over to the washbasin and poured some fresh water into it from the jug.

Jean bit his lips. It was dangerous to get Catherine angry. She was too unpredictable. "I'm glad to see you again," he said, sitting down, watching her. "But why have you come so unexpectedly? No, don't tell me. I'm afraid of what you might say."

She slowly took off her clothes, dirty from the traveling she had done in the last week. "I must smell like a goat."

"All I smell is your own delicious scent," replied Jean, watching her strip. His body began to heat up.

She smiled at him and began washing herself slowly and sensuously with a soft cloth.

While she cleansed her body, Jean swallowed hard, trying to control himself. DuFont could feel the serpent again. "You are so beautiful," he hoarsely whispered.

After she dried herself, she brushed some of the traveling dust from her hair. "I'll wash my hair tomorrow. I'm too tired now." Droplets of water gleamed on her nude body in the candlelight as she walked over to the older man. She stroked his smooth chest, kissed the soft part at his throat.

"I have no power—or will— to resist you." He lay her down on the soft carpet on the floor of his room. Her body seemed to dissolve into his, and time disappeared in her arms.

CATHERINE

Part 9

Jean awoke to a beautiful morning. Summer in all its glory shone through the window. The first roses were coming into bloom in his garden. He pushed the lace curtains aside so he could see. "It must be quite late. People are walking to Mass on the main road." He heard a little yawn behind him.

Catherine was awake and looking at him with eyes that revealed nothing. A half smile played on her pink lips. "My darling, I am famished. Do you plan on starving me as well as keeping me a prisoner here?"

DuFont smiled at her joking. "I am glad to see you feel so well this morning." He began kissing her fingers. "I was afraid to look at you. I thought perhaps you were just a dream that made its way into my room last night like a spirit."

Catherine began stretching like a cat, making little moaning sounds as she did. "I feel terrifically well. I feel good enough to be two people!" And she laughed a melodic laugh.

He smiled a broad smile, relaxing a bit.

"When I first arrived, you looked like you were three steps from the grave. I am glad to see you looking like your old handsome self." She stroked his face, letting her fingers linger, then slid them down his neck, his chest, until they stopped just above his navel.

Jean's face lit up. He cupped his hands around her face, and drinking in the words, then pulled her to him.

The hunger of his touch made Catherine wince. "Don't...force me...to love you. When you do that, it is like trapping a wild bird. I want to fly away when you touch me like that." She pushed his hands away.

"I'm sorry, my sweet Catherine, my love. You don't understand. I don't intend to be forceful with you. You mean so much to me, I get afraid."

"Afraid of what?" asked Catherine, slipping on Jean's dressing gown and rolling up the sleeves.

"Of losing you."

"How can you lose what you don't have?"

His face darkened. His formerly cheerful mood disappeared.

"My darling, I am so sorry. I must be irritable from hunger." She slipped over to him and put her arms tenderly around him and kissed him deeply, rubbing her breasts against him, moving her pelvis next to his leg.

He melted as the snake coiled. Catherine relaxed and kissed him quickly on the ear. "Let us find something to eat. Then we can attend the second Mass."

Jean started. "What are you talking about? Going to Church? Except for Holy Days, I have hardly been to Church in years since my Mother died and then I was with your mother." He found it difficult to believe that Catherine had ever been inside a church.

"Come on, hurry," she urged him.

In a daze Jean allowed himself to eat, then dress for Church. The spell was only broken when Pierre stopped him at the door to inquire when they would be home. "After church," said Jean.

Pierre's eyes narrowed. "But, sir, you cannot take her..."

"Silence!" ordered Jean, and taking Catherine's arm, they walked to Church.

The bells in the steeple began to ring.

"Why do they sound ominous?" In the warm morning he felt rivulets of sweat drip from under his arms.

Catherine on the other hand seemed cheerful and energetic, almost giggling under her breath. "Hurry up, Jean, or we will be late!" She tugged at his arm.

As they walked up the brick walkway to the Church entrance, Jean felt the blood rush from his head. Vertigo came in waves. *Why am I afraid? What am I sensing? Is it the villagers who will stare at us and gossip? Or something else?*

Catherine felt him wavering and squeezed his hand. "I am here beside you." She smiled at him.

Jean's head cleared. "I am being ridiculous. Sometimes I feel like I am young enough to be Catherine's child, rather than old enough to be her father." He looked at her, her dark silky hair blowing in the morning breeze.

A shadow played around her mouth as if she were resisting laughing. Her heavy lids with their luxuriant lashes were veiled.

As they approached the front door of the Church, several townspeople turned to stare at them, shocked looks spreading across their faces. "It is the Magistrate, arm-in-arm with that wench!"

"How could she be so brazen as to show her face here?" One of the women slipped inside to spread the malicious news. Within seconds the church was buzzing with chatter.

As Baron DuFont and Catherine stepped inside, a silence louder than any voice followed them. Genuflecting to the altar, they walked to the special seats reserved for his noble family.

Some of the parishioners stared in open disbelief or frank curiosity. Some stood to get a better look.

Jean felt his face become hot, being the object of so much controversy. "Sit down, Catherine."

She sat demurely, a smile playing around her cherry lips.

What is her game? Jean felt a fear. *I wonder if Adam felt this way after eating the forbidden apple.* An urge rose to hide himself from the terrible face of an angry God.

The ritual of the Mass began, and little by little duFont's face returned to its normal color. His breathing deepened and he relaxed a little, watching the priest and the altar boys as they participated in the liturgy.

Then came time for the Communion. Jean and Catherine knelt at the rail before the Holy Father.

There was a boyish, innocent look to the priest that made his thin face glow.

"He is so young. It is a sign of old age when authority figures seem like children." DuFont sighed and rearranged his stiff knees.

Catherine kept her head down like a saintly schoolgirl as the tall priest approached them. Then she looked up and gazed directly into Father Montremarte's face.

Jean could not believe the sudden transformation of the holy man.

"It is you!" The Priest seemed to forget himself for a moment, as he stared adoringly at Catherine.

She smiled, as one greets an old lover, "It is I, Father," then opened her mouth sensuously to receive the sacrament.

The priest's face blanched whiter than his robes. "Merciful God in Heaven, forgive me."

The buzzing began again as the villagers watched and heard the exchange.

DuFont turned his head and retched violently on the flagstone floor.

"Monsieur Magistrate, you are ill." The Priest immediately gained his composure. "Come, let me help you." He held duFont's arm, assisting him to his feet.

Catherine made a move to come closer.

"Stay where you are, Mademoiselle," ordered the Priest.

Pale and shaken, Jean turned his head and said to Catherine, "Go home. I'll be there shortly."

Catherine regally strode out of the Church, holding up her long dress so she wouldn't trip on it, ignoring the horrified looks of the parishioners.

Father Montremarte helped duFont past the altar and into the anteroom, where he often received visitors. "Please Monsieur, help yourself to some wine. I will be back after I finish the Mass." The priest handed him a towel. With more control than he felt, the priest went back to finish the Communion and Mass. The altar boys had cleaned up the mess. Head held high, the priest silenced the murmuring by raising his hand and offering a prayer of thanksgiving.

When the villagers had filed out and he had said good-bye to the last of them, the priest rejoined duFont and sat next to him. "I am glad to see that you are looking better."

"Father, I am terribly sorry that I disrupted your Mass," said Jean, rising to his feet, his hands turned up in apology.

"There is nothing to be sorry for," the Priest replied as he motioned for his esteemed guest to sit down. "I am honored, Monsieur Magistrate, for you to take time from your many duties and obligations, to pay homage to God."

"It was not my idea to attend Church today, but Catherine's. Damn her! Pardon me, Father."

The priest sat with his hands folded tightly in his lap.

Burning jealousy filled Jean. Trying to regain his composure, but with a voice that shook, he asked, "You must tell me under what circumstance you know her."

The Priest quickly made the sign of the Cross. "God forgive me," he mumbled. Memories of Catherine flooded through his mind. "I met her several years ago, before I joined the priesthood. It was a balmy spring night. The full moon was just rising. It had drawn me to the river, where I liked to walk and think." He fingered the material of his robe. "That night as I strolled, feeling the night breezes, it seemed that the moon followed me along the winding water's path. That's when I saw her on the soft new grass along the river's edge." He licked his dry lips.

"She was lying on her back, staring up at the tangerine-colored moon, her arms behind her, supporting her head. She turned ever so quietly when she heard my footsteps. Her eyes sparkled in the moon-light."

DuFont repositioned himself in his chair, growing ever more un-comfortable, and cleared his throat.

"'Oh, mademoiselle, I beg your pardon,' I said. 'I did not mean to disturb you.'" Jacques Montremarte had forgotten the Magistrate and was lost in his memories. "She raised herself up on one elbow and said, 'Come over here and sit by me. We will share the moon together.'"

"Almost without my will, I walked over to her, as if in a dream. I sat next to her, looking into her face by the pale light. She reached over and lightly stroked my cheek."

A hot-cold shiver raced down the priest's body, desire awakening at the memory. "I touched her in return. My hands found skin softer than a baby's, warm in the cool evening. Then I drew away." He sat up very straight, his hands clenching and unclenching.

"'Don't you like touching me?' the dreamy vision asked me. 'I like your touch. It is so...manly, so strong.' She snuggled up against me, a young, wild thing against my chest." Father Montremarte stopped his reverie suddenly and looked at duFont. "I cannot continue. I am so ashamed."

DuFont's jaw tightened noticeably. "You must tell me what you know. I give you my solemn word that I will not disclose this to any-one."

The priest studied the Baron's eyes, satisfied by what he saw. "I met Catherine many times in that same secluded spot by the river, always at night. It was as if she was a river sprite, emerging from the cool water to fulfill my manhood, which would soon be locked away from womanly embraces forever. We were lovers, even before I knew her name."

DuFont gasped.

Father Montremarte became dismayed again, seeing the pained look on the face of the older man. "Do you wish to confess something to me?"

"Yes," said duFont, then hesitated.

"What people tell me from the depths of their soul is a secret only known to me—and God."

"She is my mistress."

The Priest closed his eyes wearily. "God have mercy on us both. I will pray for both of us, good and honored Sir," he said abruptly.

"What do you mean?" asked Jean.

Montremarte wanted to change the subject, hoping to avoid this topic, painful to them both. He looked unseeingly at the wall in front of him. "I believe she enchants the souls of men." He stopped and looked down at the sacred loop of cloth around his neck, played with the fringe for a moment. "I venture to say that someday she will find herself in deadly trouble."

"What..." wheezed duFont, "are you talking about?"

"I can help you, but not if you continue to be with her. If you want to break off the relationship, come to me and we will perform special exorcism rites."

"Exorcism? She is no devil," returned Jean vehemently.

"I will pray," the priest continued, "hoping that someday you will seek me out for help from our Divine Lord. I need to visit some of my ailing parishioners. If you will excuse my rudeness, I must go now."

Father Montremarte abruptly stood up to go, but the nobleman rose also and gripped his arm.

"She must be protected at all costs. Do you understand?" Jean's eyes, flashing with anger, glared into the priest's.

"If you mean, will I notify the Inquisitioner, the answer is no. I will not turn her over to that Authority. Perhaps I will be damned that I do not." He crossed himself slowly, still savoring his tainted memories.

Baron DuFont reached into his purse and drew out several coins. He held them in his hand. "This is for the poor and for you to continue your blessed work." The Priest opened his hand and Jean dropped them into his palm.

Holding tightly to the valuables, and with a determined step, the priest walked out of the anteroom. When he closed the door, he leaned against it, shaken from the conversation. He walked outside, and down the dusty road. Young Father Montremarte finished his narrative, for himself. *For almost a month, I met Catherine on the banks of the Moselle, and we made love each time. It was a fantasy out of every young man's desires. Then one evening I went to our meeting place, but she did not come. Catherine disappeared from my life as suddenly as she had appeared. Until today, when she stepped to the rail to receive the Sacrament. Why did she come? Did she hope to shame me? What is her game?* All questions for which he had no answers. He stumbled along like a blind man, grateful he had sick parishioners to see that day.

DuFont dragged himself slowly from the Church. "How could she have humiliated me like that? At least the Inquisitor will not be notified. I could not help her then."

Although the sun was shining and the birds were warming themselves in its rays, Jean felt cold, slumped over like a very old man. As he walked through the street of Quimont, he imagined the townspeople peering at him around their doors. "I have been a solitary man, hiding my private life. That was my choice. Now I will be forced into complete seclusion." He thought about what the priest had told him. "I wonder what other secrets she has that I don't know about. The more I know her, the less I understand."

A pain tugged at Jean's chest. "I love her. Perhaps that is dreadfully wrong, as the priest said. Yet I would do anything, give up anything to be with her." He shuddered when he remembered Antoinette and pushed the thoughts of that good woman out of his mind.

"Catherine may not love me the way I do her, but I don't care! I'll take whatever she gives me." His body, which seemed to have aged greatly that day, sagged even more. He staggered up the driveway and, with effort, climbed the steps to his front door.

Catherine was waiting for him there. "My dear Jean, you do not look well." She seemed contrite and gently helped him take off his cloak. Taking his hands in hers, she tried warming them. "Come, let me care for you."

Allowing himself to be taken upstairs, duFont felt empty. *I have no emotion left, no anger, no jealousy, just a void.* He let Catherine undress him and put him to bed, tending to him gently. He looked into her face, but it was unreadable as usual.

She wordlessly gave him a concoction to swallow, rinsed down with some sweet well water, and after a few minutes, she gave him a cup of warm herbal tea. He fell deeply asleep.

It was late when he awoke. Catherine was lying beside him, her eyes glowing in the dark.

"I feel almost young again." The awful events of the day had melted away. He touched her cheek lovingly.

She gave a cry of relief. "I was afraid," she said simply, "for the first time in my life."

He put his arm around her, gently caressing her cheek with his other hand. "You are safe from any danger."

She sighed deeply, relaxing into his arms, stroking his chest, thighs, and kissing him over and over.

"Do you love me after all?" he murmured.

"I don't know," she said slowly. "When you looked so terrible at church, and then again at the front door, I felt small and cold. I wanted to make sure that you would stay well and whole. I need you to be strong." She buried her head against his chest.

"You do love me," he affirmed quietly.

Catherine slid out of his grasp and walked to the window and looked out. There was a sliver of a moon and her naked body was silhouetted in its cold glow. "I have never pretended to be anything but what I am. I'm not sure what that is exactly. I know that I am different from other women. Sometimes I think I act more like a man. And I know that I have a ...power... It talks to me, and I can do whatever I want. I don't think I am capable of love. I want to, and my heart is dead somehow." She turned around and walked back, rubbing the wooden bedpost with her hand. "I promise you one thing. I will do what I can to keep you healthy and strong." She lapsed into silence, reaching for him.

Jean gently took her hand. "You and I are entwined forever. I will never stop loving you."

She lovingly bit the fleshy part of his palm. An electric surge of energy raced through his body, making him feel like a young man again. The events of the day were erased as though they never occurred. Venom of unholy passion dripped into his heart, poisoning the goodness that had once been there.

Several weeks later two men called on the Baron Jean duFont on official business. Monsieur le Magistrate invited them into his library. The impressive room, surrounded by his leather-bound books on ancient wooden shelves, exuded a sense of stability and power. The officials were duly impressed.

"We are inquiring about the death of a man named Michel Lamont. We were told that a dancing girl named Catherine was somehow involved with him and might know about his unfortunate, untimely demise." The man looked around with frank envy at the luxurious surroundings.

The Sheriff of Roubaix spoke directly to duFont. "Let me tell you bluntly. The woman Catherine is suspect in his death if the story I heard about her is true. A certain individual knows about Michel Lamont and Catherine, and told us that this young girl is a sorceress, a witch. She may have used black magic to inspire the fight, leading to Lamont's death." The Sheriff observed the nobleman's countenance.

Catherine's lover swallowed, willing himself to relax, so as to appear unconcerned. "Gentlemen, I am sure there is a grave mistake. I know Catherine of Quimont intimately. Very well, I mean," he corrected himself. "I have known her mother for years and I am their Protector. Two more god-fearing people you could not find." He looked to see if they believed what he was saying. He continued. "There can be no truth to this allegation and it could only be made by someone who is jealous of Catherine's beauty, talent, and intelligence. Perhaps a jilted lover?"

The two men exchanged meaningful glances.

"Furthermore," he continued, "Catherine is overcome with grief. The doctor has advised a long rest in this quiet countryside to still her delicate nerves over the tragic death of her young man. They were betrothed to be married, I believe."

"We were informed by a woman named Maxine that Catherine had been involved with this Lamont and she went missing after his murder. When we questioned some others from the troupe, we were told that Maxine, not Catherine, was due to marry Michel."

Jean wiped the sweat from his face. "A warm day."

"Yes it is," the Sheriff agreed.

"Would you care for something cool to drink?"

"No, thank you," then he continued. "As far as we are concerned, none of those gypsies can be trusted. They lie to everyone." He sighed. "It is probably as you say. A jilted lover wanting revenge. Thank you, my lord, for your help in this matter." They stood up.

"It is my duty to the King."

Jean left the room and came back with a bag heavy with silver. He handed it to the Sheriff of Roubaix. "This is for your time and trouble. I am deeply sorry that you were sent on a fool's errand by some resentful vixen. I know how women can be when infatuated with another woman's man." He laughed for what he hoped would pass for lightheartedness. He led them to the front door, opened it, and stood aside to let them pass. "Are you staying at the Triple Cross Inn here in town?" he asked them.

"Why, yes we are," the official replied.

"Make sure to tell the owner there that you are guests of the Baron DuFont and I will pay for your rooms and food."

"That is most gracious of you," said the sheriff, smirking. Normally such courtesies were not extended to men of their position. "Either the Magistrate is very generous or very guilty," he whispered to his associate. A large haunch of venison had been roasting at the hearth when they left the Inn that morning, and he salivated, thinking what a delicious dinner he could get tonight. "I will be more than willing to accept your fine offer, Monsieur." He licked his lips. *Wine, too*, he thought. *I'll have the finest wine they offer.*

He bowed to duFont, as did his companion, and they left.

The Sheriff contemplated the interview as they walked back to town. "Perhaps I am mistaken," the official mused to his colleague. "The Baron did not seem nervous. I wonder what this Catherine looks like. A beauty I hear. The Magistrate is probably not guilty, just protecting his own interests, I venture to say." Getting hungry, he urged his companion to walk a little faster.

Jean closed the large oaken front door, leaning against it, feeling weak. *I have lied to officials of the King.* Conflicting thoughts rushed through his mind. *Yet, I couldn't let the Inquisitioner's office get their hands on Catherine. She must be more careful, if she wants to avoid a fiery ordeal.*

CATHERINE

Part 10

Catherine was watching through the small upstairs window when the caravan rolled past the estate into town that summer. *Therese has come back for me!* The early morning sun shone on the painted wagons, although the colors were faded.

The traveling players had arrived at Quimont. The villagers were excited. The acrobats, jugglers, and minstrels relieved the monotonous drudgery of their tedious, uninspiring lives. They could go to the farces and laugh at the antics performed there. But the merchants and innkeepers welcomed the players as much as farmers welcomed locusts. "There will be fights and picking pockets, stealing silver and chickens, and general havoc," they complained to each other.

Catherine remembered old Therese's clever words. "The prettiest girls must always sit in the front of the wagons when we arrive. That way the men can see them, and will come to spend money to see them."

Catherine's heart beat fast. It had been months since she left the troupe, after the fight. She thought about Michel, handsome, virile Michel. *His body is rotting in a grave in Roubaix, she thought. What a waste. Men could be such fools over a woman, especially when there is so much of this woman to go around.* Catherine hurried to get dressed.

Downstairs in his library, Jean was trying to help two local farmers who were squabbling over property lines. Out of the corner of his eye, Jean saw a flash of color. He glanced out the open window. "Catherine! Where are you going?"

As the two men argued, Jean watched Catherine running down the dusty road, heading towards the south end of Quimont. As he watched her disappear, he noticed he was holding his breath. In a sharp exhale, he turned back to complete the business at hand, powerless to stop the young woman.

The wagons had pulled up next to a small stand of trees, close to the Moselle River. The horses pranced with impatience, longing to taste the young, tender grass, while the men unbridled them.

Women were pulling out cooking utensils and pans, while children foraged by the trees, looking for fallen wood for the campfires. They would set up temporary wooden stages in the center of Quimont later. Now they just needed to get unpacked.

"Therese!" There was a mixed reaction when Catherine ran into their midst. Her face was red from exertion, her long black hair flying wildly behind her.

Men went to greet her, hugging her in turns. "Walk with me to Therese's wagon," she insisted, and many complied.

The women did not turn around, but continued their chores, ignoring her. One woman in particular had a very tight jaw when she spied Catherine walking through the encampment.

That witch! thought Maxine. She burned with hatred. Maxine had been in love with Michel and she hoped he might have loved her, too. Michel was a faithful lover and a good provider for almost a year. *For a while there was talk we might get married. But all that changed when he met HER!*

Maxine remembered the fateful day that Catherine had come to see a performance in Quimont. Michel had been acting in a play on Virtue that fateful afternoon. Catherine had watched and had followed him back to Maxine's and his wagon after he had finished and introduced herself. Maxine could remember the words spoken, as she listened from inside.

"I want to learn to do that," Catherine said in her low, husky voice.

"What is that, young one?" replied the attractive actor.

"I am not young!" said Catherine, fiercely. "And I want to be on stage, to act. Will you show me how?"

"Get some of your belongings together. We leave Quimont the end of the week. You can travel with me and I will teach you... everything," he finished meaningfully.

Michel gave me away to the Spaniard, Jose, and took Catherine into our wagon. Maxine could feel her rage increase as she mused over the past. *He should have stayed with me! He would still be alive, instead of dying over that whore!* She put a pan of water on the fire, as red and hot as her face.

The white-haired old crone cried out when she saw Catherine. Wiping her soiled hands on the front of her dress, Therese strode over and hugged Catherine like a long lost daughter. "Catherine, my child. I have missed you!" The undisputed leader of the troupe welcomed the girl.

Catherine smiled at her and hugged her in return. *Therese might be old, but she can help me. After all, she is the leader*, she thought. "I have longed to be part of all this again," she said to Therese. She cast her eyes down in homage before the matriarch.

"Look at me," commanded the ancient woman. Therese scrutinized her and was satisfied with what she saw. "You have done well and are cared for, I can see." Then she asked loud enough for everyone to hear, "Are you coming back? I have missed you."

"Yes," said Catherine. "That is, if you will let me," she continued coquettishly.

"Of course. The past is past. We go on."

Catherine smiled a look of gratitude at Therese. "I missed you, too."

"Hah!" said the old woman, pretending to disbelieve her. "It will be good to have you here again. You can help with my aches and pains. My joints bother me now that you weren't here to help with your unguents and remedies."

"I will be honored to help you as before."

"That is not the only misery I have witnessed. The men greatly pined for you. Ha, Ha, Ha!" Therese cackled at her own joke. Then she lowered her voice, whispering conspiratorially. "Beware of sharp-clawed cats, though. They will draw blood if you give them half a reason. Especially Maxine. She will never forgive you, I think. Leave her to me."

They walked arm-in-arm around the camp, the old woman gossiping about the towns they had visited, the feuds that had been resolved, the coinage that had been garnered. Then she pushed Catherine ahead. "Go now and help with the chores." And she gave Catherine's voluptuous bottom a swift pat.

Maxine had watched the two women as they walked and talked. Her heart throbbed wildly, one hand tightly holding a large cutting knife. *She had better take care,* Maxine thought, *if she wants to stay attractive!* To assuage her anger, Maxine began to cut up a newly-dead chicken for stew. The blade of the cleaver rang out for all to hear, loudly hitting the wooden cutting board.

* * *

Jean watched the sun setting in the west, casting purple shadows across the sky. The farmers had left hours ago, the disagreement resolved, due to his impartial and tactful ways.

"Would you care to eat now, my Lord?" asked Pierre, standing at the library door.

"Where has Catherine gone?"

"She has gone to the camp of the traveling performers, Sir," he replied disdainfully.

DuFont's face contorted. "When will she return?"

"I hope she never returns!" declared the servant vehemently.

"Pierre, how can you say that?"

"She only brings you misery and unhappiness."

"No, Pierre, you're wrong. I love her."

"As you say, Sir."

The Baron let the subject go. "I'm not hungry just now. Perhaps later." He turned back to the window. "Bring me a bottle of wine and a glass instead."

Pierre bowed and returned to the kitchen. *How I detest that woman! She brings sorrow to this house. If only I could protect him from her.* He told the cook, "Master will not be eating tonight. Prepare some broth for the morning. He will probably have a headache then." He grimaced.

A stab of jealousy pricked Jean's heart. *So the gypsies have returned to Quimont. Will she leave with them again? What possesses her?* he wondered. *Could it be that she truly loves to perform and dance? Or does another man entice her away from my safe and warm house?* He rashly flung one of his valuable law books across the room, its leather binding ripping apart, pages flying.

Since she came into my life, I discovered feelings I never knew before, a profound hunger that will not be satisfied elsewhere. He picked up the torn volume, putting the pages back tenderly. *And other darker emotions.*

Pierre returned with the wine.

"Thank you, my friend," he said warmly. The servant left.

What if I went looking for her? No, she would only despise my possessiveness. I must wait for her return of her own accord.

He poured some wine into the glass. It will numb the pain and help me sleep a little. The deadly serpent slithered deeper into his vital organs. Had Catherine been romantically involved with Michel Lamont? Did she love him? Had she...?

DuFont didn't want to think anymore. Thinking only brought pain. He gulped down some more wine. *When will she return back to me?* He gulped the rest down in a single swallow. The old familiar heat warmed his throat, and he poured another. Jean's thoughts continued to torment him until he lost consciousness.

***

Almost two years had passed since Catherine had left duFont and Quimont.

A man with a pock-marked face from the troupe peeked in the back of her wagon. "Hello, Catherine," he said shyly.

"Francois! Will there be a big crowd today?" she asked the man who was both crier for the theatrical events and part-time actor.

"Oui, many people asked me where the plays would be held," replied Francois. "The peasants are in a cheerful mood. Crops are growing well; their masters treat them to the festival of Midsummer's Eve. Noblemen have escaped the confinement of their wives and have come for excitement here in Bordeaux."

"I can feel it. I am excited, too."

He glanced at her costume. "Why are you dressed in your costume so early? It is hours yet until you perform." He gazed admiringly at the red velvet vest over a low-cut, soft white blouse, tightly laced around her full breasts and cinched at her narrow waist. Catherine's womanly hips flared out generously and her red velvet skirt hung almost to her bare feet.

"I've decided to walk through Bordeaux. I'm restless; the play can begin on the streets."

Francois, puzzled, wrinkled up his face. "With your stage makeup, too?" Her makeup was heavily exaggerated, rich in color and design.

"Of course. That is part of my character." She flounced and her breasts jiggled.

He smiled longingly at her.

It is too bad he had the pox when he was a child. It left his face badly scarred. But scars don't show up too much in the dark, Catherine thought. She kissed his disfigured face in response.

Francois felt a warmth radiate through his body. "Other women hate me because of my appearance, but you are not like that. Do you love me, just a little?"

"Of course, I love you, Francois," she said brightly and, to show him she meant what she said, hugged him tightly to her.

He could feel her lush body next to his. "You are Catherine, the Goddess," he declared.

"Sweet Francois."

"You are sweet, too, Catherine. I don't understand why people say you are a trouble-maker." He bristled thinking about the nasty things he had heard about her. "Can I see you later?" he asked, looking at the hem of her skirt. Looking into her blue eyes made him dizzy.

"Not today. There are too many sheep just ready for shearing and I only have a limited time," she smiled. "I might even find a wealthy ram who would be willing to exchange his gold coins or jewels for being with me."

"I don't care if you are with other men, so long as you find time for me."

"I will, because you don't try to possess me as so many men want to do."

"Some things are meant to be shared," the man said.

"Want to know what great fun is? A man joins the audience the day after he and I have been intimate. We wink and wave to each other, knowing our little secret." She quivered with excitement.

Francois tingled at her shared confidence.

"If his wife or friends attends the play with him, unaware of our rendezvous, the mystery becomes even more tantalizing."

"What if the wife should find out?"

"She won't," and Catherine shrugged dismissively. "Anyway, I am not trying to steal her husband. It is all in the spirit of pleasure and fun."

"You are perfect for the part you play," said Francois softly.

"I consider that a compliment," she replied, thinking of the character she would display to the audience, Evil's Mistress. "She is more fun to act than Morality or Prudence." Audiences, especially the young men, enjoyed her antics in the morality plays. Catherine got many laughs from the audience with her vast repertoire of facial expressions and broad, comedic body movements. She loved being with the troupe, with all eyes turned towards her when she performed. It was an exhilarating feeling, as though she could command people's lives, if only for a short while.

"When we leave Bordeaux, may I drive your wagon for you?"

"Of course, Francois." She beamed at him until his head began to spin.

Francois whistled a jaunty little tune as he left her wagon.

Catherine left to mingle in the thick crowds. The Midsummer festivities were rowdy, ale and wine being drunk profusely. *I wonder where there are plums ripe for picking. A man won't notice if a coin or two turns up missing. If he does, I will be long gone.* She noticed an elderly gentlemen, his heavy velvet purple doublet bulging. "Pardon me," she said, as she slid herself along his body, smiling flirtatiously, while her swift fingers checked his clothing.

His manhood tingled a little at her touch, something that hadn't occurred in a long time. He reached out to feel her softness, but Catherine had disappeared, along with the pouch of his coins. Later when he tried to pay for wine he would note his loss. "I must have lost my money again," he mumbled absent-mindedly to himself, "somewhere in the dusty street."

Catherine returned to her wagon much later, after her worthwhile and prosperous adventure. She hid her stolen booty inside the wagon. Then she shook the dust out of her long black hair, brushing it until it shone like silk, humming to herself.

An older man called her name from outside. "Catherine!" He sounded urgent.

She stuck her head out of the doorway of the wagon. "What is it, Rene?"

"Oh, there you are," said Rene, relieved at seeing her. "Maxine told me you had gone off somewhere. I didn't believe her, but she was right."

"I am always here on time," she said. "Maxine likes to make trouble for me."

Rene did not want to get in the middle of the two women's rivalry. "It is getting close to performance time and I wanted to make sure you were ready. There will be a lot of people today. Some look positively wealthy." Rene laughed heartily.

Catherine walked to the edge of the step. "Wonderful muscles," she said to him, stroking his strong arms and his bull neck, reddened from many afternoons in the hot sun. She could smell his manly scent, mixed with sweat. "Some say you are past your prime, Rene, but I say you are still quite a catch." She ran her fingers through his black hair, thickly flecked with grey.

Rene threw his head back and laughed again in his thundering voice. He grabbed Catherine from the wagon, set her down and hugged her tightly. "Woman, you excite me as much as if I was a young knave! Therese warns me about you. That one of these fine days I'll lose my heart to you and then all this will be lost. Ha, ha, ha," his voice boomed.

"I don't think Therese has anything to worry about. You have been Therese's man for so many years that no one can remember when you hadn't been."

"True. She doesn't mind sharing me, though. She knows that I am bonded to her, even though we have never wed, nor had children." He tone became more serious. "I owe her my life, Catherine. She took me in when my family died of plague and I had nowhere to go."

"I never knew that."

"No one does. I was a young lad, and she was an older woman, smart in the ways of the world. She taught me this business, so that I would always have a livelihood. Now I manage the traveling group, settle fights, and take care of her. Even though she's old now, I would never leave her." Rene genuinely cared about the old woman he had lived with for so many years. "I must see to it that everyone is tended to in cold weather, sickness, or old age."

"She is lucky to have a man such as you."

"Therese has known many seasons, many men before me. She knows that men, like birds, cannot be caged, or they struggle to be free. She gives me lots of room and I always come back."

"Therese is a wise woman."

"That was why she came back to Quimont to find you. You bring a lot of silver to the company. She is no fool when it comes to money, but it is not just money that interests her. She regards you as her own kin."

"I am fond of her, and you, too."

Rene nodded, a sideways grin on his lips. "I understand you, Catherine, and how I figure in your life. I am merely part of a large circle of admirers. I would be willing to wager you will have your hands full tonight," he said, beginning to joke again.

"I believe that is true," replied Catherine, smiling so that her face dimpled slightly. "There's going to be such a crowd that we all will be busy. What about you?"

"Well, you know what they say. One stallion in a herd can handle all the mares." He threw back his head and laughed loudly again. "The crowd is getting noisy, impatient to begin."

Catherine felt her temperature rise watching the muscular man walk away. "Rene is a joy to be with. He doesn't take anything seriously, including himself. He gives me pleasure, and never interferes with the way I want to live my life." She went back into the wagon to double-check her makeup and costume.

The audience was anxiously and eagerly awaiting the small group of traveling performers. The jugglers, the mimes, the jesters and buffoons came on. Breathlessly the audience watched as the acrobats performed impossible feats.

Finally the uncomplicated, short plays began. Sometimes as many as three or four morality plays and farces were performed in the span of a day. Each of those plays would run once every day for a week or two, depending on how many came to be entertained.

The last play of the day was about Good and Evil. Evil was fighting against Good in the play. Catherine as Evil's Mistress inflamed Evil against Good, rewarding his evil behavior.

When Catherine made her slow, sultry entrance, an adolescent boy in the first row stood up and shouted, "I love you, Mistress of Evil!" He was joined by his fellows, who whistled and stamped their feet. They were hushed by some of the audience, pummeling them with hats or open hands, or loudly yelling, "Quiet!"

During the play, Catherine tried to seduce Good but, unlike real life, she was unsuccessful.

Some of the audience secretly wished that Catherine had been victorious in her seduction. "Good's virtue is not always perfect," one man whispered to his neighbor.

However, according to the play, the Master of Evil was overthrown by Good and died, as Good triumphed at the end of the short play.

Mistress Catherine's final line to the audience was, "I steal off into the unknown, to find another Master, yet more Evil."

After the play was over, the men in the audience went wild. They clapped their hands together, and made lewd, hooting noises. They whistled. The ale and mead they had drunk gave them inebriated forwardness. "Send us the Mistress of Evil. Send us the beauty!" They pounded on the wooden planks of the stage.

Rene said to Francois, "Tell Catherine she will be dancing."

Dancing was Catherine's passion, even more than acting, and she shook with excitement as she readied herself. She added a veil and pieces of jewelry to change her appearance.

Rene strode onto the stage, his powerful presence calming down the mob. "You will get what you have asked for. Catherine will now dance for you."

The mob pressed in closer to the stage to get a better look, the smell of sweaty, unwashed bodies making the air close. Two men, holding a large, brightly painted cloth, walked onstage. Someone began playing a tambourine. Slowly the stagehands let the cloth drop.

With her back to the audience stood Catherine, ribbons in her long black hair, beaded necklaces around her neck. She had exchanged her heavy velvet skirt for one that was soft and light.

With one voice, the audience cried, "Ahhhh." Some threw coins onto the stage.

Drums, a tambourine, and a recorder joined in harmony to her dance.

Catherine moved slowly to the music, twisting her hands like snakes to the side, above her head, and then turning around to face her audience. Her arms and hands moved rhythmically, while her hips and thighs undulated in harmony with them. The movements appeared smooth, as though she had no bones in her body. Her breasts jiggled with the movement, flowing with her body. Her hips motioned to the audience suggestively.

The young man who had made a scene before the play climbed onto the warm boards of the stage. He was reeling from too much wine. "Let me fondle your flowing mountains." He reached out to touch her.

Rene was there first. "Let me dampen your enthusiasm, boy," and he roughly dragged the boy offstage.

The audience applauded the interruption; it made her dance more intriguing.

The Duke of Casale Monterrato, known as Emilio Fialdini, was especially hypnotized by her dance. The weather had turned extremely hot in Venezia and he had desperately taken to the road with his manservant. The middle-aged noble had arrived in Bordeaux during the festivities, and eagerly joined in the entertainment.

He handed out money to the vendors as though coins were mere flowers, gave orders, and drank profusely.

Catherine watched the short, stout man blaze with desire as he watched her dance. *The Duke is generous. His ample stomach tells me that he freely indulges his senses. I wonder how much he might give me for his pleasure.* She danced down the steps of the stage and onto the street, feeling the uneven cobblestones with her bare feet.

Emilio reached out but she eluded his touch. His lust was more than apparent. "I want you very much."

She smiled in answer to his statement.

The life force in the Duke swelled, until he yearned for release, and he felt dizzy. "It is the warm sun, blazing on my head," he reasoned with himself. He smiled back at her with the assurance of a hunter, not knowing that he was instead the prey.

The music grew more rapid and her dance became more frenzied. Perspiration stood out on Catherine's forehead and chin, while rivulets trickled down the cleft between her breasts, until the music and her wild dance ended simultaneously.

Catherine bowed deeply, exposing her cleavage. Then she passed around a basket, collecting money for her dancing. *It grows heavy with coins. I have been a great success today.*

Fialdini stood up, rather unsteadily. The Duke headed for her, weaving a little. "Mademoiselle, one moment."

She finished her collection and turned to him. "Yes, my Lord, do you wish to provide for my future?" She held out the basket to him, in order that he might place large golden coins in it.

He pushed her hand away. "Put away these tokens from peasants. You will accompany me to the Inn where I am in residence at present."

Catherine nodded her head. "My dance is complete. I can go wherever I please." She hurriedly ran to Rene, handed him the basket of coins, then went to her wagon, and grabbed a shawl. She quickly walked back to where the Duke was waiting impatiently. "Here I am, your Highness," she flattered him. She flung the shawl around her, moving her dark mane of luxuriant hair off her shoulders.

The Duke took hold of Catherine's arm, more for his own support, and began walking. He chuckled to himself. *This woman is quite a conquest.* In his drunkenness, the Duke seemed more like an adolescent than a nobleman, in his wine-stained shirt, leering and giggling at her. "You are beautiful beyond measure," he said, his breath reeking of wine and garlic.

"Thank you, my Lord," she replied, looking away for a moment.

She is modest, too, the Duke assumed, not realizing she was merely avoiding his bad breath.

The two of them strolled to the Inn, and went up to his suite of rooms. The suite consisted of Fialdini's large bedchamber, with an adjoining small room for his servant, plus a sitting area furnished with a well-scrubbed wooden table, sideboard and chairs.

Catherine scrutinized the room. *The mattress is goose down. It* will be plump and comfortable after the small, lumpy one in my wagon.

A vase of flowers was set in the middle of the table, along with a bowl brimming with fresh fruit. A decanter of wine with four tankards was set on the sideboard.

"Meals can be taken in the dining room, or up here," he explained suggestively.

"I will be quite comfortable here."

The Duke struggled to remove some of his heavy clothing.

"Here, let me help you," she offered.

"No, just let me watch you for a while," he replied.

Catherine took off her shawl then poured some wine for the two of them. "Would you like some fruit?" He nodded, and she sliced up some apples, removing the core and seeds.

"You are the kind of woman with whom I could be happy," he said, sitting on the bed. "I am glad I undertook this journey."

"I am, too, Sir, and I hope that you will enjoy Bordeaux and all its many pleasures." She walked over and slid a piece of apple into his mouth, brushing his thick lips with her fingers, and smiled broadly.

Dawn's sunlight streamed through the narrow window of the Inn. The Duke lay snoring next to Catherine. Blankets were flung off and hung in disarray around his feet.

Catherine shivered a little in the early morning air. The room was damp, chilled from the breezes that blew in from the coast, as well as from the cold, stony walls.

She stretched her arms and legs, indolent from the wine they had drunk the night before. *Everything is a blur.* The remains of their evening meal was sprinkled across the table in the next room. *I indulged myself greatly, but the Duke is a ferocious eater.* She looked over at his corpulent body. *He's nothing more than an overgrown white slug.*

Catherine sat up, ran her hands through her long, black hair and rubbed her eyes. She slid off the overstuffed mattress, onto the carpet laid over the polished wooden floor. She rubbed the bottom of her feet on its soft surface.

I need to wash last night off me. She began splashing water on her face, arms, and breasts. She poured water into a goblet, and drank some. She sipped a little more, rinsed out her mouth, and spat it into the basin.

Emilio Fialdini is a man who enjoys life to the fullest. Food, wine, and women, and not necessarily in that order. He has a way with horses, too. Thank God he does not wish me to join him on his morning rides. Horses intimidated her and she hated being weak in any manner.

As Catherine sat in the morning sunshine at the dressing table, she reflected on the Duke. *Over the last few days he has become obsessed with me.* She brushed her luxuriant tresses, fastening the thick strands with ivory combs that he had given her. She picked up the looking glass with a tortoise-shell handle to examine the effect, also a present from the generous Duke.

She recalled the night before. The ensuing discussion after dinner had disturbed her greatly.

"My darling, *mi amore,* how beautiful you are," Emilio had said, nuzzling his nose into the nape of her neck, taking out the combs, watching as her hair fell to her waist. Catherine did not respond.

He turned her around. "You frown," he said in a low voice. "Are you displeased with me? With the combs? With anything I have given you?"

Catherine replied in her husky voice. "Honorable Duke, I owe you my obedience and forever am grateful for your warm generosity these last few days. I am pleased and appreciative of all the presents you choose to give to me. I only regret that I have so little to give you in return." She sighed and hung her head to show her respect, the mischievous look in her eyes veiled by her thick eyelashes.

The Duke lifted her chin with her hand and glanced up into her face. He could feel himself become aroused again, as he had been so often since his stay in Bordeaux. "You are indeed the most exciting woman I have ever encountered."

She tried to move her face away.

"I want to give you much more. Perhaps n*ell' autumno,*" he said, lapsing into Italian, "I mean in the autumn," you could come with me to Casale Monterrato and I could establish you permanently as my mistress."

Catherine's eyes gleamed for a moment, thinking of what being Fialdini's mistress might mean to her. *Riches, more clothes than I could possibly wear in a year, jewels, and servants. Emilio Fialdini is a man of great wealth and power. I would be of no trouble to his wife and family. Men of his station take mistresses all the time.*

Then she looked at his fat, hungry face leering at her. "I don't deserve what you promise me," she replied so quietly that he had to bend his ear to her mouth to catch all her words.

Fialdini could hardly believe that this woman, little more than a lowly prostitute, would dare defy his offer. "I have known women like you before and appreciate your talents and charms. Yet you insult me! What a wicked woman you are. You are not in the least worthy of all I lavish on you. I should kick you back into the street where you came from right now!"

Catherine patiently waited for the outburst to end.

"Don't you understand what I am offering you?" he almost shouted at her. His humiliation turned to purple rage that Catherine had not seen before in him.

"Yes, my dear Sir, I do. Perhaps I am only an ignorant village girl," Catherine said quietly, almost modestly. It was an act, like so much she did and said. "But I must be free, to act and dance and…" She paused, registering the angry look on the middle-aged man's face. "Perhaps I have said too much."

Then suddenly, much to her surprise, Emilio dropped to her feet and began weeping, more from wine than emotions.

She let him cry for a few minutes. Then she knelt on the floor beside him. "Don't be sad. I am a cold-hearted woman as anyone can tell you. Perhaps it is unfortunate that you wish more of me than I can give you. Maybe it would be best if you left this town quickly so that you could forget any pain or unpleasantness that has occurred from knowing me."

Fialdini continued to blubber, his face stained with tears. "But you are the last great love of my life. I may not live many years longer. I want to spend them in bliss, with you. You give me great pleasure and I want to cherish you not only as my lover, but care for you like a daughter, too!"

Catherine stood, impatient with the Duke and unable to restrain her disgust any longer. "Get up. You'll catch cold on the floor. I stay with you as long as I will, but no longer. When the troupe leaves, I leave also."

"No, no," cried the Duke, hanging onto her hands, "My darling. *Mi amore, mi impassionati.*"

But Catherine pulled her hands out of his grasp and left his suite abruptly. She walked through the town for a long time, hoping the Duke would calm down. He had fallen asleep again, snoring soundly, when she returned long past midnight.

***

The Duke was sleeping soundly. Catherine put the unpleasant memory of the night before out of her mind. She had not yet dressed for her performance. The day was warm as the sun rose higher. *I will not be expected until later, which gives me time to dress, eat, and walk.* She heard him beginning to stir. *If I can elude Emilio, with his greedy eyes and grasping hands...I feel caged when I'm around him. He wants to totally possess me and I cannot allow that.* She hurried to get into her costume.

The crowds have been good all week and the festivities continue. That means we'll be here in Bordeaux for another week, maybe even two. Today at least I have some time to myself while the Duke is recovering from his drunkenness. I hope he sleeps late into the afternoon and during the performances. How I detest his loud, vulgar comments from the first row! She gave him a hateful glance. His snores deepened.

She grimaced, looking at the rich and powerful man. *I'll make sure that he gives me gifts and money before I leave, to support myself during the winter.*

Catherine glanced around at the Duke's clothing and personal effects. His jewelry and clothing lay scattered on the floor. His gold medallion and chain were cast off as well, the one his Prince Protectorate had given him as a symbol of his ducal office.

The disagreement from the night before kept pushing itself into her awareness. *It will be difficult to get rid of him though. He wants to follow me everywhere I go. I can never allow that!* Catherine shuddered. *Then I must separate from him before the troupe leaves Bordeaux.*

The Duke snorted in his sleep. Catherine pulled her clothes on faster. Quietly she let herself out of the suite. The other guests of the Inn had been up since dawn, enjoying the jovial atmosphere of the summer festival time. Many of them had gone to watch the jugglers, have their fortunes told, shop at the open marketplace or take a swim in a river nearby. Some chicken was left over from dinner the night before, as well as fresh fruit and cold porridge, sitting on the dining room table. Catherine picked up some fruit to eat on the way and set off for her wagon.

The crowds are still thick, as Rene predicted. Good pickings. But Catherine knew she didn't have to pick any pockets while the Duke provided so well for her. She smiled at the men's faces, both old and young, as she undulated past them. Some tendrils of hair hung in curls around her face, unable to be tamed by the ivory combs. Although she had on no face powder or rouge, she looked extravagantly beautiful, her white, silky skin framed by her black mane. Arched eyebrows framed her deep blue eyes; the long lashes lazily curling around them.

Some men recognized her from the plays and dancing, and waved. Catherine waved back, sometimes throwing a little kiss the man's way. *It is more fun to have a hundred minnows nibbling on a hook, than to catch one fat fish,* she smiled to herself.

When she got to the encampment, there was quite a hubbub going on. The wives of several of the town's officials were complaining volubly to Therese and Rene about Catherine's conduct, both onstage and off.

Therese noticed Catherine and motioned to her, while Catherine quickly ducked out of sight.

"That woman Catherine is a disgrace," complained one whiny-voiced woman.

"You need to put her under lock and key," protested another stout woman. "She shouldn't be allowed to prance around. She is dangerous to my sons."

Two officials, who accompanied the women, were also arguing with Rene. "You must remove Catherine from the plays, and keep her locked in her wagon, while the troupe is in Bordeaux."

"What you have heard about Catherine?" Rene insisted. "What has she done that you attempt to take away her livelihood?"

The town's highest official, the mayor, sputtered and stammered to Rene. "Well, I don't know exactly the nature of her crimes, but I understand that her bodily movements are—suggestive—to say the least. Also the young boys are being encouraged to make wild statements." He paused and wiped his face with his linen kerchief. Although the day was still young, the sun was hot and sweat dripped down his beefy face.

Rene cut in. "My dear mayor," he replied soothingly. "Is being beautiful a crime nowadays? Nor can I prevent young men, carried away by their youth, from forgetting that she is simply acting in a play. Play-acting is not real life."

"Yes, yes. I know all that. You don't have to explain plays to me. It's just that, my wife, and some of the women..."

Again Rene interrupted. "Ah, yes. The ladies. They have fragile sensitivities. Perhaps our farces are a bit too immodest for ladies to attend." He patted the mayor on the back as he herded him away from the wagons, while continuing to mollify the mayor's ruffled pride.

A merchant, walking with them, piped up. "Your Honor, many people come from outlying areas, villages, hamlets, even other big towns, to join in the merriment during the carnival. Local wine is purchased, the inns are full, and wares are sold by local artisans, all of which support families in Bordeaux. Life is hard. You will make it even harder by forcing these players to leave Bordeaux, thus discouraging our visitors and their money."

The mayor nodded reluctantly in agreement.

When Rene and the townspeople were out of sight, Therese went to Catherine's wagon, where the young woman waited. "Have you done anything that I should know about?" she queried, her old eyes squinting at her.

Catherine smiled a full, genuine smile for Therese. There wasn't anything that Catherine could sneak by the old woman. "No, Madame, you know everything that I know. Fialdini, the Duke, still ardently pursues me. He's sleeping off the wine from last night. Some of the local boys have been friendly. Just the usual. You know."

"Hmm," said Therese. "Either these wives are more sensitive than most, or you are have hurt them in some personal way. Do you know why they would be upset with you?"

"No. I can't think of anything."

"Are any of these young men their lovers?" The elderly woman was wise in the ways of the world. "One of the fifteen-year-old boys bragged about his making love to an older woman. I wonder if that has something to do with all the fuss? Watch your back carefully. It wouldn't do to find a slender stiletto plunged into it by a jealous woman, now would it?" Although Therese smiled, there was no amusement in her eyes, just concern for Catherine. "You have blossomed into an exceptionally beautiful woman, one that men find very attractive, and that women easily become jealous of—or worse."

Prickles of fear raised the hair on Catherine's head and gave her arms gooseflesh. "I promise you, Therese, that I will be careful."

"Good girl." Therese left to find Rene.

Catherine turned and went into her wagon to apply her heavy make-up. As she sat in front of the warped old piece of silvered bronze, Catherine took stock of the woman she saw reflected there. The jaw and chin were feminine, but firm. Catherine tensed her throat a few times to strengthen the muscles. Her steely blue eyes gazed uncompromisingly back at her, will and power lay within them. She smiled with her full, ripe lips, her cheeks dimpling a little. Her teeth were white and even. She removed the combs that Emilio had given her and let her hair fall. The warm locks brushed her face, and she luxuriated in the feeling of her hair. Then she took a brush and brushed it until it gleamed.

Her red velvet costume was cut daringly low across her bosom. It needs mending. *Soon the holiday will be over and we will move on. Then I can repair it.* She began to apply the thick greasy make-up. This smell has become a part of me, and liberally applied it to her creamy skin. Burnt cork for her eyebrows and eyelashes, and red face paint, which made her cheeks look higher than they were.

She dabbed a scent behind her ears, smelling of orange blossoms, that a previous admirer had given her. *The mayor wants to lock me away to protect his town. Ha! I must be very powerful!* She hummed a little tune, the fear she felt earlier dissolving.

As she left her wagon, she bumped into Rene. He was still chuckling over the visit from the mayor. "There's absolutely nothing to worry about. Just a group of catty wives, worrying about their husbands' and sons' morals—or lack of them," he told her. "It's happened in a hundred towns and villages." He knew from experience. "Just be careful until we leave Bordeaux."

But Catherine wasn't paying attention. Her face was flushed beneath the rouge, and her eyes had a wild, thrilled look to them.

"You have never seemed as desirable as now." He put his arms around her and bent over to kiss her, but she pushed him away.

"Not now, Rene. I've got other fish to catch." She laughed at her own private joke. And before Rene could say another word, she was gone, walking purposefully through the crowd.

A jealous Maxine watched Catherine leave. She smiled grimly to herself. "Be very careful, Catherine." She disappeared into the wagon she shared with the temperamental Spaniard after the death of her lover.

***

The sky was becoming blacker. Thunder could be heard in the distance. The actors walked onto the small, wooden stage. Thrilled, the crowd began applauding noisily. Catherine prepared for her entrance.

Just then the mayor of Bordeaux came striding up. "Stop!" he demanded, interrupting the entertainment.

The audience was astonished, and several boys jumped to their feet, insisting that the mayor let the play finish.

But the mayor was adamant. "I'm here for the woman known as Catherine." His authoritarian voice boomed across the crowd. "She has murdered the Duke of Casale Monterrato!"

Catherine heard the reverberating words of the town's official from her wagon, accusing her of murder. She ran to her wagon, changed out of her costume and wiped off the heavy makeup. She stood there, indecisive and trembling. *I can't believe it. Emilio can't be dead.*

Rene motioned to Therese, who was standing offstage, to go to Catherine's wagon. She understood in a flash the message he was trying to convey.

Then Rene stepped out on the stage to face the irate mayor, taking hold of the man's arm. His grip was firm and helped the town official calm down. "Catherine hasn't been seen today, sir. Perhaps I could talk to the other players, to see if she told anyone where she was headed."

"Talk to them then. I want this woman found and brought to justice. The Duke was a rich, influential man. Rumors will spread and ruin our good reputation."

"Yes, of course," Rene spoke quietly and soothingly. The mayor was noticeably relaxing. "I can't imagine Catherine able to accomplish such a crime, though. She is flirtatious, but not capable of murder, I assure you."

The mayor became agitated again. He was determined to find a culprit and all evidence pointed to Catherine. "She was the last one to see him alive. He was stabbed in the chest with a stiletto, the kind a woman would use. Then robbed of all his valuables. This woman may act flirtatious, but I know a fortune-hunter when I see one, and this woman was obviously after the Duke's money."

When Therese opened the door of Catherine's wagon, she was assailed by the scent of drying flowers and herbs that Catherine had gathered in their travels. The young woman was standing in the middle of the wagon, a traumatized expression on her face.

Therese's eyes were wide with alarm. "You must leave quickly. The mayor is after your neck," Therese told Catherine. "Take my brown horse. When you leave, lead the mare by the bridle until you are well away from here. Then ride to your Protector for all you are worth."

"I didn't do it, Therese. When I left the Duke, he was asleep, but alive." Catherine looked with anguish at the old woman.

"I believe you. But that doesn't matter now. If the mayor thinks you are guilty, then you will be punished. Go back to your Baron. Ask him to take you in again. It is your only chance."

"But I want to stay here, to act, to dance. I am innocent." Catherine's anger surged. "I am innocent!"

"Yes, yes, I believe you are," replied Therese quietly, trying to hush the agitated woman. "But if you stay, I am certain you will die. I can feel it. I knew something bad was going to happen today. Please—leave quickly."

Catherine pulled up a plank, uncovering a small dark opening. She cried out in distress. "The money I hid is gone. Someone took it!"

Therese handed her some coins. "I hope this will be enough to get you home. *Bon chance!"* She gave Catherine a quick hug and left.

Catherine crept out of the wagon, found Therese's saddled horse, and began leading it out of town. Her heart pounded. *This is so unfair. Who would do this to me?* She thought of the Duke. *Who would want to kill him? He wasn't bothering anyone. Maybe it was just a robbery after all, and the thief killed him when he woke up.*

Catherine mounted the brown mare, far away from the wagons and the turmoil. Suddenly Maxine's face flashed through her mind. *It had to be her. That conniving bitch! She's never forgiven me for Michel!* Catherine galloped away into the countryside, seething with dark hatred for the vengeful, jilted woman.

Therese was right. Some cats have very sharp claws, so sharp they can cut a man to pieces. Even a powerful man like the Duke.

Her jawline grew hard. *I've learned my lesson. I will be sure to protect myself from animals like Maxine from now on. Men are fools mostly, or act like ones. They are helpless when their organs dictate to them. But women are powerful. They are patient and devious, and cunning.* Catherine saw her enemy clearly now.

Catherine rode into the night. *In the morning I will have to find something to eat. The horse can forage on grass, but I will need something more substantial.* She and the old horse were tiring and her legs and backside were getting sore. *I've never liked horses, or trusted them either. Therese's elderly brown mare snorted. What if the horse steps into a rut or burrow hole and breaks its leg? What would I do then?*

After the sun had set, she reined the horse to a stop. She dismounted and walked into a thicket of birch trees, and tied the horse to one of them. She was exhausted but remembered to remove the saddle. She laid her head on the tough old leather and attempted sleep.

Now I will not be able to get the money Emilio promised me. Yet she was relieved to be away from him. *Therese is right. Jean will take me back. He must take me back. How far am I from Quimont, anyway?*

She longed to curl up with some strong man right then, who could protect her. *Too bad Rene couldn't make the journey with me. I wonder if I will ever see him or the troupe again?* Catherine fell into an uneasy slumber. It was the first time in ages that she had slept alone.

CATHERINE

Part 11

The next morning Catherine woke, stiff and aching from her long ride the day before. The sun was shining brightly on her face. *It's going to be very hot again today.*

The brown mare was tired and sore, too, and whinnied when she saw Catherine. The horse had been busy eating grass around the tree Catherine had tied it to.

Catherine's stomach rumbled. "It's time to find something for me to eat. Well, Grand'Mere, we have to go on."

The horse snorted in reply.

Catherine attempted to put the saddle on, but it was heavy and awkward, and Grand'Mere kept sidestepping. Finally she backed the mare against the tree, and managed to swing the old leather saddle onto the horse. Holding tight to the cinch, she kicked the horse firmly in the stomach.

Grand'Mere let out her breath and the cinch tightened. *Hah! I am smarter than you think.* She tightened the cinch a few more notches and climbed on the mare, hunger urging her forward.

Hours passed. The day was hot and still, but there was no sign of a village or even a farm.

Catherine felt faint from the heat, lack of water, and hunger. The mare was foaming at the mouth. "We need to find a town soon, old lady."

The sun was high overhead when the road began to widen and show signs of recent use. She passed several dilapidated farms. *I'll turn around and beg a meal from one of those farms if I can't find a village inn.* She suddenly arrived in the small town of Chinon, which consisted of one short dusty street with a few struggling shops and a roadhouse.

Grand'Mere perked up her head when she saw a watering trough in front of the tavern. On wobbly legs, she cantered over and began drinking in great gulps.

Catherine dismounted and tied the reins to a log on the ground while the horse drank. She sat down on the log in a dizzying rush.

A girl came out of the front door of the inn. Her hair hung in greasy strands around her face. Her dress, ragged and strained, was too big for her and was gathered with a cord around her waist. She spotted Catherine and the exhausted horse in the shade.

"Are you a traveler?" she asked, in a nasally, simpering voice.

Catherine ignored her question. "Do you have some food I can buy?"

The girl nodded.

Catherine pointed north. "Am I going in the right direction to get to Quimont?"

The girl nodded again, and wiped her runny nose on her sleeve.

Catherine wrinkled her nose in disgust. "Do you know how long it will take me to get there?"

Without a word, the girl ran back into the tavern.

Catherine shrugged her shoulders in frustration.

The girl returned, pulling an older man by the arm from the dingy building. He was coughing a deep, phlegmy cough. His short nightshirt revealed his spindly legs. The slovenly man scratched his unshaven chin. He was more repulsive than the young woman. He eyed Catherine appreciatively. He wiped his slavering mouth on his arm. "She says you're heading to Quimont."

"Yes, on my way to Lorraine province, where I live."

"Why you be traveling all alone?"

Catherine drew herself up and looked down on the short, scrawny man. "That is no concern of yours," said Catherine. She hated looking at his repulsive countenance, but she needed his help. "I want some traveling food first. How far is it?"

"It's two, maybe three more days. You'll see a crossroads. There should be a stone marker, if the rains haven't washed it away. Ha, ha." He laughed a humorless laugh, which turned into a spasm of coughing. When he was done, he spat a thick, brown stream in the street.

"How far it is to the next town where I can sleep and rest?"

"You should get to Orleans by nightfall, if your horse lasts that long." He looked at Grand'Mere.

"Well, then, if you could fix up some food for me to take with me, I will pay you for your trouble."

The man held his hand up. "No need, mademoiselle. I am amply paid by your beauty." He and the girl went back into the inn.

Catherine shivered with revulsion, then went to the trough and scrubbed the grime of traveling from her face, neck, and arms. The man's daughter came out and handed her a greasy package wrapped in thick brown paper. The girl fed Grand'Mere a bucket of grain which gave the old horse strength.

Catherine thanked the untidy girl, got astride the mare, and trotted off. *I pray the next town will be larger and cleaner.*

The day was still hot, but a cooling breeze had come up. By dusk she and Grand'Mere had arrived in Orleans, bustling with tradesmen and farmers selling their crops. There were two inns and Catherine chose the larger of the two. *I will be less noticeable there.*

The brown horse's head was drooping and exhaustion showed in the animal's shaky, thin legs. Catherine spotted a blacksmith's shop. *I hope Therese forgives me, but I must sell the horse. You wouldn't make the rest of the trip anyway.* The owner paid her a hundred sous for the horse.

An older woman was standing by the door when Catherine walked into the lodge, an innkeeper's wife with years of experience dealing with people. *A gypsy wench, I'm sure,* she thought.

Catherine boldly walked up to her. "I want a room for tonight, possibly tomorrow as well. I need to bathe myself and get fresh clothing."

"Fresh clothing, mademoiselle? Surely you have a trunk with you?"

"No, I have no baggage. It was, uh, stolen from me, yesterday. I have only what is on my back."

"Oh," said the older woman, obviously not believing her for a second.

Catherine confronted her directly. "Is there something about me that you question?" she asked, gazing aggressively into the older woman's eyes.

"Oh, no. Everything is fine," the other woman relented with a shrug. "I have a small room upstairs I can rent to you. There is a bathhouse out back where you can clean up. I will see if I have a dress or two which might fit you."

Catherine nodded agreement.

"That will be twenty sous for the room. We are serving dinner now."

Catherine gave her the coins.

The woman left, muttering loudly.

A young man, possibly a farmer's son, was sitting by himself at one of the long tables, looking at her.

With uncanny accuracy, Catherine could size up a man, even from across a room, to determine if he was interested in her. A man must want to be captured before she could make a conquest. Boys and older men were particularly susceptible to her wiles. She approached his table.

The boy looked up at her, and gulped. His protruding Adam's apple bobbed up and down.

Catherine smiled languorously at him. In her quiet, husky voice, she asked, "Would you mind terribly if a weary traveler shares this table with you?" She gazed directly into his eyes.

The farm boy looked to be about sixteen at most. His clothes, although crudely made, were sturdy and more formal than clothes he wore at his family's farm, but had become too small for his maturing body. Long, unruly hair, tied in back, was coming undone and he pushed it back out of his eyes. He tried to hide the evidence of his growing attraction. "Please sit down," he invited her.

Catherine touched his arm gently. "Thank you for your courtesy, Sir. I am in your debt," she flattered him.

He stood up quickly and knocked over his goblet of wine. He dabbed at the pool of liquid on the table ineffectually.

The other diners, who had been watching, snickered to themselves, watching him making a fool of himself in front of the woman.

He returned his goblet to its upright position and remained standing while Catherine sat down. He was intoxicated, even without wine.

She moved close to him. "Let me help you clean up the wine." When she leaned over, she let her breast brush his arm.

He quivered. In his most adult voice, the boy said to Catherine, "I am called Philipe. I would be honored if you would share your meal with me." His recently maturing voice cracked, and he cleared his throat.

When she nodded, Philipe shouted for the serving girl.

The other guests glanced at each other knowingly. "The boy will be a man before the night is over," one man murmured.

"Order whatever you like. It will be my gift to you. I heard what you said to Madame Le Coeur, about the robbery."

Catherine touched Philipe on the cheek, softly stroking it for a moment. *His blonde whiskers are still scraggly and fuzzy, not yet a man's beard*, she thought. "You are terribly kind. I don't know how I can repay you, but I will think of something." She looked at him with a meaningful glance. "You may call me Catherine."

"Catherine," he repeated. "What a beautiful name." He trembled a little, but picked up her hand and gallantly brought it to his lips and felt a thrill of expectation. *It will be worth spending some of father's cabbage money to pay for her dinner,* the boy thought.

After dinner, the innkeeper and his wife approached their table. Catherine looked up.

The woman was holding several dresses, worn but still usable. "Here. You can have these. If they don't fit, I will look for others."

Her husband was unabashedly staring down the front of Catherine's low-cut dress.

His wife poked him in the ribs with her elbow and he looked away nonchalantly.

Catherine stood up and took the garments from the woman. "Thank you. If you could tell me where my room is...?"

"First door to the left of the stairs."

She excused herself and went upstairs. She looked down and saw Philipe watching her. She nodded to him and went into her room. In a few moments, Philipe followed her into her room, and quietly shut the door, sliding the bolt.

Catherine was lying naked on the lumpy old bed, waiting for him. *I wonder what I can squeeze out of him,* she thought.

***

Philipe insisted on seeing Catherine off the next morning after paying for her room, dinner and a coach as well. After safely tucking her into the conveyance, Philippe held her hand until the coach was ready to leave.

"Good-bye, my love," he said in a sorrowful tone. "I will never forget you."

"Good-bye, Philipe," she replied airily..

As the coach began moving, he ran alongside until it moved far away from him. The coach vanished into the distance in the hot morning sun, and Philipe began to worry. "What will I tell Father when I return?" He had spent all his father's money on Catherine.

Catherine leaned back against the seat. "He's a young boy. He will get over me," she told herself.

The horses hooves clip-clopped as they cantered along the road to Quimont. She looked out at the moving landscape. Insects buzzed around the window.

There was only one other passenger, an old German gentleman, on his way to the border. His clothes must have been fine once, but had seen better days. He was odiferous and Catherine made sure to stay upwind of him.

The monotony of the trip lulled Catherine into a dream-like state. She ceased to notice the old German man, and only waited for meals and rest stops. Villages passed in a blur. *When I get to Jean's I'm going to have Pierre heat up lots of water for me to bathe. Then I'll sleep for days.* She lapsed into her daydreams, fatigued and feeling ill.

She began to recognize the passing scenery. *I am almost home.* Her excitement grew with every passing mile. Then she saw the outskirts of Quimont. The coach passed over the river on a narrow wooden bridge that creaked and groaned with the weight. *I can almost feel Jean's strong arms around me.* The carriage rounded a bend and came to a stop in front of his manor house.

Catherine flung the door open and jumped out, without waiting for the driver to open it for her. She scampered up the steps to the front door, opened the door and ran into Pierre in the hallway. "Pierre, it's so good to see you." She almost hugged him in her excitement.

Pierre, on the other hand, was quite dismayed to see the dusty, travel-worn woman in the hall. "What are you doing back?"

Catherine ignored him. "Where is Jean?" she asked.

"He has gone to settle a dispute in town, and is expected back this evening. He told me he would be having dinner here alone."

"I need to bathe before your master gets home," she told him. "Heat up some water for me now."

Pierre did as he was told, but grumbled as he prepared her bath.

"I'm starving," and she strode into the kitchen, found some fruit, and ate her fill. Then she quickly went out into the garden, picked some roses and arranged them in a vase for Jean.

After she ate, Catherine sprinkled rose petals and dried lavender in the warm water Pierre had heated and luxuriated in the soothing bath. Then she dried herself and went to Madame DuFont's armoire, where she found a beautiful soft nightgown. She put it on, feeling the smooth, soft cloth next to her equally soft body, then she lay down on Jean's bed to wait for her lover. She fell asleep and slept deeply, exhausted from the trip.

It was late when Jean arrived. He looked spent from the day's exertion. The wrinkles around his eyes and mouth were etched deeper than ever. He was dusty from the day and tired.

Pierre went to greet him but didn't mention Jean's guest.

"What do we have to eat, Pierre?" he asked.

"There are baked vegetables from the garden," he said. "We have green beans, summer squash, cabbage, carrots, and peas cooked in butter. There are some cut up tomatoes and they are chilling in the wine cellar. Cook baked some of your favorite bread with dill and grated cheese baked in it."

Jean smacked his lips. "It sounds like a feast for kings, Pierre," he said. "Thank you, my friend." Pierre bowed.

Jean walked into the library where a candle had been lit. There were roses in a vase on the massive desk. "Pierre!" he called.

"Yes, my Lord," said Pierre as he came into the library.

"Thank you for the roses. They are a nice touch."

"You're welcome, Monsieur."

A feeling began to stir in him. "Did you pick these flowers?"

"No, sire." Pierre was truthful to a fault.

"It's Catherine. Who but Catherine would do this?" he shouted wildly. "Where is she? Where is my darling girl?" But before Pierre could reply, Jean was running up the stairs, two at a time, like a young man.

Pierre shook his head in loathing.

Jean dashed into his room, which looked like a vision out of a fairy tale. Catherine had lit candles and they shimmered in the night air. Roses filled the room with their scent and their beauty. But most beautiful of all was the woman lying upon his bed. She woke up, opened her arms to him.

With a cry he flung himself upon her. "My darling, my love." He kissed her everywhere, her mouth, her face, her hands, and her throat. "It is you. You have returned!" He was delirious with happiness.

She kissed him in return. "*Mon Cher,* I have missed you so much. I have thought about nothing but you, my darling."

His hands sought to find her warmth.

She groaned at his touch. "Not now, my sweet. I am very tired from my long journey. You must be tired and hungry as well."

"You're right. I am famished. We have a superb dinner waiting for us."

"I know," replied Catherine. "I told cook what to prepare."

"I can hardly believe my eyes. When did you arrive?"

"At noon. I have been traveling for a week, maybe longer, I'm not sure any more. I know one thing, though. I am glad to be home." And she hugged him to her.

"Glad to be home," he echoed, and he thanked God for the miracle.

***

Catherine woke Jean early the next morning. "Jean, my head is burning." Her eyes were glazed and she alternately shook and sweated with a high fever.

"Are you ill?"

"I have never been sick in my life—until now."

Jean became frightened. "I'll get Antoinette. She will know what to do, what herbs to give you."

"No!" replied Catherine, becoming agitated. "She must hate me"

"The doctor then. But a question first." He took a deep breath and expelled it before continuing. "When you were away, did anything happen? Are there any problems I should know about?"

"Yes," she said quietly. "But I am afraid to tell you."

A momentary pain came over him. "I suspected as much. Tell me. That is the only way I can help you."

"I stayed with a Duke in Bordeaux during the Midsummer festival. Maxine, I think it was Maxine, killed him with a stiletto and I was blamed. The authorities were going to arrest me, but Therese gave me a horse and I got away and came here." Her voice trailed off.

Jean reached for Catherine's hand and stroked it. "Maxine is the same woman who sent the authorities to see me."

Catherine put her arm over her head and moaned.

"Her jealousy and hatred must be strong indeed, to work such vengeance." He fondled her hand. " You only come back to me when you're in trouble." He choked on the bile that rose from his stomach. "To seek refuge from yet another problem. Yet here you lay, so helpless, needing me. I could never refuse you." He kissed her hot forehead affectionately. "Catherine, it is best that no one knows you are here."

"I understand," murmured Catherine. Her eyes were filled with such pain, that Jean fell deeper in love with her at that moment.

"I must treat you myself and hope for the best. We don't have any choice."

After a week, the fever had subsided and Catherine's strength slowly came back. She was able to bathe herself and wash her thick hair, which had become stringy and greasy from her long illness.

She was unable to make love. Even drinking caused her mouth pain. "I must wait until the sores heal."

"Of course, my darling, we will wait as long as we have to."

She began to look like her old self, but more subdued. Winter fell, the snowdrifts heaped around the house, and still Catherine remained with Jean.

One warm spring evening Catherine paced like a caged lioness. There was an edge to her mood that made the Baron feel uncomfortable.

The next day Catherine was gone from his side when Jean woke, instead of sleeping late like the lazy cat she was. None of the servants had seen Catherine leave that morning.

The clock was chiming ten o'clock two nights later when he heard footsteps on the stairs and rushed down to greet her.

Catherine was springing up the stairs two at a time. Her appearance was quite disheveled, hair in disarray, and feet blackened with dirt. There were twigs and moss clinging to her dress. She stopped when she saw him on the landing. "Oh, hello," she greeted him casually.

"Where have you been? I've been worried..."

"You're always worrying. I'm fine, I tell you." She flounced up the rest of the stairs on the way to her room.

He reached for her arm.

She pulled her arm away with a snarl. "I don't belong to you. Please remember that," Catherine glared at him.

DuFont's head was spinning. "Have you been with another man, Catherine?"

She stared at him with a hateful look, but refused to answer and continued up the stairs towards her room. Then she spun around.

The insane expression on her face sent prickles down duFont's back. Looking at Catherine was like facing a hungry tiger that was sizing him up for dinner.

"Yes," and she laughed a sardonic, mirthless laugh.

"Is it always going be like this? Not knowing when you will leave, or when you'll return. Wondering whose arms are holding you." His face was red with emotion.

She walked over to him and put her arms around him, pulling him to her.

He stiffened, but didn't break contact, his body starting to tingle and responded as he always did to her touch.

"I am the way I am. You have always known that," she breathed into his ear. "Yet you want to hold me and crush me like a butterfly."

"Why can't you stay and make a life with me here?"

"I can't." Her tone and attitude took on a persuasive tone. "Don't be angry. Be happy that I am here with you now." She reached inside his hose and began to stroke him. Jean became instantly erect, and in return began kissing her neck and her breast.

She twined her leg around his, rubbing her warm body against his groin.

"I'm sorry, my dearest," he said, his voice muffled by her flesh. "I'm a jealous man. Forgive me."

"I forgive you," replied Catherine happily, abruptly breaking away from their embrace. "I'm hungry. Let's go find something to eat." And she dashed down the stairs towards the kitchen. Her shawl lay on the steps.

"I must be mad," he sighed to himself, picking up her shawl and slowly followed her down the stairs and into the kitchen.

"Here, drink some wine. I want you to be happy—like I am."

DuFont drained the glass.

She drank from her own glass then kissed him deeply, moving her tongue around his mouth. The taste of grapes swirled around her lips. The scent of orange blossoms emanated from her.

"She is intoxicating." Lingering in the kiss, warmth crept through his body. His anger dissipated, Jean could feel her power take hold. He cursed his weakness silently, but at the same time remembered how much he had missed their love-making.

"I am healed, Jean. Do you want me?"

"Yes, my darling, I want you very much," he moaned. He laid her on the wooden table there in the kitchen and the night swallowed the lovers.

***

Catherine's evening forays intensified.

The Baron was miserable and prayed for some way to keep her at home. "I have been asked to preside at a complicated trial in Paris." With sudden inspiration he asked, "Would you like to go with me?"

"Oh, yes!" she cried. She jumped up and began pacing the floor, quivering with excitement.

"Come to bed. You'll catch cold." He worried about her all the time since the fever.

"I'm not cold. I don't have anything to wear, though."

"I'll have some dresses made for you."

She jumped onto the bed and playfully leaped on top of the magistrate. Her hair hung in his face and she giggled. "We'll have so much fun. Where shall we stay?" "

"We'll stay in the most wonderful place and we'll make a holiday out of it," he replied, pushing her hair out of his eyes. "It will be good for us."

"Let's pack!" she cried with enthusiasm.

"We won't be leaving until next week." He slid out from under her and left the room. When he returned, he had many small parcels to show her. "I will bring these for you to wear in Paris." He opened the packets of family heirlooms of jeweled bracelets, rings, and elaborate necklaces. Amethysts, rubies, emeralds, and diamonds glittered in the candlelight. Strands of pearls gleamed.

"You are very wealthy," she said, her eyes opening wide.

"These have been in my family for generations."

A strand of dark blue beads with little flecks of gold appealed to Catherine. She reached out to touch its smooth coolness. "What is this?"

"That is lapis lazuli, it belonged to my mother. It is said to have mysterious powers."

"Oh, really?" She fingered it with a growing appreciation. "I want to try it on."

"Of course. Here, let me help you. This will display your breasts wonderfully." He fastened it around her neck.

Catherine gasped as the cool necklace touched her warm skin and stroked it with her fingertips. "It is lovely."

Once it was hanging around her neck, she caressed it again and again. "It feels wonderful."

"Then I want you to keep it as my gift."

She hugged Jean so fiercely that the two of them fell down on the bed, locked in her strong embrace. "Thank you," she breathed in his ear. "I will wear it always."

"Then I thank you," he declared. "If it makes you this appreciative, I always want you to wear it." He laughed out loud. "Perhaps you will remember me more."

"I... will.. always.. remember...you," she said accentuating each word separately. I will always find you. And we will always be together."

"I can never forget you, either, my dearest one."

Catherine kissed him many times, then climbed on top of him. Jean was already erect, and she slid him into her, rocking back and forth, laughing and giggling. After a few minutes they came together, and she fell asleep next to him, happy and tired.

"This is a good idea," he thought to himself. He turned over and touched her soft roundness. *Life is good,* he told himself. Then he too, drifted into sleep.

The house that Jean brought her to in Paris was elegant and beautiful. "I had hoped to take a bride to this house many years ago." He brightened. "I can pretend that you..." He stopped in mid-sentence.

"Don't despair, Jean. Here I am here, in these amazing surroundings, the daughter of a poor peasant woman." At the mention of Antoinette, a chill passed between them. Catherine shook it off quickly.

During their stay, Baron DuFont was usually gone until dark. A relative of the King was being tried for witchcraft, and Jean attended to his duties for his king, Louis XII, by way of law counsels and conferences for the upcoming difficult trial. The royalty was spared the humiliation of a public trial when the offender hung himself in his dank cell. No one knew how the nobleman had procured a rope while imprisoned, or at least weren't telling. The dead man's body was spirited away, buried in unconsecrated ground and quickly forgotten. Jean was secretly relieved that the matter was so easily settled.

The last evening Jean and Catherine were in Paris, a party was to be given in his honor.

His Eminence, Cardinal Malplaquet, who had accused the now-dead nobleman of sorcery, was in attendance. He had heard much from the Baron regarding Catherine. He speculated about duFont's fiancé. "Considering that Baron DuFont is still without an heir, it is good that he will announce his engagement tonight," the Cardinal mused, as he munched on a sugar treat. The Cardinal required many yards of the red material to cover his massive bulk and his florid face matched the scarlet robes of religious office. A number of officers from the Cardinal's special guard, some related to nobility, were also in attendance.

When the couple arrived, Catherine was trembling. "Are you cold, my love?" Jean asked. "Would you like to put my cape around you?"

"No, I'm excited, that's all."

As they made their entrance, all guests hushed and turned towards the couple. Many stared at Catherine, unable to take their eyes away from her ravishing loveliness. Then the chattering began anew. "Who is that?"

"Have you ever seen her before?"

"That is the Baron's Catherine."

"No, it cannot be."

"Look at her dress! The gold embroidery."

"Her jewels!"

Madame DuGard, the hostess, dressed in a soft green velvet gown, welcomed her, and announced the two of them to the rest of the gathering.

Catherine curtsied, smiled enigmatically, and then walked towards the music, drawn to the dancing.

Jean watched her leave, proudly yet with some hesitation, then turned to talk to some of the guests.

The Cardinal had watched them come in and saw something in Catherine that disturbed him. *She is mystifying but in time I will understand.*

There was an immediate stir when Catherine joined the dancing. A number of men strove for Catherine's attention including soldiers, surrounding her, clamoring for a dance, a walk in the moonlight, or hints of other pleasurable pursuits.

"All I want at this moment is to dance. Musicians, strike up a lively tune."

A handsome trooper, Lt. Jean-Claude DuPree, was first to ask her hand to dance. The lieutenant was an exceptionally tall, elegantly slender man with long, wavy blonde hair, with a blonde beard and mustache. He had light, dreamy blue eyes, almost grey by the light of the burning candles.

Yet his dreamy eyes hid his immense strength. As he led her to the dance floor, Catherine could feel the muscles ripple in his arms, and she stroked his solid arm appreciatively. She could imagine his powerful thighs pressed against hers or running her hands over his bare muscular chest and taut belly.

Jean-Claude in turn was becoming infatuated with her. "You're not like the simpering ladies that I am used to. You look me in the eye like a man."

Catherine laughed while she moved sinuously to the measured steps of the dance.

"You are a marvelous dancer," he whispered in her ear.

"I love to dance. The music enters me and moves me," she whispered back, lightly touching his ear with her lips.

Her touch sent a thrill through Lt. DuPree. "Meet me later," he whispered again.

"Perhaps," replied Catherine. "But do not trifle with me." She looked him in the eye without flinching.

"I am utterly at your command." He bowed slightly.

She held her fingers to her lips in a lingering kiss then brushed Jean-Claude's lips with them.

The effect was electric. She watched his pupils dilate with excitement, his lips parted.

He bowed. "Until later?" And he strolled away with a nonchalance he only pretended.

Someone tapped lightly on her shoulder and she turned around. A man stood before her, accompanied by the hostess Madame

DuGard. He was short, with a medium build and slightly paunchy. Almost fifty years old, he was not aging gracefully. His pinched face and sharp, pointed nose gave her the impression of a weasel with brown eyes so dark that the pupils could not be discerned.

"May I present Colonel Robert Pouissent, Commander of the Cardinal's Special Detachment," announced Madame du Gard.

Catherine nodded and held out her hand, unimpressed.

The Colonel bowed stiffly and kissed her hand, never taking his eyes from hers.

"Col. Pouissent is distantly related to Charlemagne," added Madame du Gard.

Catherine shrugged without interest. "Do you know Lt. DuPree, Colonel?" she inquired about the handsome young man.

"Yes, he is under my command, Mademoiselle," the man replied with irritation, then changed the subject. "Will you honor me with a dance?"

She hesitated, then politely nodded her head and coolly offered her hand.

He grasped her hand so tightly it made her wince. Pouissent was a shrewd and powerful man. He had used that power to command for the last five years.

Catherine sized him up instantly. "You are like me. You cannot be manipulated or controlled."

The Colonel smiled slyly at her then led her out to the dance floor.

When the dance had finished he announced, "Meet me in the garden by the statue of the angel—in one hour." He bowed again and left.

"I have no intention of meeting with him. Not ever." She wiped her hands on her dress, to remove the unsavory feeling of him. She walked out into the cool night air of the balcony.

"Warm tonight, isn't it?" asked a husky voice behind her.

She jumped, and turned to see yet another officer who was standing on the balcony. The rounded tops of her breasts gleamed whitely in the moonlight and he stared at them.

The officer tore his eyes away with difficulty. "A thousand pardons, Mademoiselle, for startling you. May I introduce myself? I am Captain Henri Martel, at your service." He took off his hat and dipped deferentially to her. His open, boyish face belied his maturity and years of service to the Cardinal and the King.

"Enchanted," she replied, with an elegant air. "Monsieur, you seem flushed. Are you ill?" She put her warm hand to his damp forehead.

The touch had the effect she wanted as Captain Martel shuddered under her touch. Catherine smiled in the dark. "Are you sure you do not need to lie down—and rest?" she asked with mock concern in her voice. She enjoyed teasing the awkward, easily aroused man.

"No. I'm fine. It must be the warm weather."

"Ah. I see."

"Are you enjoying the dancing?"

"Very much. Are you?"

"Oh, I don't dance. I'm too clumsy."

"I would like to...dance with you." She leaned closer and whispered, "Perhaps we could practice out here, until you feel more comfortable." She offered her hand and put her other hand on his shoulder.

Martel was profusely and utterly flustered. "Maybe we had better not. I would be upset if I stepped on those delicate feet or hurt your pretty hands."

"You're a kind man," she whispered again. The movement of air from her deep, melodious voice into his ear made him giddy and he utterly forgot himself. He took hold of her around the waist and kissed her deeply.

Catherine kissed him in return, her arms around his neck, her body pressed hard against his.

He moaned with pleasure deep in his throat.

His hands slid down to her round bottom and pulled her closer to him.

Catherine enjoyed the kiss, and stroked Henri's cheek. Suddenly her hair stood on end, feeling a presence behind her. As she turned, she gasped to see a figure looming in the shadow. Cardinal Malplaquet was watching them.

Henri stepped away from her as if he had been hit by lightning. "Your Eminence!" he cried.

"Good evening, Captain," Malplaquet replied sardonically. "And who is that charming lady with you?"

"Oh, pardon me. Mademoiselle, I would like to introduce you to His Eminence, Cardinal Malplaquet. And this is....I'm sorry. I didn't get your name." His mortification was complete.

"I am called Catherine, your Worship," said Catherine, ignorant of the proper term to call the large, pious man.

"I am charmed to make your acquaintance, Mademoiselle." He smiled politely but his eyes probed into her very being.

Catherine felt as if she was in the presence of a large boa constrictor who could, without warning, wrap itself around her and squeeze the life from her. Her head ached suddenly.

She took Henri's hand and said, "Come, Henri. You promised me something to eat. Au revoir, Cardinal. So happy to make your acquaintance," and immediately turned her back on the Churchman.

Henri chaperoned Catherine to the dining hall.

"I hate how he looks at me," replied Catherine. She rubbed her temples, which still ached from the experience.

"Yes. It is said he can look into people's souls."

Catherine shuddered. She shifted in her chair. "Well, I don't want to talk about him anymore."

"Of course. I want to know more about you, such as where you live, so I may see you."

"I am a visitor. I'm supposed to leave Paris tomorrow."

He sighed in dismay.

She continued without interruption. "I want to remain in Paris but I have nowhere to stay," she lied. She looked at him hopefully. "Could I room with you?"

"That would be difficult. I am headquartered at the garrison, just outside the city, and I have no other lodging."

"Oh," said Catherine, disappointed.

"Don't worry. I can find a place for you to stay. In fact, I will go make arrangements this moment."

"No, remain with me a while."

Henri sat down. He took her free hand and kissed it gently. "You are the most beautiful woman I have ever met. The most kind, the most pure. I love you, my darling."

Catherine groaned inwardly. "The fool is falling in love with me already." She stroked his hand and assumed an adoring look. Then out of the corner of her eye, Catherine noticed that Lt. DuPree had entered the dining salon. "Perhaps now would be a good time," she said quickly. "I will meet you later to discuss what you have arranged." She pushed him into movement.

"Certainly, my dear one." He bowed and left to search for his friends in the crowd, to organize a meeting place.

Catherine stood up. Jean-Claude spotted her, an enormous smile lighting up his attractive face. With a few strides of his long legs, he was standing in front of her. "I have been looking for you. My aunt has agreed to let us stay in the east wing of her home temporarily. It is hardly used anymore, now that my uncle is dead and she travels a lot. Would you accept residing there with me?" Hope reigned supreme in the young lieutenant's face and he held his breath anxiously.

"Yes, I accept," she replied cheerfully, and stood on tiptoe, but his face was higher than she could reach.

He bent over and met her face with a light kiss. As he straightened up, he looked down and saw her bulging breasts, eagerly trying to break free of the bodice of her new dress.

His young, muscular body ached with yearning. "Let us go now, before we are missed."

With excitement pounding in her veins, Catherine took his hand and they escaped through a back door.

When Captain Martel re-entered the dining room, Catherine was nowhere to be found. "She left with Lt. DuPree," reported a soldier, standing by the table, and who had watched the couple leave.

"Tell no one," replied the man, suddenly jealous and angry. Seething, he left to return to the barracks.

Henri wasn't the only confused and unhappy man. The Baron had searched for his lady, but she was gone. He inquired but was told she had left with a soldier. DuFont returned to the lavish house he had shared with her in the city. Catherine was not there and some of her clothing was missing. All the jewels were intact however, laid out for the Baron to see, except for the lapis lazuli necklace that he had given her as a present.

"I have not seen Mademoiselle," replied the maid sleepily, when he woke her with a rough shake.

He took the gold ring he intended to give Catherine as an engagement present and returned it to its velvet packet. "That woman is impossible!" he cried out loud, while he paced up and down the room. Periodically he would sit, drink wine, and think. Then pace. Dawn's pink glow was peeking through the window to find Jean still awake and pacing.

***

That same rosy glow illuminated Catherine's face on the pillow, as her lover, Jean-Claude, kissed her breasts. The only thing she was wearing was the beaded lapis necklace.

"Touch me again," begged Jean-Claude, to Catherine.

"My head hurts," she complained. "And I'm tired. I'm going to sleep now."

"Oh, no, you're not," he laughed, and began kissing her again.

"I mean it," she said sharply and roughly pushed him away, trying to crawl off the bed.

"I can never get enough of you." He grabbed one of her shapely ankles and tried to tease her out of her foul mood.

She yanked her foot away and pulled the intricately quilted cover over her head.

"Even when you're angry, I love you."

In a muffled voice she muttered, "Go away or go to sleep. But leave me alone!"

They were interrupted by a servant lightly tapping on their bedroom door. "Monsieur, a Captain Martel wants to see you downstairs."

"What does he want?" Jean-Claude put on a cotton nightshirt and went to talk to his superior officer.

Captain Martel was in a fury. "You have insulted me, and I will not tolerate it!"

"What is the matter, Captain? Why are you so angry?"

Captain Martel struggled for control of himself. "Catherine. She promised to be with me, but left with you."

"My Catherine? Are you sure? Maybe you have her confused with some other woman."

"There is no confusion." His eyes narrowed into slits. His rage and hurt pride erupted. "I challenge you to a duel for the right to possess her!"

"I'm sure there is some mistake, Captain." The tall man feigned a calmness that he did not feel.

"There is no mistake! I will meet you tonight in the clearing behind the barracks—for satisfaction." He left, slamming the heavy door behind him.

Lt. DuPree was stunned. "Catherine? With him? Impossible. Where would he get such a ridiculous idea?" He ran upstairs and shook her awake.

"Hmmmm? Is it night already?"

"Did you promise to leave with Captain Martel last night at the party?"

"Who?" she replied.

"Henri Martel, my company commander."

"Is he a shy sort of man, blushes easily?"

"That's the one. But he's only shy around women. He is ferocious on a field of battle."

She shrugged. "I think I did promise. But then you came to me with your own proposal. I preferred to be with you."

"Because of your promise, Captain Martel has challenged me to a duel, with you as the prize for the winner," he said between clenched teeth.

Catherine sat up instantly. "A duel! No, you mustn't." She remembered Michel, the one who had lost his fight. "Can't you share me?"

"I don't want to share you, and neither does he. Are you mad?"

"You might get hurt, or worse."

"I promise I will emerge the victor. He has more experience with the sword, but I'm younger... and ... I have longer arms," he bragged with the impetuous voice of inexperience.

"Don't go, Jean-Claude," she begged. "I'm afraid."

"I will come back to you."

"No! Take me with you. I cannot bear to wait here, to wonder what is happening."

"All right," he agreed. "It will be night soon. Hurry and get dressed. I will get the carriage."

The full moon was rising bright orange in the east when the two men strode out to face each other.

Martel wore a grim expression as he drew the saber with which he would fight. The passion of battle was rising within him.

DuPree made a great show of bravado. Catherine could hear him joking and laughing. As he stripped off his shirt, she could see perspiration on his chest glimmering in the moonlight.

Col. Pouissent, who was also watching in the crowd that had gathered, detected Catherine standing in the clearing. *The vixen who stood me up. A cunning smile creased his face. It doesn't matter who wins the duel tonight. I will be the ultimate winner.*

The two men faced each other and saluted with their swords. "En garde, Monsieur. The night is young and I wish to spend it with company other than yours." And with that, Martel lunged at DuPree, who could barely gather his wits in time to parry the stroke.

DuPree counter-attacked yelling, "The only thing you'll sleep with is the cold earth!" His wide slash was easily deflected by Martel's expert swordsmanship.

Catherine watched the two opponents go through their formal dance of challenge and counter-challenge. Time seemed to take on a slow-motion eerie quality, as if the scene was being recorded in the memory of the universe.

Col. Pouissent watched the woman from a distance, his tiny snake eyes narrowed with anticipation.

DuPree was clearly outmatched. His smile had deserted his face and he was breathing heavily with the exertion.

Martel pressed his advantage, forcing the younger man backward step by step. Martel's eyes gleamed with a bloodlust that came from the certainty that a kill was imminent.

DuPree's exhausted blows were deftly brushed aside as the master swordsman toyed with the young Lieutenant who had insulted him so severely.

Martel knocked DuPree's sword from his hand. "I may think of you this night as I lay with Catherine." With that, he drove his heavy saber into DuPree's chest and pulled it out again quickly. It was covered with blood. As the young lieutenant fell to the grass, Henri bent over to examine the young man. His lunge was sure and death had been nearly instantaneous. A savage cry of exhilaration broke from Henri's mouth and he turned to find his prize. Martel strode over to Catherine, put his arms around her, and kissed her roughly, blood on his hands.

She broke away from the embrace. "Don't leave the body lying there, you fool!" and she pushed him towards the lifeless DuPree.

Col. Pouissent took decisive action. Stalking over to Catherine, he said, "I have a small house not far from here. You may stay there as long as you want. To recover," he added hastily.

"No thank you, Colonel," she replied, haughtily, and proceeded to ignore him, as she watched Martel and several others carry off her now-dead lover.

"I never take no for an answer." The meaning and tone of his voice sliced through the night air.

She turned away from him and walked back to DuPree's carriage.

He signaled to one of his junior officers. "When Captain Martel is finished tidying up from his night's work, send him to me," he said grimly. His face was mottled and ugly.

"Yes, sir!" replied the officer. He thought, *I would hate to be in Martel's shoes. The Colonel is in a foul mood tonight.*

When Martel left the Colonel's office he found Catherine waiting in DuPree's carriage. "Colonel Pouissent has ordered me to take charge of fighting at the border. We leave at dawn. He will take care of you while I'm gone. I will return as soon as I can. I shall miss you." His shirt was stained with DuPree's blood. He kissed her deeply and then returned to the barracks.

Catherine jumped when an armed guard suddenly appeared at the carriage with Pouissent in the lead.

The Colonel had a pleased smile on his face. "The evening has worked out better than if I had planned it myself." He touched her hand but she moved it away. "I am sending you to safe quarters, my dear." The smile turned to a leer. "I wouldn't want you to be delayed—again."

He reached out and took her hand firmly. She tried to pull away again but his grip tightened. He brought it roughly to his mouth and kissed her palm. Then he bit the fleshy part of her hand until she cried out. His iron-hard eyes watched her reaction.

Apprehension tightened Catherine's jaw muscles. She squared her shoulders, steeling herself. Her temples throbbed with fear.

"Until later," he said softly. "Guards," he called, "take her to my house immediately and watch her closely."

"Immediately, sir," they answered. They took hold of Catherine's arms, daggers gleaming at their sides, and escorted her to Pouissent's conveyance.

Catherine leaned back against the leather seat and rubbed her head. "These headaches seem to be getting worse," while she tried to avoid thinking being alone with the Colonel.

***

Captain Martel's death was announced at the barracks less than a week after he and his detachment had been dispatched to the border. There had been a skirmish and he had been killed.

Meanwhile, Catherine had been kept a virtual prisoner. During the day Pouissent had an armed guard surround his house. In the evening he sent the guards away, lest they hear the ferocious sounds of the Colonel's version of lovemaking.

At first, the Colonel had been repulsively charming, ingratiating himself with small gifts of food and clothing. But when Catherine continued to defy him, he went mad. He was a strong man, used to getting his way with soldiers and women alike. The evidence was the purple bruises that covered her body.

"I hate you!" she yelled to the empty house after he had left one morning. "You make me sick!" She shook her fist at the door. "Touch me again, Pouissent, and you'll wish you had never been born!"

A young soldier unchained the door and looked in, alarmed at the noise from within.

"Let me out of here at once!" she shouted hysterically.

The soldier drew a sharp knife. "Get back. You're here under the Colonel's orders."

"The Colonel," she jeered. "The Colonel is a maniac, a wild man, and he is holding me captive against my wishes."

But the guard was more afraid of the Colonel than her hysteria.

Catherine changed her tactics. Speaking in a soft, silky voice, she edged closer to him. "Let me out for a few minutes for some fresh air, then you can bring me back. I will reward you for your kindness." She smiled, reaching out to caress his groin.

"He warned me about you," but her fingers were expertly fondling his erection that rose against his will.

Catherine moved close to him with her body, and he relaxed his grip on the knife. Her face was tilted for him to kiss. He closed his eyes and bent over her mouth.

With the speed and strength born of desperation, Catherine snatched the knife from his hand, slashed at the young soldier and ran out the door.

She had wounded him, but he would not die—not by her hand. "Come back!" he cried. "The Colonel..."

Catherine ran as though demons were after her. She raced toward duFont's ornate house, hoping that he might still be there, and banged on the heavy door of the house they had stayed at an eternity ago.

The door opened slightly and Yvonne, the maid, peeked out.

Catherine thrust the door open and bolted into the room, looking around. "Where is Monsieur DuFont?"

"He's gone, miss. He waited for you but then he was taken home very ill."

"Do you know anyone who can help me? Please! I'm in terrible trouble."

She noticed Catherine's bloody hands and the maid screamed.

A servant appeared in the doorway, brandishing a large pole.

Without a word Catherine turned and fled, fleeing for her life to Madame DuGard's house.

"Catherine, my dear, what has happened?" asked Giselle duGard, as she escorted the young woman into her house. She examined Catherine's disheveled appearance, bloody hands, torn dress, uncoiled hair, wild look, and purple bruises on her neck and arms. "Sit down, please." She patted her arm, clucking like a mother hen. "We have been so worried. Especially your fiancé. And when...."

"Fiancé?" interrupted Catherine.

"Yes, the Baron, of course. He wanted to wait for you to return, but was too ill. He insisted on staying but we sent him home." The older woman babbled on in her nervousness.

"Can you help me get home to him?"

Giselle duGard hesitated. "I will have to talk to my husband."

"Madame DuGard," Catherine said breathlessly. "I am in terrible danger. And if I don't get to him immediately, Monsieur DuFont may also die. Do you want two deaths on your conscience?"

Automatically Madame DuGard crossed herself, and left to make arrangements for a coach to take Catherine. In the meantime Catherine cleaned herself and put on a dress loaned to her from Madame DuGard and waited.

Fearfully, Catherine curled up in the corner of the duGard's coach as if Pouissent's ruthless hands could somehow seize her, while the driver whipped the horses into galloping. *I'll bet Pouissent's beaten half of his men for allowing me to get away. I hope Madame DuGard will be*

226 LAUREN O. THYME

discreet. She slept after a few hours, while unsettling dreams punished her aching head.

When the carriage finally pulled into the long driveway, she jumped out before the coach had stopped. "Thank you, Monsieur," she called to the driver. "And remember. You have never seen me!" After her long and arduous journey, Catherine rushed into duFont's house, searching for the Baron.

Pierre tried to stop her. "Where are you going? My master is sick. Haven't you done enough to him already?"

But she ran upstairs, burst in through the bedroom door, and stopped when she saw the deadly pallor on the man's face. Sweat covered his skin and his hands lay lifelessly alongside his weak body.

"Jean, my dearest." She rushed to the side of the bed.

He opened his feverish eyes. A slight recognition passed through his mind, but he was too weak to respond. Saliva drooled from his mouth, where open sores festered on his lips. A thick crust of pus formed at the edges of his eyes. A strange rash covered his face, neck and arms.

She kissed his fingers, and his hand limply clasped hers in return.

"I'm sending for my mother," she whispered to him. "She will know what to do."

He raised his head a few inches. "No. Please...I couldn't bear..." but he was unable to continue and his head fell back on the sweat-soaked pillow.

"I will not let you die," she said firmly.

After Antoinette had examined Jean, she came downstairs into the study where Catherine waited in Jean's large overstuffed chair. Her mother had aged terribly. Antoinette's eyes had lost their luster; her hair had become gray and stringy. The muscles on her skinny arms swung on the bones. "He has the Lover's disease," she said stiffly, her face emotionless. "There is no cure, and he will ultimately go insane and die."

Catherine paled, recognizing her own fate as well.

"Give him this herbal tea, keep him cool, and the symptoms will pass. He will not die—at least not yet."

Catherine was still stunned by the shocking news.

Antoinette continued. "For a long time I hated both of you and wished God would punish you." She looked down at her gnarled, arthritic hands. "You see what my hatred has done to me."

There was no response from her daughter.

"I hoped he would come back to me, but I never saw Jean again...until today." A tear rolled down her mother's cheek.

Catherine's jaw tightened.

"I will not live long, and I want to go to God with a clean soul. I must forgive you. Perhaps it was my fault that you turned out the way you did. Or maybe the midwife was right after all. That you were born with the mark of the Devil over your face." She sighed. Antoinette got up, weariness showing in her stooped body. "I'll go now." Wordlessly she left.

Catherine ran from the room, hurried up the stairs, and bolted the door behind her in the room she had taken for her own. She lay down and, like a small child, cried herself to sleep.

***

Monsieur DuFont convalesced slowly, as if he had no will to get well.

Catherine prepared the special herbal teas and gave him cooling baths, but his spirit was weakened. A new distant look had appeared in his eyes and she was frightened.

One afternoon when she brought him his remedy, he was sitting up in bed. "Put that down and sit beside me," he ordered.

Catherine did so silently.

"We have a lot to talk about," he said, meaningfully.

"Yes," she agreed.

Shadows around her jaw and chin marred her good looks. She

looked like she'd put on weight, too. He touched her belly reluctantly. "You're not expecting a child are you?"

"Of course not. I take herbs to prevent that."

"Good," he replied coldly.

"Is that what you wanted to talk to me about?"

"That, and other things. I used to believe that you would mature and settle down eventually. I have been deluding myself for a long time." He paused. "How long has it been since we met? Ten years?"

"But..."

"Be quiet. I don't have enough energy to argue today."

She nodded grimly.

"I was going to announce our engagement at the ball that last evening in Paris. But you surprised me first. I waited, hoping you would return. I couldn't look for you because it would only harden your heart."

He slid down on the pillows, closed his eyes, and rested for a moment. "I was hurt, then very angry, then I became too sick to care anymore. When I was taken home, I wanted to die. I almost succeeded."

"Are you finished with what you want to say to me?"

"Not yet. I don't understand who you are or why you do what you do. You are a cruel woman and perhaps God will punish you for that someday."

Catherine remembered similar words from her mother. Anger and defensiveness rose to her lips.

"I take care of you, only to have you leave with whatever man you become interested in. One day I will be unable to protect you. Then only God can help you." He crossed himself.

Catherine had never seen Jean make that religious gesture. Cold prickles traveled up her spine, making the hair on her head stand on end.

He chuckled morosely. "But I cannot help myself. I am under your spell. The priest told me that you are a witch and have enchanted me. If that is true, God help me."

"I cannot help myself," she replied. "Maybe someday I will be forced to change my ways." She laughed harshly, without humor, then suddenly nauseated, remembering the Colonel, and she tried not to retch.

Jean watched her expressions with concern. "I know some other authorities will come looking for you and I will have to lie again." He shook his head. "I'm glad my father is dead so he cannot watch my decline." He changed the subject abruptly. "I dreamt that I saw Antoinette, but she was greatly changed."

"She helped me with your illness."

Guilt pangs overran duFont. "Sweet Jesus of Nazareth, she looks terrible."

"Yes."

Tears fell from the sick man's eyes and he wiped them away. "I wish you and I could be together with no one getting hurt. And that you didn't have your terrible sickness with men." He sighed in frustration. "Did Antoinette diagnose my sickness?"

"Yes. She called it the Lover's sickness. You and I are doomed. Little by little we will go mad, until we die."

"I have heard of it. It is passed from one person to another through lovemaking. Which man was it?" He sounded remote, as if he were talking about someone else.

"I will not endure your questions!" She leapt off the bed and onto the floor, pounding it with her fists.

Jean watched patiently, unable to be of much help in his weakened condition.

Slowly her hysterical fit subsided.

"You had better go now. Have Pierre bring dinner up for me."

"I want my mother." Her pupils were dilated and her face was agitated. Catherine left the house and walked into Quimont. When townspeople saw her, they whispered among themselves, turning away from the shadow she cast, afraid.

When Catherine approached the lane to Antoinette's house, she was appalled. The wretched hovel was burnt almost beyond recognition, and her mother had vanished.

What has happened here? She wondered as she looked around, stumbling now and then on the wreckage. *What happened to my mother? Did she die here? Or did she burn this place down and leave?* No one was around to answer her questions.

She turned and ran all the way back to Jean's house. She knelt on the floor beside his bed. "I have nowhere to go," she said in a little girl voice. In her diseased mind she watched a parade of apparitions pass in front of her, grimly marching past her to their graves: Michel, the Duke, Jean-Claude, Henri Martel, and now her mother. She squeezed her eyes to shut out the hallucinations. "Do you love me?" she asked her lover.

"God help me, I will love you throughout time itself."

***

Catherine was becoming increasingly careless about her appearance; most days she didn't dress carefully or brush her hair. Dirt gathered under her ragged fingernails. Her mind was slipping as the disease took its toll.

Sometimes duFont would be awakened in the night as Catherine paced back and forth in their room, unable to sleep, pressured by unseen forces. She would cry for no reason, then become angry when he tried to console her. She talked out loud to herself, carrying on animated conversations with unseen figures, sometimes scolding, sometimes begging. Her eyes had lost their intelligent brilliance and became dull and lackluster.

She was savage in bed, only becoming calm as she tired. Her seductiveness was replaced by a sadistic humor, luring him to excitement only to stop in the middle of their lovemaking and laugh.

Jean became afraid that Catherine was nearing the edge of her sanity. *I can't bear to watch her crumbling apart.* His old pain of the past paled in comparison to the new agony of the present.

Her nightly forays began again. Sometimes she wouldn't come home for days, and then only to eat, sleep, and disappear once more.

"You must send her away. She is bringing dishonor upon your house," Pierre advised him. "The town already gossips maliciously about her—and you. You must stop protecting her."

"I can't, Pierre!" the nobleman cried. "I can't get her out of my soul."

As Jean had feared, the authorities did come to visit. His old friend, Cardinal Malplaquet, accompanied by Colonel Pouissent, paid him a call early one morning while Catherine was away.

"My dear Baron," began the Cardinal, after they had been seated in duFont's library. "We are looking for Catherine. We have heard rumors that she has taken refuge in your home. You must give her up, as she is wanted for murdering a soldier."

"You must be mistaken!" duFont exclaimed. "Catherine wouldn't harm a soul. Furthermore, I haven't seen her since I left Paris."

"I was responsible for looking after her," added Colonel Pouissent. "One day she flew into a rage, lured a guard into her embrace, killed him and fled. It was most unfortunate." Pouissent looked appropriately distressed.

The piercing gaze of the Cardinal seared through duFont. "My dear Baron, she is unworthy of you, born of peasant stock, her mother a midwife." He lowered his voice, "She is suspected of witchcraft as well."

Jean's eyes dilated in apprehension. "Excuse me," he said, standing up. "I will have my servant get us some wine and cheese."

"Sit down, duFont!" The Cardinal spoke in a booming authoritarian tone.

Jean obeyed without hesitation.

The Colonel spoke up. "Because of your noble family heritage and your service to the Crown, we want to avoid disgracing you. I, that is, we, are only interested in finding Catherine. To bring her to justice." His nostrils flared and he scowled at Jean. The threat was unmistakable.

Pierre is right. I have deceived myself, thinking that my authority, power, and family name would protect me, Jean thought glumly. Then he forced himself to smile, stalling for time. "I am fatigued. Come back tomorrow and we will continue this discussion."

"No!" shouted the Cardinal losing control. He stood up, his massive frame overshadowing duFont. "We have come for Catherine, and if you stand in the way, we will take you as well!"

No longer an implied threat; the peril was now clearly defined.

"We have soldiers outside, waiting to take prisoners. Will you cooperate with us?" The Colonel lounged in his chair, fondling his chin hairs. He was obviously delighting in the Baron's hazardous situation.

"Search the house then," Jean said loudly. "She is not here. If I see her, I will take her into my custody and advise you at that time." He hoped they wouldn't suspect his ruse.

The Cardinal's eyes narrowed as he studied Jean's face. "Very well. We will search the house, though I doubt she is here. But we will remain close at hand, to make sure that you turn her over to us." Looking down at him he said, "As you know, I am not a man to be trifled with."

He motioned to Colonel Pouissent to order his soldiers to search the house.

When the soldiers were done searching, the Cardinal and Colonel Pouissent found duFont in his study, sitting behind his desk, looking more composed.

"My soldiers are camped outside, in case you decide you need to suddenly visit a sick relative or take a long trip. You may consider your-self under house arrest." Pouissent chuckled in delight.

"She is not here, as you said. But I think you are not telling us everything," said the Cardinal. "I will return for you in three days, if I haven't heard from you first." They left, the Cardinal's ponderous weight creaking down the polished wooden floors in the hallway.

Jean's shivered at the idea of being arrested, with the Colonel as his warden. "Catherine stayed with *him*. What a nightmare that must have been." His flesh raised in goosebumps. When he saw the Colonel and Cardinal Malplaquet drive away in their elaborate coach, Jean left the window and hurried to find his servant.

"Pierre, I am a dead man before too much time elapses."

"No, Master, I have been..."

But Jean cut him off. "It's too late, Pierre." He put his hand firmly on the servant's shoulder and squeezed it affectionately. "I want to thank you for your years of faithful service. Pierre, my stalwart friend, there is one request I must make of you before I die."

Pierre shook his head stubbornly, fearing what would be asked.

"You must listen! This house is heavily guarded, and I cannot leave. So you must find Catherine and take her to some safe place, where that foul demon Pouissent cannot find her!"

Pierre's expression clouded.

"I know how you feel about her. But with her safely away from here, I have fulfilled my last obligation to protect her."

Pierre looked at the floor, his teeth grinding against each other, his mouth set firmly.

DuFont continued resolutely. "The other servants should leave. Have them go one by one, as if on errands for me. I will get coins and jewels to send them on their way. Thank them for me for their years of service to myself and my family."

"But what about you?" Pierre's voice broke.

For long moments neither of the two men spoke, as each attempted to gain control of his emotions.

DuFont recovered his composure first. "The Cardinal said he would return in three days. That means you will have three days to find her and take her to some remote area, as far away from here as possible." His eyes glazed over, remembering the many witchcraft trials he had presided over, the broken men and women, suffering unspeakable agonies at the hands of the French Inquisition.

"As for myself, I have seen too much to allow myself to be taken alive. I am still a strong man, and I could withstand torture longer than I want to think about." His stomach turned with the recollection of past atrocities. "I prefer a quick, painless death." He turned to Pierre. "I need you to help me."

"In what way, Master?" His voice was subdued, surrendering to duFont.

"Call me Jean. I am no longer your Master, only your friend, a friend in need."

Pierre attempted to say the familiar name, but could not, out of duty and respect. "How do you want me to assist you?"

"Kill me quickly. My love of life, my powerful need to survive, keeps me from doing it myself. I want you to send me to God, or eternal damnation, I don't know which." He took his sharp dagger out from his waistband. The family crest was engraved on its hilt. "When that is done, locate Catherine and take her to safety."

Pierre protested. "I can sneak you out of here, Master. I have everything prepared."

Jean shook his head. "It is better this way," thinking also of the terrible disease that was consuming his body. He stood up.

Pierre realized the conversation was concluded and he would not be able to talk duFont out of his decision.

"I will come for you when I'm ready." Jean looked tired, but calm.

He wanted to say something more to Pierre, but couldn't decide what it was. He patted his shoulder as he walked by.

His servant was stunned by the sinister turn of events, mentally watching his secure, small world being twisted inside out. Emotions swirled within him, fear, anger, but most of all, misery for his friend and master. He picked up the ancient dagger and, being careful not to cut himself with the blade, sharpened the metal to a razor's edge.

When duFont had finished his preparations, he called his servant to him. He had a number of packets made up. The largest he pressed to Pierre. "Take this to my Catherine." Pierre could see jewels bulging from the velvet bag. "The rest distribute among the others and keep some for yourself."

Pierre could not hide his stricken look.

"Don't dismay, my friend. I'm sure God won't punish you for this. I bless you for your loving service to me." For the first and last time in his life, duFont hugged Pierre to him in a fierce embrace.

Pierre numbly accepted the affection.

Then duFont clambered onto the bed that had been in his family for four generations and arranged the pillows around him. He lay down, closed his eyes, put his hands next to his body and took a deep breath, steadying himself. "I'm ready, Pierre. Farewell." He looked utterly at peace, as though he was dead already.

Pierre took the dagger with both hands and plunged it deep into duFont's chest. The body jumped wildly at the blow. Reverently Pierre removed the blade, wiping it clean on the ancient quilt. Then he laid the dagger next to his master. He put his head next to Jean's mouth and listened for breathing, but there was none.

DuFont's vital organs had ceased. Blood poured out of the wound, staining everything around it, soaking the mattress.

Pierre closed the wide, staring eyes and lovingly arranged Jean's hands across the broad chest.

Then one by one the servants filed in, tears of mourning washing their cheeks. Pierre watched without emotion, unaffected, in shock. The reality of the situation wouldn't truly register for some days.

Pierre handed each of them a parcel from their dead master. He reminded them, "Pretend as though you are leaving for town on an errand. Act as normal as you can. Take nothing but this packet. And God go with you." After they had all left, Pierre sat down for a short mourner's vigil.

He thought of the wagon and the supplies he had hidden under the hollow seat before the soldiers had searched the house and grounds. The bag bulged under his shirt. He patted it for luck. "I will leave tonight by sundown. By then, the rest of them should be gone. And there will still be plenty of time."

A deathly pallor replaced duFont's robust complexion. Pierre touched a cooling hand. It would be quite a while yet before the body became stiff. "I will find her," he promised the lifeless figure.

Several soldiers were cooking some of duFont's chickens over a spit on the grassy area beside the house when Pierre harnessed the horses to the wagon and drove out of the driveway. They had also helped themselves to food in the garden and fruit orchard, only respecting the privacy of the house itself. Colonel Pouissent had given the troopers strict instructions regarding the nobleman duFont, and they were taking extreme precautions to follow it. The tension made them edgy and irritable. The soldiers rudely stopped Pierre to inspect the back of the wagon, to see if Jean was concealed. But the Baron was not there. They allowed the servant to drive off, and returned to their conversations and dinner.

I fooled them, Pierre thought. He was careful not to look back, afraid that any unusual action, however slight, might alert the guards to stop him with questions and then search the house. He couldn't allow himself to be deterred from his mission. The dead man's last wish must be carried out, regardless of the hardships.

He went to Antoinette's house, only to find the aftermath of disaster. The damage was now complete; the wreckage had been reduced to ashes and unrecognizable rubble. *She can't be too far,* he reasoned. He decided to try the tavern. *Catherine draws men to her like moths to a flame. There are a lot of men there.*

He flogged the horses in the darkening evening, the bit making their mouths bleed. When he got to the tavern, he looked around the main room but didn't see her. He took the owner aside.

"She does come here sometimes," Pierre was informed. "A weasel-faced officer was here earlier, asking about her, too. Something about that man made me afraid, so I told him nothing."

Pierre clapped the man on the back. "Her life is in peril by that man and others. The Baron has sent me to find her and take her to safety."

The innkeeper nodded his head knowingly. "I suspected something like that." He looked around furtively, making sure no one could overhear him. "On the outskirts of town, there is a settlement of paupers and vagabonds. You might try looking for her there."

"Thank you, good sir. Here is something for your trouble." He pushed a small silver coin into the tavern keeper's hand. "I would appreciate it if you would continue to be close-mouthed for a while longer. But do not put yourself in jeopardy. The man you described is dangerous and will stop at nothing to achieve his goal."

"No," the tavern-owner said to Pierre, giving him back the money. "Keep this. If what you say is true, you will need it for your journey." He smiled. "When you return, give the good Baron my greetings."

Pierre lowered his eyes. Lying was new to him; even simply withholding the truth was difficult. "I will," he finally replied, palming the coin.

Without another word, Pierre walked rapidly but unobtrusively to the wagon, and headed for the north side of Quimont.

When the loyal servant found the encampment of homeless men, plague survivors, and beggars, he was appalled. The area smelled of unwashed bodies. Many small fires burned, silhouettes of ragged people were outlined in the light. He looked around but couldn't see Catherine.

He stopped the horses, got out, and then led them to a tree, to which he tied the reins. The horses shook themselves and snorted, being so close to crowded humanity. He patted their necks until they calmed down. Then he walked through the encampment, peering into each group he found.

Towards the edge of the camp, he heard a woman's shrill laugh mingling with deeper male voices. As he edged closer, he saw a small group of men, passing a jug from one to another. Catherine was in their midst. He stopped short, repulsion rising in his throat, replaced quickly by rage.

Catherine had obviously been partaking of the contents of the jug and was intoxicated. Her bodice was ripped, and a pink breast was exposed. One of the men had his grimy hand on it. Her coarse laughter broke through the night again.

He stepped into their midst and held out his hand to her.

"What are you doing here, Pierre?" she asked, slurring her words.

"Monsieur DuFont gave me orders to take you away from here." He spoke roughly, glaring at the men around her. It was too dark, though, for them to see his angry expression. "Come with me."

She didn't move then she laughed again. "I don't take orders from *him* anymore. You may tell him..." but she didn't have an opportunity to continue.

With the energy of his wrath giving him great strength, Pierre grabbed her arm, and pulled her up. He adjusted her clothing to cover her nakedness. "You *will* come with me. Now!"

He led her half walking, half dragging her to the wagon. Pierre could hear the men shouting behind him as he strode away.

"Ow! You're hurting me," she cried, but he disregarded her.

She hit him with her free arm and clawed his face with her nails.

He turned his body to offer the least amount of unprotected skin.

The horses whinnied when they saw him. Pierre untied the reins, rudely shoved Catherine onto the seat and climbed aboard himself. He ignored her threats and blocked her wild blows as he whipped the horses to a hard gallop.

Catherine gave up protesting, crawled into the back of the swaying wagon, and passed out.

Pierre sat on the hard wooden seat, rage keeping him alert. "She is beyond saving. How could he have ever loved her?" He clenched his teeth together, lashing the horses harder in his righteous anger, as they rode away into the dark night.

When Catherine woke up on the hard floor of the wagon, sunshine was glittering through a green, leafy canopy above. She looked around, her head throbbing, painful to the touch. "Ohh," she moaned.

Pierre, normally a sound sleeper, was awake instantly at the sound. He rolled into a sitting position on the uneven ground he was lying on, then walked over to the side of the wagon.

Catherine, shabby and unkempt, glared at him. "I'm hungry." She crawled to the back of the wagon and clambered out, then went behind a tree and vomited. When she was done, Pierre handed her a pouch of water and she drank thirstily.

He stopped her. "Don't drink too quickly," but she pushed his hand away, gulped some more, gagged, then handed him the pouch.

"Where are you taking me?" she whined.

"My master wants me to take you far away from Quimont, to somewhere safe. Men are looking for you."

Catherine's eyes opened wide in terror. "Is one of them a very dark, evil-looking military man?"

"Yes, he came to duFont's house, to arrest you for murder."

"He lies!" she replied hotly. "It is he and not I that should be punished for murder. He is a devil." She saw Pierre's disbelieving glance. "But what do you know—or care?" She pushed up her dress, which had slid off her shoulder. "How far will we travel?" she asked, changing the subject.

"Many more days, perhaps to the ocean."

"I like the ocean," she remembered. The breeze blew the leaves and the sun gleamed through, making her eyes water. She turned away, her headache still pounding.

"Let us leave then," he commanded. He picked the blanket up off the ground and tossed it into the back of the wagon. He wiped off the lip of the pouch and drank some water. Then he broke off a piece of bread from the basket hidden under the boards of the seat, and got aboard the wagon seat while munching the crusty loaf.

Catherine got onto the seat next to him with some difficulty.

They rode for a long way in silence.

At noonday, Pierre stopped the wagon to let the horses drink from a stream and nibble at the grass along the banks there. He offered Catherine some food. She took it hungrily, and ate with her back turned to the servant.

Her mind was involved in plans of escape. "Returning to Jean is obviously out of the question," she rationalized. "Pouissent will be waiting for me to return." She grimaced. "He'll never leave me alone." As she thought about the Colonel, an intuitive shiver raised the hair on her head. She finished the cheese she was eating. "Do you have any wine?" she demanded haughtily.

"Yes," he answered abruptly, but he didn't stir.

She rummaged around until she found a bottle and drank from it greedily.

Pierre grabbed it out of her hand. "That's enough for now," he admonished.

Wiping off the red rivulets of wine dribbling down her chin, Catherine glared at him in silence.

As they rode, her backside ached. The seat was hard and the man sitting next to her even harder. She studied him but knew she could not make him change his mind. Time hung heavily in the warm afternoon, the horses kicking up dust on the road.

Pierre refused to stop at any of the towns they passed through and kept a tight grip on her wrist until they were safely beyond any town's borders.

"DuFont would not treat me so cruelly," she complained.

A sudden pain ached in his chest. "Shut your ungrateful mouth!" and he backhanded her across the cheek, leaving a red stinging welt. They rode on in mutually hostile silence.

Finally the trees thinned out and only bare sandy fields surrounded the road. The air was getting cooler. Catherine believed she could almost smell the salt in the air. "We must be getting near the ocean," she cried out.

Pierre smiled to himself grimly. *I am almost done with this distasteful duty.*

Catherine craned her neck, squinted her eyes to see if she could make out any details, and tried to stand up.

"Sit still," he ordered her.

But Catherine squirmed in her seat, anxious to terminate her dreary trip. "There's a town up ahead."

The road widened at a crossroads. Other wagons were traveling across the road. Pierre slowed the horses to avoid a collision. Before he realized it, Catherine had hopped off the wagon and was running down the road before them, avoiding horses and the cursing drivers.

"Catherine!" he shouted, but she disappeared from sight. He shrugged, feeling the heavy pouch in his shirt that duFont had entrusted to him for the woman's safety. He was exhausted and didn't want to chase the repulsive woman he detested any longer, even with the promise to the Baron fresh in his mind. She was like a wild animal, a nightmare he could not awaken from. He resigned her to whatever fate lay in store for her. With an expert flick of the reins, Pierre turned and began the long trip back to Quimont, intending to bury his Master, whatever the cost. A burial was his promise to himself. All thoughts of Catherine were gone from his mind now. He shuddered as he thought of Pouissent, a feral beast, not quite human. Pierre wasn't sure how he could deal with the Colonel, but he would have to try.

***

Catherine ran eagerly down the dirt road, grateful to be away from Pierre, breathing heavily. She slowed down somewhat as she ran through the town gates. Ahead was the main square, brightly colored wagons decorating the area. The stages were awash with acrobats and jugglers. Excitement flooded through her. *Therese?*

The audience was packed close together on that warm summer day, the plays ready to begin. Catherine pushed her way through the crowd to get a better look. She searched the players' features. Her face fell with disappointment. *I don't recognize a soul.* She stood there for a few minutes, trying to catch her breath and to decide what to do next.

Several men in the audience next to her eyed her appreciatively and licked their lips, even with her ragged and disheveled appearance. She hugged her ripped bodice tightly to her chest, momentarily aware of her tattered dress. One reached out to touch her round bottom.

Catherine felt the pressure on her backside and looked to see who was fondling her. A young farmer grinned at her. The stench of animals was strong on him. She wrinkled her nose in distaste. He reached out to grab her hand as she left but she yanked it away and quickly moved to the area behind the wagons.

She gasped as she spotted a rather muscular man, his back to her, signaling the performers. "Is it Rene?" she asked, hoping vehemently that her journey was over and she would be safe again.

The man turned, a huge scar from an old knife wound cut deeply into his cheek and across his nose. The stranger stared at her, angry at her intrusion. "You there, get away from here!" When Catherine didn't move, he boldly walked up to her.

She stood her ground, unafraid, a slight smile playing at the corner of her lips, remnants of her flirtatious days flitting through her memory.

"This is off limits," he said in a low-pitched voice.

"I was looking for Therese Lefevre."

The stage manager narrowed his eyes, taking a closer look at her. "How do you know Therese?"

"I traveled with her for several years," she explained, staring into his eyes in her peculiar hypnotic way.

"Hmmph," was his only reply. "We don't have need of any new performers just now."

"I can do anything, dancing, too," Catherine said emphatically. "I am particularly good—between acts," she added suggestively.

"Stay here," he motioned. "Let me see what I can do." He scratched his neck, sweating under the coarse woolen shirt he wore. He gave her a final appraising look and returned to his group.

Catherine looked around and found a large stone to sit on. She watched him interact with several other men. The whispered conversation was lively, with many gestures, until he finally pointed in her direction. His companions glanced at Catherine, then nodded their heads in assent and left the area.

The sun was very warm. She realized she hadn't eaten since morning and her stomach was complaining loudly. After a few minutes, but what seemed like hours, the big man returned to her side.

"I have decided to watch you perform, then I will make a decision. Business has not been good lately." He paused. "They call me Marmot." He looked at her disheveled appearance. "I will find you some decent clothes to wear and maybe a costume. Come with me."

"I must eat first. I'm starving," she complained.

"Yes, I will get you food, too." He felt an uncomfortable twinge in his belly and searched her face once again. "You are in trouble, aren't you?"

Catherine was taken aback by such forceful directness. "Yes," she replied. "Trouble with a man. He is looking for me."

Marmot said, "I can believe that, with your looks. If you were cleaned up, I think you would be most attractive." He edged up close to her.

Catherine could smell his stale breath.

His hard glare was unmistakable. He scratched his head. "I want no trouble from you while you are here. Do you understand me fully?"

"I understand," replied Catherine, returning his gaze.

The two wordlessly stood face-to-face for a few heartbeats. Finally Marmot turned away, satisfied for the moment. "If I find that you are not worth your keep, I will turn you out immediately."

"I am worthy!" Catherine spoke hotly. "I will make you money. You will see."

Soup was cooking over a fire at the campsite. One woman got a wooden bowl, ladled some of the soup into it, and wordlessly handed it to Catherine.

Grease floated on the top and the broth was peppery, but she was grateful to have something to eat. Catherine sat down on a tree stump and began eating the hot soup slowly.

A man sidled up to her, his face vastly wrinkled like a dried-up potato. He put his arm around her soft waist, giving her a squeeze.

"What's a young thing like you doing wandering alone?"

"Get away, old man, before I dump this hot soup on you and dampen your ardor."

The elderly actor pulled away hurriedly and disappeared into a dilapidated, faded wagon nearby.

Marmot watched the interaction, his face red with suppressed anger. "She had better bring in a *lot* of money!" Then he returned to oversee the performance.

That afternoon, after Catherine had cleaned up and changed into a borrowed dress, Marmot forgot his inner warnings. Her voluptuous body was thinner, but still round and inviting. Her long hair, freshly washed, gleamed in the twilight, its black highlights shimmering around her face. A slight breeze blew some of the silky strands, and they floated in the wind behind her. Marmot had an overwhelming urge to stroke its smoothness, but held back.

Women whispered among themselves, afraid of the newcomer in their midst.

"If she touches Noel, I will slit her throat in her sleep," said one woman jealously.

"Hush," replied her friend, "Marmot will hear you."

"I don't care," spat Maxine. "I know what she is capable of. I have known her a long time. She will only bring trouble to us."

"Be careful," Anna urged. "Your talk is dangerous. And you haven't been with us long yourself."

Catherine had heard the women's conversation, but pretended not to. She made a great show of stirring the cooking pot and smelling the delicious aroma of rabbit steaming from it. She had recognized Maxine and trembled, smelling danger as a deer smells a wolf.

When she bent over the cooking fire, several of the younger men hurried out of the glare of the campfires, embarrassed at the way their bodies responded to her. She was totally aware of the furor her appearance was making and it secretly delighted her. *I wonder which one is Noel,* she mused.

Marmot walked up to her. "I want to see you dance tomorrow," he said loudly enough for all to hear.

"Of course." Catherine nodded, smiling at him.

Marmot felt uncomfortable, as if a great predatory cat was stalking him. He wanted her to leave the gathering immediately. Yet at the same time he wanted to take her into his arms and kiss her on the mouth and take her to his wagon and fill her with his fire. He took a deep breath to bring his raging feelings into control.

"You better stay away from that new woman," Maxine informed her man Noel a few minutes later, "or you will both be sorry."

"Leave me alone, woman!" His eyes blazed at Maxine, but, undaunted, she glared back. He reached his arm back and slapped Maxine soundly on the face, the sound ringing in the still night air, knocking her to the ground. "Remember your place. I am the man here! I agreed to take you in but I can just as easily boot you out." He quickly looked around and saw approving looks from the other men.

She lowered her head; angry tears welled up in her eyes. But she held her tongue.

Marmot was instantly at their side. "What is the matter here?"

"Nothing," growled Noel. "Just a stupid woman trying to tell a man what to do."

Marmot took Noel by the shoulders and walked him a few feet away, out of earshot of Maxine. "Stay away from the new woman. She is..." He stopped, not knowing exactly what else to say. Just—stay away."

Noel nodded. He understood that Marmot wanted Catherine all to himself.

Marmot took Catherine by the hand and led her to his wagon for the night. She had observed the interplay of the three people and was both fearful and excited. Marmot would take good care of her, if she took good care of him.

In the morning when Catherine emerged in her costume and make-up from Marmot's wagon, she turned a number of heads. She asked Marmot who was following her. "Will I be able to have a wagon of my own?"

"Maybe We'll see if you dance as good as you say you do. So far I have no complaints."

Noel was eating breakfast when he heard the commotion and looked up to see what was causing it.

Catherine was walking through the campsite, hips swaying, her breasts bouncing under the low-cut fabric. The smell of wine was strong on her.

His mouth fell open at the sight, food still on his lips.

As she headed towards the performing area they had cleared, Catherine could see the gathering crowd. Midmorning was already hot and humid and many would stay home instead.

Catherine could feel the excitement rise within her. She felt tall, beautiful, and more powerful at these times. Her excitement made her shiver a little, as she waited behind the wagons, unsteady on her feet.

She heard music. It wasn't much, just a lute and a tambourine but it was enough for her.

Marmot appeared. "It's time. You had better be a very good dancer."

She smiled broadly and walked up the stairs and onto the stage. When she appeared, a shout was heard from a rowdy man in the first row. "Let's see the bitch dance."

Without understanding why, the words made Marmot's blood run cold, and he watched anxiously.

Catherine was the most lithe, sensuous dancer he had ever seen.

Her movements looked as though her bones had turned to water, so graceful and easy were they. He turned his head away for a moment to look at the audience. They were as entranced as he. Many stood to get a better look.

Catherine held the audience in her power. When she swayed, they sighed. When she moved her shoulders, breasts jiggling, they gasped. "She is incredible." Marmot said smiling to a helper. "She will bring in a lot of money."

The music got stronger, louder and wilder. Catherine's movements increased with the music. The audience began to clap their hands in time to the music, as she moved and twirled. Then dripping with perspiration, she ended her dance.

The audience roared with approval, and clapped. They threw coins and flowers at the stage. Catherine bowed deeply, showing her cleavage to its full advantage.

Albert Jouer, a pig farmer, was the man who had called for her to dance. He impetuously reached for her arm and pulled her off the stage. He fell on top of her, kissing her drunkenly. The audience shouted in one voyeuristic howl.

"Get off me, you drunken fool!" she cried.

Marmot strode over to the couple, and pulled them apart roughly, pushing Catherine aside.

She looked at the pig farmer for a moment with narrowed eyes. "How dare you!" she exclaimed. She pointed her first and fourth fingers at him, while her eyes widened and she said something unintelligible. It was the sign of the Evil Eye, the Maloick.

Maxine stood watching. "She gave that man the evil eye curse," she said, speaking to Anna standing behind her. "She is a witch, no doubt of it." Maxine grimaced and left.

Catherine sneered, then turned and walked back to the encampment. Her forehead and temples ached terribly. The pressure made her eyeballs feel as though they would pop out of her head. She went into Marmot's wagon, gulped some wine, curled up into a ball and fell deeply asleep, her outlandish makeup smearing the old quilt. She didn't smell the farmer as he came in and lay down next to her. She woke as Albert lifted her dress and climbed on top of her, rocking with pleasure. He quickly climaxed and passed out. She pushed him off her and turned on her side to sleep. Sometime later Marmot and Noel joined them in the wagon, all ferociously drunk and an orgy ensued.

Marmot woke in the dark to hear a heated argument just outside the wagon. Catherine was snoring quietly next to him, Noel on her other side. The pig farmer was missing. A woman's voice was raised shrilly, shrieking at her husband.

Marmot put a cloth around his waist and came out to find the pig farmer Albert and his wife Madame Jouer arguing furiously in the bright light of the harvest moon.

"You cannot leave me. What shall I do? Don't you care about your three children? We will starve without you." She desperately clung to his arm.

Shaking away her grip the pig farmer replied, "I don't care what happens. The children are probably not mine anyway," he added, as a final insult.

His wife beat on her husband's chest with her small fists, hysterical and frightened.

The farmer shoved her away from him and she fell down on the hard ground. She lay there, crying pathetically.

Marmot stepped back inside the wagon unnoticed and lay down next to Catherine. She was awake now.

The wretched woman got up and ran weeping from the encampment.

Albert swung open the wagon's wooden door, and stopped, suddenly realizing for the first time that there were two other men inside with Catherine. He had been too inebriated earlier to take notice what was happening.

Catherine looked up at the figure in the doorway, illuminated by the moonlight. The two men snickered. Marmot started to get up, but Catherine shoved him down.

She got up and picked her way to the doorway. She stood tall and proud; her naked body swaying voluptuously. "What do you want now?" she arrogantly asked the farmer.

"Darling Catherine, I want you. I left my farm, my wife, and my children to be with you."

Catherine lashed out in a lightning reflex. With a quick motion, and a snarl, she clawed deeply at Albert's face, her jagged fingernails drawing blood. Nostrils flaring, the pupils of her eyes dilated with unseen power, she stood before him, breathing heavily, looking at his bloody face. Her illness had developed into madness and her actions had become insanely violent. "No one can own me."

Albert stood as still as a stone, shocked by her vicious action. "Don't you love me?" he asked in a mournful voice.

Catherine laughed loudly and hysterically. "Love *you*? You must be mad! Go back to your pigs," she spat at him. "That is all you deserve!"

He could hear her crazy laughter follow him as he stumbled through the camp and fell on the ground in a daze. Through his pain, Albert saw two feet approach where he lay.

Maxine looked down at his bloody face. She spoke derisively. "See what has become of you. And all because of Catherine."

He put his hand over his eyes.

She knelt down and put her mouth to his ear. "She practices the black arts. You can see what her evil spell has done to you!"

He groaned, but ignored her.

Maxine kicked at him a little. "Come with me. We will go to the authorities and tell them of her wickedness."

Albert got up, dazed. He was numb with grief and jealousy, sickened by what had transpired. He blindly followed Maxine through the campground and into the town.

Later the sheriff and the Mayor of Lebec, followed Albert Jouer, led by Maxine back to the wagon. Maxine shivered in the cold night, hoping the men would believe her, and not brush her problem aside as a trivial woman's squabble. She knew Albert was a vital link in convincing them. After all, he was one of them, a farmer in this farming community.

When the group arrived at Marmot's wagon, Maxine looked at Albert. "You must provide the evidence."

The farmer hesitated. He looked at Catherine longingly.

Maxine pushed him up the stairs of the wagon.

Peals of raucous laughter emanated from the wagon, which provided the final impetus for him. He threw open the wagon door. The sheriff peered in, holding up a torch, trying to see clearly in the dim light.

Catherine bounced to her feet, angry at yet another interruption. As she did so, she realized that she had made a grave mistake. The sheriff held the torch high, scrutinizing her face. Then he glanced at Albert, to make the identification complete.

Albert pointed at Catherine and said in a broken voice, "This is the sorceress I told you about." Then he turned and ran, as though demons were pursuing him.

"Arrest her," the mayor ordered.

In the flickering firelight, Catherine looked like a diabolic nature spirit, totally naked, with only her long hair wildly draped around her.

The sheriff faltered.

Marmot got up and covered Catherine's nakedness with a cloak. He stood protectively in front of her, but she pushed him aside.

"The Baron Jean du Font will make you pay for this outrage!" her rich voice reverberated in the night air. She elbowed past the sheriff and directed her appeal to the Mayor. "Send a messenger to Quimont. Monsieur du Font will clear me of this false and dangerous accusation."

"The Baron is dead and can help you no more," snarled a familiar voice out of the darkness.

Catherine recognized that voice, and froze.

"The Baron's servant was...*kind* enough...to tell me where you had fled." Col. Pouissent strode up to the wagon and sneered at her. "Up to your old tricks Catherine?" He saw Noel jump out of the wagon and disappear into the shadows. "I see your taste in men has sadly declined. You should have stayed with me." He motioned to his soldiers, who roughly grabbed hold of Catherine on either side." He laughed, while Catherine, powerless, fumed on the step.

"Madame?" he asked.

Maxine stepped forward.

"You deserve a reward for helping us to find so evil a witch as this one." He handed her a bag of coins, which jingled seductively.

Gloating Maxine said, "A very careless witch." She jangled the bag of coins in Catherine's face. "You should have stayed away from Noel." She turned and vanished into the night.

Marmot spoke up. "What evidence do you have that this woman is a witch?"

Pouissent looked at him, and shook his head. "If you search your soul, you will know. Even now, she has you under her dark spell."

"That's absurd," Marmot protested. "You are wrong."

"Then you must be in league with her," replied Pouissent. Motioning to the soldiers, "Arrest this man also."

As several soldiers held him, struggling, Marmot challenged the Colonel. "I am not a witch and neither is Catherine. You are mad to believe the prattle of a jealous woman."

Pouissent motioned to his men, who then forcibly took Marmot away, yelling obscenities. The Cardinal's chief officer merely turned away from the noise, irked with the resistance.

Catherine was left alone, inside. She glared at him but kept her mouth shut.

"Have nothing to say for yourself, eh?" He mounted the steps and stroked her face. She cringed and tried to draw back from his foul touch, but her captors held her tightly.

"What you say about Jean isn't true!" she spluttered at him.

"I saw his stiff, white body, with a dagger hole through the heart. Foolish man." He shook his head in mock sadness. "He is dead all right, and cannot defend you against your long overdue, well-deserved punishment."

"No!" cried Catherine. "I don't believe you."

"I should have seen you for what you are." He threw up his arms. "But, alas, I was enchanted by you as well."

"Liar!" she countered.

"My dear, haven't you learned that a lady speaks only when spoken to, with her eyes cast demurely down?" He motioned to the men and they pulled her out of the wagon and down the steps.

Catherine strained to break free from her captors. Her fear made her strong, yet she was unable to get away. She stared at Pouissent with profound hatred glittering in her eyes, and spat at him.

"Down, I said!" He hit her on the side of the head with the handle of his dagger.

She slumped unconscious into the arms of the soldiers, who carried her off, followed by the Sheriff and the Mayor of Lebec. All but one of his troops brought up the rear.

The Colonel turned to his most trusted soldier. "Ride quickly to Quimont and return with Cardinal Malplaquet immediately. Tell him we have found the sorceress. She'll burn by All Hallow's Eve, unless I'm mistaken."

The obedient soldier bowed, then found his horse and rode swiftly to Quimont.

Pouissent looked around, examined the inside of the cabin. He thought for a moment, picked up the red dress Catherine had discarded, then left, following his prize captive.

CATHERINE

Part 12

Catherine, after many weeks in the dank prison, was convicted as a sorceress by the holy Inquisition headed by Cardinal Malplaquet, and sentenced to die by the cleansing flame. She was subsequently led to the pyre and tied to the stake. Her mouth was gagged with a sodden rag, so that no unholy words could escape from her lips.

The hooded man held up a torch and lit the wood at Catherine's feet.

The mob gasped to see the fire roar up, smoke billowing thickly, making it difficult to see the unholy demonstration. The fire licked at the hem of Catherine's red dress, catching hold, moving quickly up her body in a fiery caress, crackling in its eager passion. She twisted and turned, trying to escape the cords that bound her. Only her eyes spoke, wide with terror and unbearable pain. *They can't get away with this,* she thought. *I'll make them pay.* The flames danced higher, obliterating all else.

The crowd, watching her fiery anguish, yelled its approval and gestured wildly.

The sky, which had been murky and overcast all day since the public trial began, darkened even more. Thunder could be heard in the distance. Lightning crackled into the countryside, startling the people gathered around the bonfire, eager to watch the sorceress die. A strong wind buffeted them.

As the sorceress looked up into the roiling black clouds, her dark hair blowing wildly in the strengthening wind, she seemed to summon her demon lovers, imploring them to help her. The wind moaned its answer to her, but the freshening gale only blew the flames higher.

The bystanders had hoped for a spectacle, but today was beyond their wildest expectations. The witch displayed magnificent powers, calling the violent storm to her. Strong gusts of wind whipped at their clothing.

Smoke billowed thickly around the stake, shutting out her image from the curious eyes of those who strained to watch, stinging the eyes of priest and official, noble and peasant alike.

"Can you see her?" croaked an old man, looking over the heads of the crowd at the elevated mounds of the execution area. He coughed and choked.

His daughter-in-law shouted to him, in order to be heard above the roar, "No, the smoke blocks my view. Listen." She put her finger to her lips.

Groans rose involuntarily from Catherine's throat, due to the heated expansion of her bodily liquids. At the sound, a clamor rose from the assembled horde. Thunder bellowed loudly from the dark sky. Nearby a flash of lightning split apart a tree, alarming the on-lookers.

Suddenly rain began to pour down upon them in an unholy outburst of water. The crowd was soaked to the skin in the chill autumn air. Nobles pulled their velvet robes closer around themselves, hoping to stay dry.

The deluge extinguished the flames.

Although they were soaked, the rabble strained to see the sorceress. "Did her evil companions rescue her?"

But the redeeming rain had come too late to save the sorceress. Catherine was dead, her body charred beyond recognition.

As the downpour continued without letup the crowd dispersed, hurrying for their warm, dry homes or snug taverns.

"Our work is done here, Your Eminence," reported the Colonel.

Cardinal Malplaquet glanced at Pouissent, pulling his red hood over his face as they scurried out of the rain.

Catherine's young, broken body was dumped in a deep pit in unconsecrated ground, heaped on top of other corpses. No one would mourn her. Indeed, many from Lebec and elsewhere were celebrating her death. At the end of her short life there was only the silent void. Her charred remains gave way to worms and decay.

CATHERINE, *Lauren O. Thyme © 2019*

APPENDIX 2

ASTROLOGY

My chart is not the worst—nor the best—I've seen in my 46 years of practicing astrology. When I was in astrology class during my yearlong instruction, our teacher gave us students a chart to examine. We were appalled and speechless at the horror of what we were scrutinizing. How could this person survive?

One of us said to our teacher that she didn't know how to interpret it—it was "too awful."

Our teacher smiled grimly. "This is the chart of a baby who lived a mere three days!"

We gasped in unison.

"A soul is only given a chart he or she can tolerate or else he or she dies," my teacher summarized.

Her illustration made an impression that was deep as a chasm. I never forgot that class and what my teacher taught me.

History of Astrology

Many cultures have attached importance to astronomical events, including the Indians, Chinese, and Mayans.

Among Indo-European peoples, astrology has been dated to the 3rd millennium BCE, with roots in calendrical systems. A form of astrology was practiced in the first dynasty of Mesopotamia (1950–1651 BCE). Chinese astrology was elaborated in the Zhou dynasty (1046–256 BCE). Hellenistic astrology after 332 BCE mixed Babylonian astrology with Egyptian Decanic astrology in Alexandria, creating horoscopic astrology. Alexander the Great's conquest of Asia allowed astrology to spread to Ancient Greece and Rome. In Rome, astrology was associated with 'Chaldean wisdom'. After the collapse of Alexandria in the 7th century, astrology was taken up by Islamic scholars, and Hellenistic texts were translated into Arabic and Persian. In the 12th century, Arabic texts were imported to Europe and translated into Latin, helping to initiate the European Renaissance, when major astronomers including Tycho Brahe, Sir Isaac Newton, Johannes Kepler and Galileo practiced as astrologers. Astrological references appear in literature such as Dante Alighieri, Geoffrey Chaucer, Christopher Marlowe and William Shakespeare.

Astrology today

Modern astrologers believe there is a correlation between what is happening astronomically and what happens to individuals, nations, and the earth itself. It may be a rephrasing of an old maxim: "As above, so below." How astrology actually works and how it can be so specific to individuals and events is still an eternal mystery, not quite answered.

Before the advent of computers, a chart was "drawn" manually, which took hours and many mathematical calculations. An astrologer had to have been educated in mathematics and astronomy, as well as have a familiarity with human proclivities, personalities, social interactions, and frailties. Most of the attributes assigned to various planets, signs of the zodiac and "houses" were created long ago. Using specific software, a chart now can be cast in a matter of seconds.

Some people scoff and say they don't "believe" in astrology. It's like saying they don't believe in physics or psychology. Scientists continue to add theories and information to the growing body of scientific knowledge. The same is true of astrology. There is a basic tenet to astrology, and the rest is interpretation. The chart is an exact scientific, mathematical, astronomical creation of a precise, cosmic moment in time. The rest is analysis, clarification, theory, and explanation. For millennia astrology and astronomy were linked together as one science. Only in the last few hundred years have those been separated, and astrology became ridiculed by religions and scientists. The more I study astrology, the more amazed I become as I uncover unbelievably complex synchronicities of personality and events.

Your birth chart

I spend time studying the specifics of a chart. That's where the art of astrology comes into play. I use my own schooling, 46 years of study, along with other astrologers' interpretations, and whatever wisdom I've gleaned to make sense of a chart, plunging into depths of discovery. Every chart is unique and will not be found anywhere else in time or history. Each person is a totally unique individual in the history of the cosmos.

The birth (also called natal) chart is one's life blueprint. This chart consists of 10 planets (sun and moon are considered planets in astrology as is Pluto). The planets are projected against the cosmic sky—called the zodiac—from our perspective here on earth, containing 12 signs, each 30 degrees wide. If you know your exact birth time, then I will also interpret those planets and signs in specific houses as well as your rising sign, the sign on the eastern horizon at the moment of your birth. A chart will change significantly every 5 minutes, so an exact time is helpful. I can do a chart without a time and will use noon, which is standard procedure. The houses of your horoscope represent different spheres of your life, described in terms of physical surroundings as well as personal life experiences. Sometimes a planet is in contact with one or more of your other birth planets, called an aspect, which can be either "easy" or "challenging" to your blueprint. Easy aspects are the abilities, skills, traits, and talents gleaned from other life-times or, at the very least, are the traits, abilities, and knowledge that come easily to us. The more challenging the aspect, the more you have an opportunity to learn, grow and evolve into the lessons chosen for this life.

One of the most difficult birth charts I've ever seen belonged to Mahatma Gandhi. He had a number of challenging aspects: triple t square; Pluto opposition to Venus and Mars; Uranus square Neptune and Ascendant; with the sun in the 12th house of confinement and imprisonment.

My personal theory of life as connected to astrology is that:

— A soul chooses to come to earth to learn certain lessons.

— With the assistance of higher vibrational, enlightened beings known as the Council of Elders, a soul decides on a specific course of action.

— The soul "surfs" into life on a particular wave of energy/thought arriving at her birth moment. That moment is cast indelibly into the chart and into the history of the cosmos.

— The chart is a blueprint of that soul's current life, including personality traits, strengths, talents, weaknesses, challenges, and desires, in order to learn the lessons decided upon in advance. These attributes are neither good nor bad, but simply part of the contract in order to learn the appropriate lessons. Furthermore, the chart is not set in stone, but simply a set of possibilities or probabilities. The soul chooses from those, as life events unfold, in order to evolve.

— I've often been asked about free will. I believe we are confined within the borders of our blueprint/chart, and only able to work within its limitations, a "box" of sorts. Each of us lives within our box; I've never seen anyone move beyond one's chart. Furthermore, I believe that it's not what we "do" necessarily, but how we respond to life's challenges and other people that helps us to grow and evolve.

— Even if you don't agree with my theories, astrology can still work splendidly for you, especially if you have an open mind and curiosity about the synchronicities and correspondences found in your chart as relating to you and your life. I've had clients who told me that understanding their astrological blueprint helped them to relax, to more deeply appreciate themselves and their lives, and to stop judging themselves and others so harshly.

— One final note—astrology isn't an exact science, but an art. Astrology deals with "tendencies" rather than absolutes. Furthermore, a segment of one's interpretation may be accurate, while another isn't. Also there may be conflicting or contradictory tendencies in one's chart. That is common for everyone, and shows where there is tension and/or complexity in one's life. A person might act one way one day or in one set of circumstances, and another in some other milieu or time or relationship. The study of one's astrological chart can last a lifetime.

Charts and analyses

My father's natal astrological chart is the only one I've ever examined that shows unhealthy sexual boundaries and behavior. The planets in his chart warn of cold, unfeeling personality traits, the danger of which would be to shut down his emotional life altogether, and is what I believed happened with him.

My mother's natal astrological chart is almost as difficult as Gandhi's. She was "hemmed in" and generally frustrated by what is known as a Grand Cross, one of the most demanding of astrological configurations. The planets in her chart also warn of cold, unemotional personality traits, although not as chilly as my Father's.

My birth chart as compared to both my mother and father are painful and unaligned with having them as suitable, helpful, or beneficial parents. One of the descriptions of a comparison of one of my planets to one of my mother's planets is that we would be "enemies until death." In contrast, my sister's chart is favorable to both my mother and father, as if we are from completely different families (or different planets!). Obviously my sister and I came to earth and chose these parents for dissimilar reasons. Challenging interactions between a parent and child can indicate neglect, abandonment, even abuse. I have both parents in that configuration. When studying astrology it's easier to be forgiving and understanding of self and others from a cosmic viewpoint.

In the "blueprint of my life," I have ultra-sensitivity in mystical, psychic areas with difficulty in practical matters, along with deceit, deception, and secrets by others—Neptune square Sun, Moon, Mercury, and Mars. Ease of sensitivity, spirituality, and psychic abilities is indicated in job and career—Neptune sextile Saturn and Pluto. Mars square Neptune refers to alcoholic and drug related relationships with partners, husbands, and lovers. Yes, unfortunately.

That's a lot of Neptune for one chart!

I show various skills in communication—writing, lecturing, acting, and teaching—Sun conjunct Mars in 3rd house. Strong practical skills are indicated in this area—Mercury in Capricorn conjunct Sun and Mars.

I have Pluto conjunct Midheaven, which is considered to be an attribute of a researcher. Dr. Marie Curie, the discoverer of plutonium, had Pluto conjunct Midheaven. Pluto conjunct Midheaven is also a natural psychologist. My education includes a B.S. in Transpersonal Psychology as well as many decades of study on my own and counseling others. I "added" Pluto on the Midheaven to my blueprint so that I could research, discover, and understand my own psychology, as well as that of others.

Uranus is strong in my chart, which is considered to have a "locomotive" shape (4 empty houses in a row). Uranus is the engine of that locomotive, which translates to a person who is unusual as well as independent and self-reliant (adding my three planets in Capricorn), while interested in uncommon studies, particularly astrology.

My empty houses are: 4th house—childhood, home, and mother; 5th house—pleasure, love, and entertainment; 6th house—health and service to others; 7th house—relationships and marriage. These empty sectors mean that **none of the major planetary energies are affecting the matters of those vacant sectors.** Instead their energies are focused elsewhere.

I have Scorpio rising in my chart as well as Jupiter in Scorpio. I am unafraid of experiencing extremes and going to the depths of life. I refer to myself as a "balls to the walls" kind of woman. I willingly go "where angels fear to tread."

North node in 8th house:

> "As the Lunar Nodes indicate Karmic debts and connections with previous lifetimes, the native who has the North Node in the 8th house [me] must concentrate on developing his occult skills, and learn through transformation. The North Node always shows us what road we must follow in order to develop ourselves, and most of the times it is not the easiest one to choose."–*https://theastrocodex.com/north-node-in-the-8th-house/*

Since I was born within 10 minutes of a full moon, I have Sun opposition Moon. This refers to health problems and lack of physical energy, especially with an empty 6th house of health, as well as being as at cross purposes with myself and others. The Moon in hard aspect to Neptune indicates health problems that may be nebulous and difficult to pinpoint or diagnose. The empty 4th house relating to my moon shows a lack of a stable home and my mother's failure to nurture me. My moon has one easy aspect to Jupiter and three difficult ones to Sun, Mars, and Neptune. So my emotions, home life, childhood and mother are generally problematic but sometimes I'm "saved" at the last minute by Jupiter's beneficence. Neptune shows lies, deceit, and confusion in regards to my home life with Mars adding a sexual flavor to the mix. My moon is particularly strong in Cancer, as are my emotions. I feel everything deeply and am compassionate as well. The Elders tell me I'm a "virtuoso of emotion." With Mars opposing the Moon conjunct the Sun, I have a strong temper as well as a strong sex drive, with many detours.

Then there is Pluto.

I am what Donna Cunningham calls a Plutonian.

> "Plutonians are those people with a strong Pluto, Scorpio, and/or 8th house tendencies who have difficult childhoods that feature losses, betrayals, or abuses of power." – Donna Cunningham *http://www.neptunecafe.com/donnaC1.html*

I scored 51 points from Cunningham's Pluto questionnaire (see Appendix 3), a very strong Plutonian.

I also have Pluto conjunct Saturn, which Donna Cunningham describes:

> "...may signal tough life circumstances, losses, obstacles, and challenges that test endurance and character to the limits...

For the most part, they grew up afraid, either due to harsh conditions in their surroundings or to parents who were haunted by fear… [they] are also Survivors—they exist in survival mode much of the time, and they have the strength to endure conditions and losses that would crush the average person. While this strength is admirable, there's also a tendency… to endure a situation or hang on to a person for far longer than is reasonable to do so."

–Donna Cunningham
http://www.neptunecafe.com/donnaC1.html

This trait is known as codependency.

Transits

I have a tricky chart so anytime a demanding transit hits one of my planets it reverberates like a bowling ball striking the planetary pins.

During 2012-2018 I survived four Pluto transits:

Pluto conjunct Mercury, Sun, and Mars, while Pluto was opposing my Moon. I encountered: death of my partner of a 21 year relationship; death of my best friend; major financial losses; sold all my possessions and moved to Santa Fe to be with my lover; then after one month was abandoned by my lover; major upsets and needing to stand up for myself again and again. I left still another dysfunctional, karmic relationship four years later, in 2018. Here are the details below:

1. **Pluto conjunct Mercury**—communication, writing, research, and study projects; loss of a sibling (my sister and I broke contact for over two years).

2. **Pluto conjunct Mars**—standing up for myself, often in explosive and not-so-gentle ways; anger, aggressiveness, and assertiveness. Thank goodness I know how to make amends. My

sexual energy expanded to 10,000 levels (at 65 years old), as my kundalini burst forth, without hardly any sexual satisfaction.

3. **Pluto conjunct Sun**—health and personality transformation; body and self-esteem changes; death of an important male figure (my partner died and two lovers subsequently left me).

4. **Pluto opposition Moon**—transformation of childhood issues. This was an extremely painful time as it brought up all unhealed areas to be rehabilitated. I had emotional flashbacks almost every day during this period. I learned about complex PTSD and worked on myself: mother; childhood; family; memories; death of an important female figure (my best girlfriend of 37 years died). I had two romantic relationships during this transit that mirrored my difficulties with each of my parents, so I was healing parental issues through each of those men. I bless them!

5. **2017 – 2021 Pluto sextile Jupiter**—positive (dare I say stress-free?) energy towards publishing; transformation through publishing; expansion in my career and work. Thank heavens I'm on a more enjoyable path as of November 2018, while publishing a lot of books.

My soul chose everything that shows up in my astrology chart, which were imprinted at the moment of my birth— in order to learn, grow, and evolve. Everything is perfect, no matter what it looks like.

I've now become a Pluto expert for astrology clients.

APPENDIX 3

HOW STRONG IS YOUR PLUTO?

"Would you be considered a Plutonian person? You would if Pluto, the sign of Scorpio, and the 8th house are strong in your birth chart. Below is a test to give these chart features a score and then a description of what that scores says about you. While there aren't any scientific measurements of a planet's strength, I've assigned number scores to certain chart factors, based on 40 years of doing charts professionally. This test is Skywriter's [website created by Donna Cunningham] most popular post of all times, with over 50,000 taking the test as of January 2015.

In order to find these elements of a chart, you'd need to be at least an intermediate student [of astrology] or know someone who can do it for you. In each of the categories below, add the total score of all the factors that apply to that item, and write the total on the line next to it. Then add all the items up to find out how your Pluto ranks.

Limited degrees for aspects: 8° for a conjunction or opposition, up to 6° for a square or trine, 3° for minor aspects. The only exception would be a conjunction or opposition to the Midheaven or Ascendant which can be up to 10°. Minor aspects, for 2° each, include the sextile, septile, semisextile, quincunx, quintile, semisquare, and sesqui-quadrate.

Here's the test:

Pluto in aspect

Pluto conjunct, square, trine, or opposition the Sun, Moon, Ascendant or Midheaven	10 ea	____
Pluto conjunct, square, trine or opposite other planets	5 ea	____
Pluto in minor aspect to the Sun, Moon, Ascendant, Midheaven or other planets	2 ea	____
Part of major configuration like a stellium, T-square or Grand Trine	5 ea	____
Stellium planets – lead planet, first in series, or Alpha Dog	5 ea	____

Pluto/8th house features

Pluto in Scorpio	10 ea	____
Ascendant in Scorpio	10 ea	____
Sun, Moon, or Midheaven in Scorpio	5 ea	____
Other planets in Scorpio	3 ea	____
Sun or Moon in the 8th house	5 ea	____
Other planets in the 8th house	3 ea	____

Bonus:

Add 2-5 for each factor such as Pluto aspects to the Nodes or Part of Fortune in Scorpio or the 8th house	2-5 ea	____
	TOTAL	____

Score: 0-10 would be considered low, while 15-30 indicates a moderately strong influence. 30-60 strong. Scores as high as 70 – very strong indeed. You're definitely a Plutonian.

What does being a Plutonian mean?

Pluto has a wide range of expressions. At the unevolved level, Plutonians can engage in manipulating or coercing others, abuses of power, battles for control, resentments or grievances, failing for spite [a self-destructive way to get even with someone], and being a target of other people's projections.

At the evolved level, the expressions can include transforming, healing, and empowering themselves and people and conditions they care about. Plutonians can have a natural gift for psychology, the healing arts, and understanding what makes people tick.

Pluto issues include: power and control; trust; to discover and analyze what lies beneath the surface and eliminate the undesirable; separateness; holding on to things or feelings; revenge; death and endings; rebirth; healing; and transformation.

Worldly matters associated with Pluto/Scorpio: healing; psychology; sexuality; wealth; uses and abuses of power; corruption and dirty dealing; secrets; exposés; occult; death and the afterlife; national and personal debt; stocks.

Examples of Plutonian occupations: psychotherapist; healer; medium; past life therapist; researcher; grief counselor; OB/GYN staff; cancer treatment; sex therapist; insurance agent; financial planner; stock broker.

If you had a high score, you're an over-achiever in the matters of Pluto. You're probably a Plutonian and therefore extremely strong in some of the qualities listed above—the positive ones, the negative ones, or more likely both ends of the spectrum at once. You may alternate between isolation and being joined at the hip in obsessive relationships. In the worst of times, you could be controlling; mistrustful; have emotional intensity; bitter; vengeful. And/or you may be dedicated to healing yourself and, as you learn how to do that, can become a natural healer and catalyst in the lives of people around you.

If you had a low score, you may be an under-achiever in the matters of Pluto. If your score is down in the single digits, you may be lacking in some of the qualities listed above. You may not often look deeply within and may be missing important psychological insights that could help you change undesirable patterns. When you've had a bad setback, you may take longer to mobilize yourself to come back from it. On the bright side, you're probably pretty easy-going and not likely to carry grudges or harbor plans for revenge. Unless you're challenged by Pluto transits, you might not give a rat's behind about transforming yourself or your world.

Example of a Plutopalooza:

Actor Matt Damon, who has 3 planets in Scorpio, 4 planets in the 8th house, and a Grand Trine that involves Pluto, is a big time Plutonian with a score of 50.*

© *1-16-2010, revised 5/2012 by Donna Cunningham, MSW*
Lauren has a score of 51

APPENDIX 4

Healing Modalities; Books; Workbooks; Websites

Some other healing modalities—in no particular order
Psychotherapy—inner child work; Complex PTSD; Borderline Personality Disorder; and many more
Rebirthing (conscious breathing)
Hypnosis
Bodywork, exercise, yoga, tai chi, qi gong, Egoscue method
Nutrition—diet, supplements
Holistic, preventive, alternative medicine, Naturopathy, homeopathy, Ayurveda
Forgiveness
Surrender, including 12-step programs
12-step groups—ACA (Adult children of Alcoholics & Dysfunctional families); Alanon (family and friends of alcoholics); Co-dependents Anonymous; SIA (Survivors of Incest Anonymous); AA (Alcoholics Anonymous); NA (Narcotics Anonymous); OA (Overeaters Anonymous)
Past lives therapy
Astrological counseling
MDMA—pharmaceutical grade ecstasy coupled with intensive psychological therapy due to be available to the public in 2020-2021
Ketamine coupled with psychological therapy – for drug-resistance depression, anxiety, PTSD and complex PTSD
Abraham-Hicks workshops and Youtube

Books

Pete Walker, *Complex PTSD: From Surviving to Thriving*

Judith Herman, *Trauma and Recovery; Father/Daughter Incest*

Christine A. Courtois, *Healing the Incest Wound: It's Not You, It's What Happened to You*

E. Sue Blume, *Secret Survivors: Uncovering Incest and its Aftereffects in Women*

Bessel van der Kolk, T*he Body Keeps the Score*

Dr. Jim Hopper, et al *Mindfulness-Oriented Interventions for Trauma*

Patrick Carnes, Ph.D. *The Betrayal Bond*

Mic Hunter, *Abused Boys: The Neglected Victims of Sexual Abuse*

Donna Cunningham, *Healing Pluto Problems*

Caroline W. Casey, *Making the Gods Work for You*

Robert Hand, *Planets in Transit*

Eckhardt Tolle, *The Power of Now*

Lola Jones, *Everything is Going Great in My Absence*

Gerald Jampolsky, M.D., *Love is Letting Go of Fear*

David R. Hawkins, M.D., *Power vs. Force*

Pete Egoscue with Roger Gittines, *Pain-Free: A Revolutionary Methhod for Stopping Chronic Pain*

Lauren O. Thyme with Sareya Orion, *The Lemurian Way: Remembering Your Essential Nature*

Liah Holtzman & Lauren O. Thyme, *Forgiveness Equals Fortune*

Lauren O. Thyme, *Cosmic GrandmaWisdom; Alternatives for Everyone*

Workbooks

Twelve Steps of Adult Children

The PTSD Workbook, Mary Beth Williams, Ph.D.; Soil Poijula, Ph.D. (including complex PTSD)

The Dialectical Behavior Therapy Skills Workbook, Matthew McKay, Ph.D.; Jeffrey C. Wood, Ph.D.; Jeffrey Brantley, M.D.

The Twelve Steps & Twelve Traditions Workbook, Co-Dependents Anonymous

Some websites

Pete-walker.com

Jimhopper.com

Drchriscourtois.com

Survivormanual.com

https://besselvanderkolk.net

Drjudithorloff.com

Myersbriggs.org

Abraham-hicks.com

APPENDIX 5

STAGES OF RECOVERY

Section 1: Judith Herman's Stages of Recovery, *Trauma and Recovery*
Section 2: Mic Hunter's Stages of Recovery, *Abused Boys*

Section 1: Herman's Stages of Recovery

(reprinted by permission from Dr. Jim Hopper
https://www.jimhopper.com/) Jim Hopper has worked closely with
Judith Hermann and Mic Hunter and has permission to use their concepts.

"In her classic book *Trauma and Recovery*, Judith Herman presents a
three-stage model of recovery which describes in detail the healing
process of people who struggle with a combination of problems related
to unwanted, abusive, or traumatic experiences.

The problems may include:

- Difficulty regulating emotions and impulses

- Emotional numbing

- Anger and aggression

- Substance addictions

- Behavioral addictions (porn, anonymous sex, gambling, etc.)

- Self-harming behaviors (cutting, burning, etc.)

- Dissociation (spacing out, blanking out, losing time, etc.)

Stage 1

The first stage of dealing with and overcoming such problems, and of any helpful therapy or counseling, is about:

- Getting a 'road map' of the healing process.

- Setting treatment goals and learning about helpful approaches to reaching those goals.

- Establishing safety and stability in one's body, one's relationships, and the rest of one's life.

- Tapping into and developing one's own inner strengths, and any other potentially available resources for healing.

- Learning how to regulate one's emotions and manage symptoms that cause suffering or make one feel unsafe.

- Developing and strengthening skills for managing painful and unwanted experiences, and minimizing unhelpful responses to them.

Most important, the key to healing from traumatic experiences in childhood is achieving these 'stage-one' goals of personal safety, genuine self-care, and healthy emotion-regulation capacities. Once these have become standard operating procedures, great progress and many new choices become possible.

Importantly, the first stage of recovery and treatment is not about discussing or 'processing' memories of unwanted or abusive experiences, let alone 'recovering' them. (For more on how the stages of recovery are related to memories of abuse, particularly recovered memories see Personal Questions under Recovered Memories.)

Of course, everything is not always so perfectly ordered and sequential.

For example, during the first stage it may be necessary to discuss the contents of disturbing memories that are disrupting one's life. This may be required to help manage the memories, or to understand why it is hard to care for oneself (e.g., the abuser acted like or even said you were unworthy of care or love). However, in this case addressing memories is not the focus of therapy, but a means to achieving safety, stability, and greater ability to take care of oneself.

Depending on the person, the first stage of treatment may also involve:

- Addressing problems with alcohol or drugs, depression, eating behaviors, physical health, panic attacks, and/or dissociation (e.g., spacing out, losing time).

- Taking medication to reduce anxiety and/or depressive symptoms, for example serotonergic reuptake inhibitors (SSRIs) like sertraline (Zoloft) or paroxetine (Paxil).

- Participating in Dialectical Behavior Therapy (DBT), a treatment for people having serious problems with tolerating and regulating emotions, interpersonal effectiveness, and/or self-harming behaviors.

Common to All Stages

Throughout all stages of treatment, it is often necessary to address psychological themes and 'dynamics' related to one's history of unwanted or abusive experiences.

Some core issues that determine the very nature and structure of treatment include:

- Powerlessness

- Shame and guilt

- Distrust

- Reenacting abusive patterns in current relationships

In the first stage of treatment, these themes and dynamics must be addressed when they are obstacles to safety, self-care, and regulating one's emotions and behavior. Therapy can help with recognizing habitual behavior patterns, beliefs, and motivations that maintain self-defeating and self-destructive behaviors outside of conscious awareness or reflection.

Increased awareness of these themes and dynamics brings greater understanding, greater ability to take responsibility for them, and greater capacities to choose new, healthier responses and actions.

Stage 2

This stage of recovery and treatment is often referred to as 'remembrance and mourning.'

The main work of stage two involves:

- Reviewing and/or discussing memories to lessen their emotional intensity, to revise their meanings for one's life and identity, etc.

- Working through grief about unwanted or abusive experiences and their negative effects on one's life.

- Mourning or working through grief about good experiences that one did not have, but that all children deserve.

After establishing a solid foundation of understanding, safety, stability, and self-regulation skills one can decide   mindful of the potential pain and risks involved—whether or not to engage in the work of stage two.

In fact, once the first stage of recovery has provided such a foundation, some people realize that thinking and talking about painful memories is not necessary to achieve their goals, at least in the short term. Some find that the memories are no longer disrupting their life and no longer of much interest to them. (And sometimes people need to teach their therapists about this!)

For those who choose to focus on disturbing memories, including because those memories are still disrupting their lives, several 'memory processing' methods can be used during this stage.

In general, these methods involve re-experiencing the memories within a safe and healing therapy setting. They can be very effective at ending the influence of such memories in one's daily life.

Most importantly, there are very effective therapy methods that have been proven, through years of clinical experience and research, to bring great relief and healing by transforming memories and responses to reminders of harmful childhood experiences.

(Please note: None of these methods 'erase' memories, and they are not designed to 'recover' memories.

One of the most research-supported approaches for processing traumatic memories is EMDR This method can rapidly transform traumatic memories into non-traumatic ones—and you don't have to talk about them in detail, if at all, making it a great option for some men and woman.

Again, the main point here is that *there are effective and relatively rapid methods for dealing with intensely distressing memories.* People do not have to be tortured by them for years.

Stage 3

The third stage of recovery focuses on reconnecting with people, meaningful activities, and other aspects of life.

I will not go into that stage here, but recommend reading *Trauma and Recovery*, which describes all three stages of recovery in depth and detail."

Section 2: Mic Hunter's Stages of Recovery

(reprinted by permission from Dr. Jim Hopper
https://www.jimhopper.com/)

Hunter's Stages of Recovery

This model is described in detail in Mic Hunter's *Abused Boys*, one of the first books written for men struggling with the effects of unwanted or abusive boyhood sexual experiences.

The model comes from Hunter's experiences of helping men and women sort out and overcome the effects of such experiences. It applies to both men and women dealing with the effects of any kind of child abuse, including emotional and physical abuse.

Hunter found parallels with the stages of grieving the loss of an important person in one's life— which makes sense, because harmful childhood experiences and their effects are often experienced as causing one to 'lose' important aspects of oneself (for example, one's masculinity or femininity, confidence, trust, or enjoyment of life).

1. Denial—'Nothing happened...'

Denial doesn't necessarily mean refusing to acknowledge something that is true, though this can be the case. Rather, it refers to a variety of ways that people can—for very good reasons—push memories of unwanted childhood sexual experiences out of their awareness. These ways range from completely 'blocking out' or 'splitting off' memories, without even realizing it, at one extreme, to intentionally, and often with great effort, trying to keep memories and reminders from breaking into consciousness, at the other.

Most people who have had such experiences, but haven't yet sorted them out or dealt with their effects, find themselves somewhere in the middle. They have clues that something happened, or fragments of memory that pop into awareness, but these are quickly pushed away or 'blocked out' whenever they come into awareness.

There are many reasons that people have for pushing such memories and related thoughts out of their minds. They can trigger unwanted feelings like anger, sadness, fear, or horror. They can trigger unwanted and disturbing thoughts—about one's masculinity, about important people and relationships in one's life (past and present), and about what would happen if such memories and thoughts were not always pushed away.... It is neither helpful nor respectful to push or try to convince a man to look at such memories or information which suggest that he may have had childhood sexual experiences that are causing him problems now.

On the other hand, as Hunter points out, it can be costly to keep such information out of awareness. In some cases, it uses 'cognitive resources' that are needed for other purposes, like one's school, work, or job responsibilities. It can keep one in constant (if unacknowledged) fear of experiencing any vulnerable emotions that could trigger unwanted feelings, thoughts, and memories about the sexual experiences. This means being unable to experience or tolerate *other people's* vulnerable emotions, which is necessary for caring about their suffering and doing the right thing to help.

Also, emotions tend to be a 'package deal.' Disconnection from negative emotions usually means experiencing few positive ones either, or not even getting close to experiencing one's potential to have fun and be happy. People in this situation often find themselves feeling like they're 'going through the motions' in important relationships—with friends, family, girlfriends or boyfriends, spouses or partners, even their children.

2. Bargaining—'Something happened, but...'

In this stage, the person acknowledges that something happened, but attempts to convince himself or herself (and others) that the experience wasn't harmful and hasn't caused them any problems—even though it has.

This is not to say that people can't have unwanted or even abusive sexual experiences that do not cause problems in their lives. This is possible, for example, if the experience only happened once and the child's life was otherwise full of healthy and positive relationships with family, friends, and other authority figures.

Instead, this stage refers to the experiences of people who are, on the one hand, no longer pushing away the fact that they had a potentially harmful sexual experience, while, on the other hand, they're not yet ready to deal with the impact it continues to have on them. These mixed feelings are often expressed in 'yes but' thoughts and statements.

The ability to *doubt* the reality of what happened, or its effects on one's current life, can be very strong at this stage. Also common is 'pseudo-forgiveness,' in which, as Hunter puts it, the person 'attempts to move from denial straight into forgiveness without experiencing any of the emotions' related to what happened. As Mike Lew puts it, "True forgiveness does not arise from denial. It can only occur when there has been a complete understanding of what has happened, including the nature of the wrongs and where the responsibility lies."

Below are some common things said by men in this stage of recovery, from chapter 5 of Hunter's book:

> *It didn't happen enough for it to matter.*
> *I know what she did, and I wanted it.*
> *I can't deny it happened, but it's my fault that it happened.*
> *She was just teaching me about sex.*
> *I can't do anything about it now. There's no sense in even talking about it.*

One last observation, and a suggestion from Hunter:

"When in the bargaining stage, many people find that a constant argument or civil war goes on in their heads: 'It really happened.' 'No, it didn't.' 'Yes, it did.' This goes back and forth, seemingly forever. If you find this happening, you may find it useful to choose a side and write a letter to yourself or someone else arguing that point, making no attempt to be objective or to see both sides. Once that is done, write another letter arguing the opposite side. Pay attention to your body during the writing of each letter, and listen to what your emotions are telling you" (*Abused Boys*, p.105).

3. Anger—'Something happened, and I'm angry about it!'

This is a third stage that many people experience. This stage begins when one recognizes not only that something happened but that it really did harm him or her.

For some people, this is the beginning of believing that what was done to them matters because they matter. For those who have squelched their anger, or been unable to feel it, this may be the first recognition that experiencing and expressing anger can be helpful and healthy.

For some, this 'opening to anger' brings fear that they will lose control and hurt other people or themselves. This fear can be valid and healthy. In fact, realistic concerns about anger's destructive potential tends to protect people from acting out violent thoughts and impulses that be triggered very suddenly.

Importantly, it's almost impossible to be simultaneously angry about something done to you and blame yourself for it. For this reason, getting angry about what happened can bring relief from self-blaming thoughts. It can be the beginning of overcoming the tendency—which is especially common—to blame yourself for ways people took advantage of you when you were a child.

For many, the recognition that they are valuable human beings, and that what happened isn't their fault, can bring a huge sense of relief. Also, the anger may also provide a lot of energy and motivation to make positive changes in one's life. In these ways, this phase can bring a great deal of healing and progress.

At the same time, this can be a risky period. Anger may become a central player in one's emotional life. It can 'spill out' in ways that are harmful to oneself or others. Or one may now feel 'justified' and 'entitled' to act in the same old angry ways one has for a long time, rather than taking responsibility for them. In addition to relief and empowerment, then, this stage can bring new challenges and responsibilities.

Another problem is that some people have trouble moving on from this stage. Whether consciously or not, they prefer anger to the sadness that is an essential part of recovery. Men especially are vulnerable to getting stuck in the anger phase, because they have been conditioned to feel safe and strong when they are angry, and fear that sadness equals weakness, even being a victim, even though, as described below, this is definitely not the case.

As Hunter points out, in this stage many people find that exercise is a great way to channel the 'energy' of anger or 'vent' angry feelings. Running, lifting weights, or playing active sports can not only channel the energy and help release the feelings but increase one's sense of being strong and powerful. Finally, for some people hitting a punching bag, or even an old mattress, can be a safe way to release anger when it wells up inside.

4. Sadness—'Something happened, and it cost me a lot.'

As Hunter writes, "Sadness comes when a man [or woman] realizes that he was wronged and that he [or she] has lost something that he can never retrieve." This is when the grieving phase of the overall grieving process described by these stages really kicks in.

Harmful unwanted or abusive childhood sexual experiences bring many losses—of innocence, of trust in others, of belief in oneself, and of achievements that never happened thanks to the effects of the unwanted or abusive experiences.

Truly facing and reflecting on one's many losses can bring a great deal of sadness. Sadness is a totally legitimate and justified response to such losses. It can be painful to experience, but coming to know this sadness can bring great strength, and deep appreciation and understanding of the suffering that are part of so many people's lives.

During this phase people can become very sensitive. Not only their own pain and suffering, but that of other people, and pets or other animals, can feel very intense. They may cry easily.

Hunter observes, "As a person moves through the sadness stage, he will notice how his tears change. At first, crying will be very difficult and painful. He may fight back the tears by holding his breath, not making any sound… or shaming himself for needing to cry. Later in this stage, the tears will seem to come from somewhere very deep and are often accompanied by a sense of being a small child. There is often a sense of great loss and loneliness.… Still later in the recovery process the tears are followed by a sense of healing, coming together, wholeness" (*Abused Boys*, p.111).

In short, in this stage of recovery one's experiences of sadness become increasingly healing and strengthening.

Hunter and others have suggested several activities that can help bring about this transformation. One is writing 'goodbye letters' to things you have lost because of unwanted or abusive childhood experiences—"for example, the relationships you never had because of your shame and fear of intimacy, or the type of parents you never had, or the loss of your spontaneity" (*Abused Boys*, p.111).

5. Acceptance—'Something happened, and I have healed from it.'
Once again, a passage from Hunter's book nicely sums up the essence of this stage:

"The final stage of grieving begins to take place when the person who was wronged has acknowledged [what happened], felt as well as expressed the emotions he has about it, and begins to put it in proper perspective. He no longer blames himself... or punishes himself for what he did or didn't do in order to cope... He becomes less and less likely to see himself as helpless, hopeless, and defective. This will make him less vulnerable to further exploitation. He will begin to accept himself and treat himself with respect and affection. Although he will never forget what was done to him, he will be able to stop organizing his life... around it. He will have a scar rather than an open wound" (*Abused Boys*, p.113).

Acceptance here does not mean failing to see that what happened was harmful and wrong. Instead, it means accepting that the past cannot be changed, and coming to peace with it rather than remaining focused on pain or sadness, anger or resentment.

While it may be hard to imagine at the beginning of the recovery process, it really is possible to experience a sense of serenity about even the worst childhood experiences and the negative effects they once had.

The acceptance of this stage brings great strength and power. The strength and power come from having faced one's life head-on, having truly experienced the worst of the past, and having arrived at a way of being that is free from either running away from painful truths or getting caught up in them. With acceptance, one can truly 'move on'— as a person of greater courage, strength, hope, and wisdom."

APPENDIX 6

TOOLBOXES FOR RECOVERY

INTENTIONS; FOR RECOVERY;
FIGHTING THE INNER CRITIC

(reprinted with permission from Pete Walker, Petewalker.com)

TOOLBOX 1: SUGGESTED INTENTIONS FOR RECOVERY

Here are normal and safe wants and needs to wish and hope for... to cultivate with mental, spiritual, emotional, and physical energy. As usual, focus on the ones that most appeal to you. Skip the ones that do not feel right for you or that you do not feel ready for.

1. I want to develop a more constantly loving and accepting relationship with myself. I want an increasing capacity for self-acceptance.
2. I want to learn to become the best possible friend to myself.
3. I want to attract, into my life, relationships that are based on love, respect, fairness, and mutual support.
4. I want to uncover a full, uninhibited self-expression.
5. I want to attain the best possible physical health.
6. I want to cultivate a balance of vitality and peace.
7. I want to attract to myself, loving friends and loving community.
8. I want increasing freedom from toxic shame.
9. I want increasing freedom from unnecessary fear.
10. I want rewarding and fulfilling work.

11. I want a fair amount of peace of mind, spirit, soul, and body.

12. I want to increase my capacity to play and have fun.

13. I want to make plenty of room for beauty and nature in my life.

14. I want sufficient physical and monetary resources.

15. I want a fair amount of help (self, human, or divine) to get what I need.

16. I want God's love, grace, and blessing.

17. I want a balance of work, rest, and play.

18. I want a balance of stability and change.

19. I want a balance of loving interaction and healthy self-sufficiency.

20. I want full emotional expression with a balance of laughter and tears.

21. I want a sense of meaningfulness and fulfillment.

22. I want to find effective and non-abusive ways to deal with anger.

23. I want all this for each and every other being.

TOOLBOX 3: SUGGESTED INTERNAL RESPONSES TO COMMON CRITIC ATTACKS

The attacks of the [inner] critic often operate below the radar of self-awareness. Unless we can identify them, we are at their mercy and helpless to deconstruct them. Once we learn to recognize inner critic attacks, the simple techniques of Thought-Stopping and Thought-Substitution are powerful tools in short-circuiting the critic.

There are two categories of attacks:

Perfectionism attacks, fueled by toxic shame, which create chronic self-hate and self-flagellation.

Endangerment attacks, fueled by fear, create chronic hypervigilance and anxiety.

PERFECTIONISM

1. Perfectionism.

My perfectionism arose as an attempt to gain safety and support in my dangerous family. Perfection is a self-persecutory myth. I do not have to be perfect to be safe or loved in the present. I am letting go of relationships that require perfection. I have a right to make mistakes. Mistakes do not make me a mistake. Every mistake or mishap is an opportunity to practice loving myself in the places I have never been loved.

2. All-or-None & Black-and-White Thinking.

I reject extreme or over generalized descriptions, judgments, or criticisms. Statements that describe me as "always" or "never" this or that, are typically grossly inaccurate.

3. Self-Hate, Self-Disgust, & Toxic Shame.

I commit to myself. I am on my side. I am a good enough person. I refuse to trash myself. I turn shame back into blame and disgust and externalize it to anyone who shames my normal feelings and foibles. As long as I am not hurting anyone, I refuse to be shamed for normal emotional responses like anger, sadness, fear, and depression. I especially refuse to attack myself for how hard it is to completely eliminate the self-hate habit.

4. Micromanagement/Worrying/Obsessing/Looping/ Over-Futurizing.

I will not repetitively examine details over and over. I will not endlessly second-guess myself. I cannot change the past. I forgive all my past mistakes. I cannot make the future perfectly safe. I will stop hunting for what could go wrong. I will not try to control the uncontrollable.

I will not micromanage myself or others. I work in a way that is "good enough," and I accept the existential fact that my efforts sometimes bring desired results and sometimes they do not. "God grant me the serenity to accept the things I cannot change, the courage to change the things I can, and the wisdom to know the difference."

5. Unfair/Devaluing Comparisons to others or to your most perfect moments.

I refuse to compare myself unfavorably to others. I will not compare "my insides to their outsides." I will not judge myself for not being at peak performance all of the time. In a society that pressures us into acting happy all the time, I will not get down on myself for feeling bad.

6. Guilt.

Feeling guilty does not mean I am guilty. I refuse to make my decisions and choices out of guilt; sometimes I need to feel the guilt and do it anyway. In the inevitable instance when I inadvertently hurt someone, I will apologize, make amends, and let go of my guilt. I will not apologize over and over. I am no longer a victim. I will not accept unfair blame. Guilt is sometimes camouflaged fear: "I am afraid, but I am not guilty or in danger."

7. Shoulding.

I will substitute the words "want to" for "shoulds" and only follow this imperative if it feels like I want to, unless I am under legal, ethical, or moral obligation.

8. Over-Productivity/Workaholism/Busyholism.

I am a human being not a human doing. I will not choose to be perpetually productive. I am more productive in the long run when I balance work with play and relaxation. I will not try to perform at 100% all the time. I subscribe to the normalcy of vacillating along a continuum of efficiency.

9. Harsh Judgments of Self & Others/Name-Calling.

I will not let the bullies and critics of my early life win by joining and agreeing with them. I refuse to attack myself or abuse others. I will not displace the criticism and blame that rightfully belongs to my original critics onto myself or current people in my life. *"I care for myself. The more solitary, the more friendless, the more unsustained I am, the more I will respect myself."* –Jane Eyre

ENDANGERMENT ATTACKS

10. Drasticizing/Catastrophizing / Hypochondriasizing.

I feel afraid but I am not in danger. I am not "in trouble" with my parents. I refuse to scare myself with thoughts and pictures of my life deteriorating. No more homemade horror movies and disaster flicks. No more turning tiny ailments into tales of dying.

11. Negative Focus.

I will stop anxiously looking for, over-noticing, and dwelling on what might go wrong or what might be wrong with me or my life around me. Right now, I will notice, visualize and enumerate my accomplishments, talents, and qualities, as well as the many gifts life offers me, like music, film, food, beauty, color, books, nature, friends, etc.

12. Time Urgency.

I am not in danger. I do not need to rush. I will not hurry unless it is a true emergency. I am learning to enjoy doing my daily activities at a relaxed pace.

13. Disabling Performance Anxiety.

I am reducing procrastination by reminding myself not to accept unfair criticism or perfectionist expectations from anyone. Even when afraid, I will defend myself from unfair criticism. I won't let fear make my decisions.

14. Perseverating About Being Attacked.

Unless there are clear signs of danger, I will thought-stop my projection of past bullies/critics onto others. The majority of my fellow human beings are peaceful people. I have legal authorities to aid my protection if threatened by the few who aren't. I invoke thoughts and images of my friends' love and support."

APPENDIX 7

VOICE FIGHTING

I learned Voice Fighting from a skilled psychologist in Sacramento, California in 1977-78. Unfortunately I don't remember his name or address although I've Googled. Nothing shows up on Facebook, Reddit, or Steemit [similar to Reddit] either. I've also looked on Amazon and other outlets to see if he has written his own book on Voice Fighting but I found nothing. So I am dedicating this chapter to a wonderful and compassionate psychologist who merits lots of praise. I hope I find him someday to give him the credit he deserves.

His clients were struggling with food problems—bulimia, compulsive overeating, and anorexia—as well as depression, anxiety, and phobias. He created Voice Fighting to help them all.

Voice Fighting was very powerful for me and I used the method for years to recover from agoraphobia.

The Voice is that of the inner critic. The Six Voice Games the Voice plays are: depression; anxiety; irrational fear; helplessness; hopelessness; and guilt. The Voice uses arguments which lead us to feel these emotions.

Step 1:
Using a journal, jot down whenever you feel any of these six emotions. Do this for a few days.
Step 2:
While paying close attention to yourself, determine what thoughts or phrases are attached to those emotions and write those down as well. Practice this for a few days.

Step 3:

Notice which comes first—the thoughts, phrases and words—or the emotion. After a while you will see that the emotion is usually triggered by the thoughts, phrases and words. These words come from the inner critic, known as the Voice. The arguments the Voice uses are the essence of the Voice Game. Continue to practice.

Step 4:

You will need to get 3x5 or 5x7 index cards and put a Voice Game and Voice Fighting messages on each card. Examples of Voice Games and Voice Fighting messages are below or you can create your own variation. You can then carry these cards in your purse, backpack, or briefcase, so you can Voice Fight at anytime, anywhere. You might want to practice these at home a few times first. You could even make more than one set of Voice Fighting cards. When one of the six emotions comes up, practice the Voice Fighting. Saying them out loud is preferable.

DEPRESSION

Voice game: I'm bad, worthless, no friends, no sex, no lover, no family, ugly, old, fat, unpopular, can't be like other people, unlovable, unlikable, damaged, or unworthy.

Voice Fighting (suggestions below or make up your own):

> Voice, I am a good, loving, and worthwhile person.
> Voice, I have friends and people who love and like me.
> Voice, What you tell me is hurtful and I don't have to pay attention.
> Voice, It's only when I listen to you that I get depressed.
> Voice, I don't have to listen to what you tell me. You are a liar.
> Voice, I can choose who I want to be with.
> Voice, I am perfect the way I am.
> Voice, I'm ignoring you now.

If the Voice persists, say—Voice, go away. Or Voice, leave me alone. Or Voice—fuck off! Then proceed to ignore the Voice and *do* something. Wash dishes. Clean your car. Take a shower. Count the cutlery in your kitchen drawer. Turn on music and dance.

EXTREME ANXIETY

Voice game: What if … (fill in blank) happens. That would be awful, terrible, dreadful, catastrophic, or unbearable.

Voice Fighting (suggestions below or make up your own)

Voice, There are no what ifs in life. That is a myth.

Voice, Whatever I worried about in the past didn't happen.

Voice, Even if the worst thing happens, it wouldn't be awful or catastrophic.

Voice, I don't have to worry about something that hasn't happened yet.

Voice, It is only you who gives me ideas about being worried about the future.

Voice, The future will take care of itself.

Voice, Facts about the future do not exist except in the words you put in my head.

Voice, I am creating my own positive future.

Voice, You are only words in my head. You're not real.

Voice, I'm ignoring you now.

If the Voice persists, say—Voice, go away. Or Voice, leave me alone. Or Voice—fuck off! Then proceed to ignore the Voice and *do* something. Wash dishes. Clean your car. Take a shower. Count the cutlery in your kitchen drawer. Turn on music and dance.

IRRATIONAL FEAR

Voice game: I am dying. I have a terrible disease, I am fainting, am having a panic attack, I am alone, I am going to be homeless or poor or bankrupt. I will die if I feel my emotions (the difference between irrational fear and extreme anxiety is that anxiety uses: what if…. and includes a catastrophe).

Voice Fighting (suggestions below or make up your own)

> Voice, I am safe in the world, in my body, and out in public.
> Voice, I am safe in my life.
> Voice, I am safe with my emotions.
> Voice, I am safe around friends, family, and other people.
> Voice, I can choose what I want and who I want in my life.
> Voice, There is no reason to believe I will be homeless or poor. Only you, Voice, are scaring me, but I don't have to believe what you say.
> Voice, I'm ignoring you now.

If the Voice persists, say—Voice, go away. Or Voice, leave me alone. Or Voice— fuck off! Then proceed to ignore the Voice and *do* something. Wash dishes. Clean your car. Take a shower. Count the cutlery in your kitchen drawer. Turn on music and dance.

HELPLESSNESS

Voice game: I can't; I'm not able to; I will never be able to; I'm not strong enough, smart enough, young enough, attractive enough, rich enough; or powerful enough.

Voice Fighting (suggestions below or make up your own)

> Voice, I am strong and smart, able to take care of my life in a positive way.
> Voice, Whatever happened in the past does not make me helpless in the present or future.
> Voice, No matter what my challenges are, I persevere.
> Voice, I can and I will live my life, expecting miracles.
> Voice, I am able to live my life.

Appendix 7 Voice Fighting   297

Voice, It is only you who tells me I cannot do anything.

Voice, There are no facts about what I can and cannot do. I can choose.

Voice, I'm ignoring you now.

If the Voice persists, say—Voice, go away. Or Voice, leave me alone. Or Voice—fuck off! Then proceed to ignore the Voice and *do* something. Wash dishes. Clean your car. Take a shower. Count the cutlery in your kitchen drawer. Turn on music and dance.

HOPELESSNESS

Voice game: I give up. There's no point in going on. The future holds nothing for me. Everything in life will continue to be bad. I don't want to get out of bed, go to work, or do anything. Life sucks.

Voice Fighting (suggestions below or make up your own)

Voice, I am strong and able to live my life the way I choose.

Voice, I am creating a positive future for myself right now.

Voice, No matter what happens in life, I will prevail.

Voice, The future is based on how I think today.

Voice, It is only you trying to convince me that my life is hopeless.

Voice, Life is wonderful just the way it is.

Voice, There are no hard facts to prove that I, and my life, are hopeless.

Voice, I'm ignoring you now.

If the Voice persists, say —Voice, go away. Or Voice, leave me alone. Or Voice—fuck off! Then proceed to ignore the Voice and *do* something. Wash dishes. Clean your car. Take a shower. Count the cutlery in your kitchen drawer. Turn on music and dance.

GUILT

Voice game: I should… I shouldn't… It's my fault that I hurt people, animals, or the world. I'm selfish.

Voice Fighting (suggestions below or make up your own)

> Voice, There are no rules about what I should or shouldn't do. I decide.
> Voice, I don't hurt people on purpose.
> Voice, If I hurt someone, I can apologize or make amends.
> Voice, I take care of myself first and that is a good thing.
> Voice, I am not responsible for other people's lives (or the world).
> Voice, The word "Should" never applies to me or anyone else.
> Voice, I'm doing the best I can.
> Voice, If I hurt someone or something, I can forgive myself.
> Voice, It is only you and your words that make me feel guilty.
> Voice, I'm ignoring you now.

If the Voice persists, say—Voice, go away. Or Voice, leave me alone. Or Voice—fuck off! Then proceed to ignore the Voice and *do* something. Wash dishes. Clean your car. Take a shower. Count the cutlery in your kitchen drawer. Turn on music and dance.

APPENDIX 8

BABAJI MEDITATION
BABAJI LUCID DREAMING

When I was 22, a new Elder popped in to replace the Chinese Elder Yuan who had been working with me since I was 15. The new Elder started teaching me every day. I didn't know who he was but I could see his image, hear his words, and feel him. We went along for a few months. Then a friend of mine loaned me *Autobiography of a Yogi* by Paramahansa Yogananda. As I looked through the pictures, I found a picture of him: The Elder. Babaji. I didn't want to believe Babaji was coming to me because I was a "nobody." I asked him why he was showing up to teach me.

"Because you listen," was his simple answer.

He's been with me ever since, along with five others whom I refer to as Lemurian Elders, including Yuan.

Two of the great teachings of Babaji were his instructions to me on meditation and also lucid dreaming, which I've never forgotten, although it's been 49 years. These were unlike anything I've ever heard of or tried before or since. I'm grateful to Babaji for teaching me these methods. This is the first time I've put these two methods in writing to share with you.

Here are the details:

BABAJI MEDITATION
Step 1:
Get comfortable in a quiet setting with no distractions. Because I had

a small child, a job, and a husband, I usually did this meditation at night in bed before I went to sleep.

Babaji told me to slowly and deeply breathe in and out for about 3-4 breaths, close my eyes, and relax.

"Review your day starting from the beginning. Remember everything of importance that happened that day, whether you liked it or not."

Focus on which of those events I would like to repeat and which ones I'd like to change. I didn't have to do anything, just focus and release.

Next he asked me to pick a simple object. I picked an orange. He asked me to imagine. Smell it, feel it, and look at it as though I had never before seen an orange. Say the name: "Orange." He suggested I pull the rind off and then to proceed to pull the segments apart. "Feel the juice dripping through your fingers," he said. "Smell it. Taste it. Say: "Orange." Look at it intensely. The orange color. The white membrane. The seeds. Remove the seeds with your fingers. Squeeze it. In other words, completely experience the "orange."

Then he told me to release the "orangeness" and let it go from my awareness. Breathe. Relax.

That's the end of Step 1. Simple? Yes, very.

He told me to wait at least 24 hours before doing another step.

Step 2:
Get comfortable in a quiet setting with no distractions.

Then he told me to slowly and deeply breathe in and out for about 3-4 breaths, close my eyes, and relax.

"Review your day starting from the beginning. Remember everything of importance that happened that day, whether you liked it or not."

Focus on which of those events I would like to repeat and which ones I'd like to change. I didn't have to do anything, just focus, and then release.

Next he asked me to pick another simple object that had a function. I picked a wooden pencil. He asked me to imagine. Smell it, feel it, and look at it as though I had never before seen a leaded pencil. Say the name: "Pencil." Then he suggested I take a pencil sharpener and sharpen it. "Smell that," he told me. "Feel the point. Feel the eraser. Feel the wooden edges. Can you take your tongue and taste it?" I did so. It had a distinctive taste and feel to my tongue. Next he told me to use it the way "pencil" would be used. I wrote with it. Printed with it. Erased the words with the eraser. Then he asked me to break the leaded point, which I did. "What does that broken point feel like?" he asked me. "Does it have a different taste, texture? Does breaking the pencil bring up any feelings in you?

Then he told me to release all of the "pencil" and let it go from my awareness, watching it disappear. Breathe. Relax.

That's the end of Step 2.

He told me to wait at least 24 hours before doing another step.

Step 3:

Get comfortable in a quiet setting with no distractions.

Then he told me to slowly and deeply breathe in and out for about 3-4 breaths, close my eyes, and relax.

"Review your day starting from the beginning. Remember everything of importance that happened that day, whether you liked it or not."

See those events I would like to repeat and which ones I'd like to change. I didn't have to do anything, just focus, and then release.

Next he asked me to select a simple word, one that would not bring up any issues or complex thoughts or emotions. I chose a word. I don't remember which one at this time.

I was to do the same thing with the word. "Smell it. Taste it. Feel it. See it. Hear it. Does it have a sound when you say the word? Does it have a feeling when you say the word? Use the word in a simple sentence, in context. Then another sentence. Then another. Can you feel the sentence? Turn the word over and over, exploring and examining it. How does it feel on your lips and tongue to say the word? Make the word yours. Own it."

Then Babaji told me to release the word and let it go from my awareness, watching it disappear. Breathe. Relax.

That's the end of Step 2.

He told me to wait at least 24 hours before doing another step.

Step 4:

Get comfortable in a quiet setting with no distractions.

Then he told me to slowly and deeply breathe in and out for about 3-4 breaths, close my eyes, and relax.

"Review your day starting from the beginning. Remember everything of importance that happened that day, whether you liked it or not."

See those events I would like to repeat and which ones I'd like to change. I didn't have to do anything, just focus, and then release.

Next Babaji told me to select a word that had a lot of meaning for me, but refrain from words like love, hate, god, sex, death, birth. I'm not sure what word I selected, but it may have been "run."

I was to do the same thing with the new, more complex word. "Smell it. Taste it. Feel it. See it. Hear it. Does it have a sound when you say the word? Does it have a feeling when you say the word? Use the word in a simple sentence, in context. Then another sentence. Then another. Can you feel the sentence? Turn the word over and over, exploring and examining it. How does it feel on your lips and tongue to say the word? Make the word yours. Own it."

Then Babaji told me to release the word and let it go from my awareness, watching it disappear. Breathe. Relax.

That's the end of Step 4.

He told me to wait at least 24 hours before doing another step.

Step 5:

Get comfortable in a quiet setting with no distractions.

Then he told me to slowly and deeply breathe in and out for about 3-4 breaths, close my eyes, and relax.

"Review your day starting from the beginning. Remember everything of importance that happened that day, whether you liked it or not."

See those events I would like to repeat and which ones I'd like to change. I didn't have to do anything, just focus, and then release.

Next Babaji told me to select a word that had a lot of meaning to me, including a word like love, hate, god, sex, death, or birth. I don't remember what word I selected.

I was to do the same thing with the new, more complex word. "Smell it. Taste it. Feel it. See it. Hear it. Does it have a sound when you say the word? Does it have a feeling when you say the word? Use the word in a simple sentence, in context. Then another sentence. Then another. Can you feel the sentence? Turn the word over and over, exploring and examining it. How does it feel on your lips and tongue to say the word? Make the word yours. Own it."

He told me to be aware of the multiple meanings and feelings of that word. To just notice.

Then Babaji told me to release the word and let it go from my awareness, watching it disappear. Breathe. Relax.

That's the end of Step 5.

He told me to wait at least 24 hours before doing another step.

Step 6:

Get comfortable in a quiet setting with no distractions.

Then he told me to slowly and deeply breathe in and out for about 3-4 breaths, close my eyes, and relax.

"Review your day starting from the beginning. Remember everything of importance that happened that day, whether you liked it or not."

This time I was to choose an event earlier in my day that I *liked a lot*. Would I want to repeat it? Would I want to share it with others? How did the event feel? Did it have a taste, a smell, a vision? How would I use that event in my future? Take a deep breath and release the event.

Next Babaji told me I could pick any object, any word, any phrase, and do the same thing I had been practicing. "Smell, taste, touch, see, and hear." I knew how to do the exercise by now.

Then Babaji told me to release whatever I had chosen and let it go from my awareness, watching it disappear. Breathe. Relax.

That's the end of Step 6.

He told me to wait at least 24 hours before doing another step.

Step 7:
Get comfortable in a quiet setting with no distractions.

Then he told me to slowly and deeply breathe in and out for about 3-4 breaths, close my eyes, and relax.

"Review your day starting from the beginning. Remember everything of importance that happened that day, whether you liked it or not."

This time I was to choose an event earlier in my day that I *didn't like* which made me uncomfortable or even emotional, or hurt someone, or someone hurt me. Would I want to repeat it? Would I want to share it with others? How did the event feel? Did it have a taste, a smell, a look? How would I use that event in my future? *Would* I use it in my future? How could I change that event into one that felt good?

Did I want to do that? If I hurt someone, could I apologize? I could imagine myself apologizing. If someone hurt me, could I forgive that person? I could imagine myself forgiving.

Take a deep breath, relax and release the event.

Next Babaji told me I could pick any object, any word, any phrase, and do the same thing I had been practicing. Smell, taste, touch, see, and hear. I knew how to do the exercise by now. Then take a deep breath, relax, and release whatever I had chosen.

That's the end of Step 7.

He told me to wait at least 24 hours before doing another step.

Step 8:

Get comfortable in a quiet setting with no distractions.

Then he told me to slowly and deeply breathe in and out for about 3-4 breaths, close my eyes, and relax.

"Review your day starting from the beginning. Remember everything of importance that happened that day, whether you liked it or not."

Then I was to choose to review an event from the day, feeling good or feeling bad, and do the instructions from Step 6 or Step 7 above.

"Take a deep breath, relax and release everything."

Then if I wanted to, I could choose an object, simple or complicated, or a word, or a phrase, simple or complicated. "Feel. See. Hear. Smell. Taste."

Next Babaji told me I could pick any object, any word, any phrase, and do the same thing. Smell, taste, touch, see, and hear. Use it in context. Take it apart and put it back together. I knew how to do the exercise by now.

Then take a deep breath, relax and release whatever I had chosen.

That's the end of Step 8.

You can practice any one of these steps every day, particularly if you are feeling down.

I practiced these steps every day for over a year. First to view the events of my day. Then to decide what I might want to repeat, do differently, or better or to refrain from repeating in the future. The exercises expanded my awareness.

BABAJI'S LUCID DREAMING EXERCISES

This process takes patience and persistence. You may achieve lucid dreaming quickly or it may take time. The point is you are training your consciousness, which is designed to follow your instructions. Babaji taught me lucid dreaming after I did the other meditation exercises above, which I think was helpful and in the proper order for me.

Night 1:

Keep a special notepad with a writing instrument to make notes *close by* for when you wake up. This will be your dream notebook.

Get comfortable in a quiet setting with no distractions, preferably *just before* going to sleep. A warm bath beforehand may be helpful.

"Slowly and deeply breathe in and out for about 3-4 breaths, close your eyes, and relax. Review your day starting from the beginning. Remember everything of importance that happened that day, whether you liked it or not. Remember. Focus. Release."

Next I was to say out loud: "I am going to have one dream tonight and I will remember it when I wake up." Breathe. Relax.

Repeat that phrase 4-5 times. Breathe. Relax.

Then go to sleep.

If you need to keep breathing and relaxing for a while to help you go to sleep, please do so.

When you wake up (either in the middle of the night or in the morning), write down any dream you can remember, even if it is just a few words. An image. A taste. A feeling.

Night 2:

Keep a special notepad with a writing instrument to make notes *close by* for when you wake up. This will be your dream notebook.

Get comfortable in a quiet setting with no distractions, preferably *just before* going to sleep. A warm bath beforehand may be helpful.

"Slowly and deeply breathe in and out for about 3-4 breaths, close your eyes, and relax. Review your day starting from the beginning. Remember everything of importance that happened that day, whether you liked it or not. Remember. Focus. Release."

Next say out loud: "I am going to have one dream tonight and I will remember it when I wake up." Breathe. Relax.

Repeat that phrase 4-5 times. Breathe. Relax.

Then go to sleep.

If you need to keep breathing and relaxing for a while to help you go to sleep, please do so.

When you wake up (either in the middle of the night or in the morning), write down any dream you can remember, even if it is just a few words. An image. A taste. A feeling.

Night 3:

Keep a special notepad with a writing instrument to make notes *close by* for when you wake up. This will be your dream notebook.

Get comfortable in a quiet setting with no distractions, preferably *just before* going to sleep. A warm bath beforehand may be helpful.

"Slowly and deeply breathe in and out for about 3-4 breaths, close your eyes, and relax. Review your day starting from the beginning. Remember everything of importance that happened that day, whether you liked it or not. Remember. Focus. Release."

Next say out loud: "I am going to have one dream tonight and I will remember it when I wake up." Breathe. Relax.

Repeat that phrase 4-5 times. Breathe. Relax.

Then go to sleep.

If you need to keep breathing and relaxing for a while to help you go to sleep, please do so.

When you wake up (either in the middle of the night or in the morning), write down any dream you can remember, even if it is just a few words. An image. A taste. A feeling.

Night 4: Getting Lucid

Keep a special notepad with a writing instrument to make notes *close by* for when you wake up. This will be your dream notebook.

Get comfortable in a quiet setting with no distractions, preferably *just before* going to sleep. A warm bath beforehand may be helpful.

"Slowly and deeply breathe in and out for about 3-4 breaths, close your eyes, and relax. Review your day starting from the beginning. Remember everything of importance that happened that day, whether you liked it or not. Remember. Focus. Release."

Next say out loud: "I am going to have one dream tonight and I will become aware *as I'm dreaming it.*" Breathe. Relax.

Repeat that phrase 4-5 times. Breathe. Relax.

Then go to sleep.

If you need to keep breathing and relaxing for a while to help you go to sleep, please do so.

When you become aware you are lucid while dreaming, pay close attention. Look at your hand. Look around. Do items shift as you look around? Is anything happening? Are any persons there with you? What are your surroundings? Notice everything.

When you are done with the lucid dream *wake up and write down* that dream in your dream notebook, even if it is just a few words. An image. A taste. A feeling.

When you wake up (either in the middle of the night or in the morning), write down any other dream you can remember in your dream notebook, even if it is just a few words. An image. A taste. A feeling.

Nights 4, 5, 6 and so on:

Keep a special notepad with a writing instrument to make notes *close by* for when you wake up. This will be your dream notebook.

Get comfortable in a quiet setting with no distractions, preferably *just before* going to sleep. A warm bath beforehand may be helpful.

"Slowly and deeply breathe in and out for about 3-4 breaths, close your eyes, and relax. Review your day starting from the beginning. Remember everything of importance that happened that day, whether you liked it or not. Remember. Focus. Release."

Next say out loud: "I am going to have one dream tonight and I will become *aware as I'm dreaming it.*" Breathe. Relax.

Repeat that phrase 4-5 times. Breathe. Relax.

Then go to sleep.

If you need to keep breathing and relaxing for a while to help you go to sleep, please do so.

When you become aware you are lucid while dreaming, pay close attention. Look at your hand. Look around. Do items shift as you look around? Is anything happening? Are any persons there with you? What are your surroundings? Notice everything.

When you are done with the lucid dream *wake up and write down* that dream in your dream notebook, even if it is just a few words. An image. A taste. A feeling.

When you wake up (either in the middle of the night or in the morning), write down any other dreams you can remember in your dream notebook, even if it is just a few words. An image. A taste. A feeling.

**Advanced—Problem solving while lucid dreaming—
Nights 7, 8, 9 and so on:**

Keep a special notepad with a writing instrument to make notes *close by* for when you wake up. This will be your dream notebook.

Get comfortable in a quiet setting with no distractions, preferably *just before* going to sleep. A warm bath beforehand may be helpful.

"Slowly and deeply breathe in and out for about 3-4 breaths, close your eyes, and relax. Review your day starting from the beginning. Remember everything of importance that happened that day, whether you liked it or not. Remember. Focus. Release."

Think of a problem you would like to solve or resolve.

Then say out loud: "Tonight I am going to work on a problem while I am lucidly dreaming. I am going to have one dream tonight and I will be aware as I'm dreaming it. *AND I WILL work through my problem in my lucid dream.*" Breathe. Relax.

Repeat that phrase 4-5 times. Breathe. Relax.

Then go to sleep.

If you need to keep breathing and relaxing for a while to help you go to sleep, please do so.

When you become aware you are lucid while dreaming, pay close attention. Look at your hand. Look around. Do items shift as you look around? Is anything happening? Are any persons there with you? What are your surroundings? Notice everything.

Remember your decision to work on a problem while dreaming and do so. If you need help to work on your problem, you can call on anyone or anything to help you. [*In my first few lucid dreams doing problem solving, I called on: 1) the Marines 2) Superman 3) Jesus 4) an elevator technician.*]

When you are done with the lucid dream wake up and write down that dream in your dream notebook, even if it is just a few words. An image. A taste. A feeling.

When you wake up (either in the middle of the night or in the morning), write down any other dreams you can remember in your dream notebook. Even if it is just a few words. An image. A taste. A feeling.

———————

Congratulations!!!

HOW TO EASILY GET WHAT YOU WANT BY WRITING A GOD LETTER

I'm not suggesting that you can get what you want. I'm telling you! I've used this method for over forty years and it works fabulously! Whenever I want something new, I sit down and do this process. It usually takes less than an hour to concoct.

I've called the method a "God letter"—although you don't need to believe in God or a higher power. You can be an agnostic or atheist and this method will still work great for you. You can call it the "Universe" letter if you want. One thing we can all agree on is that we live in the universe.

The "God Letter" consists of a few simple steps. Mostly the letter is a brainstorming device, which "e-mails" your request to the "Field of all Possibilities" as Deepak Chopra calls the un-manifested universe. You're going to be manifesting something out of nothing. A little bit like your own personal Big Bang.

HERE ARE THE STEPS:

Get out a fresh, whole piece of paper (lined is good) and a pen or pencil, whatever you're comfortable with. Hand writing is more powerful than typing your letter on the computer. Make your writing legible, neat and tidy. You want the universe to clearly understand what you are asking to manifest

1. **Current date** (day/month/year)

2. **Dear Universe:**

3. **I........... (Put your full name here) NOW HAVE the PER-FECT............. (Fill in the blank).** This could be a job, car, love relationship, house, apartment, housekeeper, employee, employer, career, vacation, health, enlightenment—or whatever you want. Limit this letter to just one manifestation, though. You can always write more letters.

4. **Details:** (here's where you're going to put your brain, heart, and imagination to work) List every single feature you can think of that would describe your perfect............. (Fill in the blank). Make this list as detailed as possible. Leave nothing out, no matter how far-fetched it seems to you. Forget your logical mind while doing your list. Your list does NOT have to make sense. Your list does not have to be "practical." Put fear on the backburner. It isn't needed here. Don't assume anything. The universe is not a mind reader. Be specific. Write it down. Include a TARGET DATE—month/day/year. This helps the universe to know when you expect your manifestation. Make your date reasonable. You'll know what that is.

5. After you've finished your detailed list, you will write these exact words: **"This or something better now manifests for the good of all concerned."**

   The reason for this sentence is:

   – You don't want to limit yourself to what you have asked for. The universe may want to give you more!

   – The word NOW is very potent. Just ask Eckhardt Tolle. Manifestation exists in the NOW.

- "For the good of all concerned"—you don't want to take something away from someone else. The phrase also protects your integrity.

- You want the manifestation to be for your own highest good as well as for others.

6. **Then finish with—"Thank you, God."** Gratitude is a very powerful, spiritual vibration, bringing good things your way. Gratitude is an excellent practice to perform every day.

7. **Sign your name** the way you wrote it at the top of the letter.

8. **Put this letter somewhere where you can see it every day,** like on the bathroom mirror or refrigerator. Although you have included a target date, you may receive your manifestation sooner—or later—than you have written. The universe operates with synchronicities, so it has to arrange and orchestrate your manifestation. Relax. The Universe Letter is a process.

I suggest you start with a simple request. This helps you become acquainted with how to do the process and to build your manifestation muscles. Not to mention it will give your skeptical mind something stress-free to work on, work up to. You may want to write a series of letters. You can then clearly see what you're willing to allow into your life by what shows up! With practice you will be able to manifest better and with greater ease. At least that's been my experience.

How can you write a beautifully crafted letter of your own? Primarily using the details on your list.

Let's imagine you want to manifest your perfect apartment. You could answer questions like those below with your list.

Price per month—would that include utilities? How about security deposit? First and last month's rent? Work exchange? Be specific with what YOU want

Locale—city, state—preferred neighborhoods if you know them—by water, mountains, desert, rural, suburban, cityscape. Be specific—what do you WANT?

Size—square footage, 1-story, 2-story, basement, attic. Lot size—age of apartment (Victorian, Art Deco, modern), condition of apartment and neighborhood —if you want an apartment freshly painted, newly carpeted, clean and bright, say that! Be specific. Include the colors of the walls and carpet while you're at it. Do you want a workroom in the garage? Include everything you want.

Amenities — which direction do you want your entrance to face? Windows (sunny or shady)? Number of bedrooms, bathrooms? Size of living room, dining room, kitchen? What kind of cabinetry? Plumbing? Electrical? Appliances? Do you want a fireplace, pool, exercise room, jacuzzi, landscaping? Bathtub or just shower? Garage? Garage door opener? Furnished or not? All the plumbing, sinks, tubs, toilets are modern and work perfectly. Be specific.

Extras —like stained glass windows, French doors, glass chandelier, indirect lighting, modern bathroom lighting, special wallpaper, skylights, whatever you can think of you'd like. Be creative.

Neighbors—close or far away, loving, kind, quiet, helpful, friendly, keep to their own business? Imagine these people in your mind. Remember your past experiences!

What kind of street and neighborhood? Quiet, attractive, tree-lined, safe, free of graffiti, close to shopping, schools, what kind of shopping and schools? What kind of children for your children to play with and be friends with?

How you (and your family) will feel in this apartment—happy, content, energetic, loving, peaceful, and creative? What do you want? **And of course include a date** for your anticipated move-in.

Do You See You are Creating a Contract? As if You Were Talking to a Realtor, a Lawyer, and a Salesperson? You are! You wouldn't go to a car dealership and merely say "I want to buy a car." You would specify make, model, year, price, extras, financing. You wouldn't call Sears and ask them to send a refrigerator without specifying what you want. You might end up with any old refrigerator. That's the point. You use the same methodology in your Universe Letter. You are training yourself to WANT what you want and GET what you want. Don't accept pale imitations anymore! Don't just put up with. Don't make do.

You are ordering from the "Sears in the Sky," and you deserve to get what you desire. In fact, the universe wants you to manifest your desires. You and the universe are one!

Over time I manifest about 90% of what I ask for. Sometimes I get 100%.

I figure if I ask for a lot, then the odds are better. Often I will get items I didn't even put in my letter. Those are bonuses. Remember— "this or something better now manifests" As you write down items you want, you may find yourself getting excited. Your excitement lets you know you are on the right track.

I wouldn't advise you to "try to figure out" how your manifestation will occur. Just trust that the universe has begun working for you already. In truth, the universe is always working for you. But this time you have special ordered a specific request, rather than longing for a vague desire. That makes all the difference in the world (cliché intended).

More helpful information:

In my article "The Complete Idiot's Guide to Enlightenment" (From

Suffering to Bliss in Two Parts)—feeling your emotions and disappearing your unhelpful stories focuses more energy into manifestation.

Another article I recommend is the "Universal Bank Account," which explains how the universe operates in giving and receiving. That essay details how to "prime the pump" to manifest what you want even more powerfully.

MANIFESTING A PERSON OR RELATIONSHIP:

You will need to be very specific. You may want to take a few days to think about and imagine the qualities you are looking for. (Twenty-five years ago I did the God Letter to manifest a boyfriend. He was everything on the list. But, I didn't read the fine print. He had several traits I didn't want—addictions and violent tendencies! Bear in mind that people are very complex.) You must think like a Divine Attorney, considering the fine print and contractual information. I generally recommend not writing a God letter for a love relationship as people and situations are way too complicated.

You must NOT try to manifest a specific individual, only qualities that you want in a person. Otherwise the universe's manifestation will either backfire on you or not work at all. That is considered magic and spell casting, which is okay if you are trained in Wicca, but is not what this method intends.

[You can write a God letter for help with health issues or even complex PTSD. I did.]

Best of luck.

Excerpt from Cosmic Grandma Wisdom © *2017*
April 24, 2012 © article first published in fatemagazine.com and galdepress.com

APPENDIX 10

13 Steps for Managing an Emotional Flashback

Pete Walker's 13 steps for managing an emotional flashback (reprinted with permission by Pete Walker, *Pete Walker.com*):

Say to yourself: I am having a flashback. Flashbacks take us into a timeless part of the psyche that feels as helpless, hopeless, and surrounded by danger as we were in childhood. The feelings and sensations you are experiencing are past memories that cannot hurt you now.

Remind yourself. "I feel afraid but I am not in danger! I am safe now, here in the present." Remember you are now in the safety of the present, far from the danger of the past.

Own your right/need to have boundaries. Remind yourself that you do not have to allow anyone to mistreat you; you are free to leave dangerous situations and protest unfair behavior.

Speak Reassuringly to the Inner Child. The child needs to know that you love her unconditionally—that she can come to you for comfort and protection when she feels lost and scared.

Deconstruct Eternity Thinking. in childhood, fear and abandonment felt endless—a safer future was unimaginable. Remember the flashback will pass as it has many times before.

Remind yourself that you are in an adult body with allies, skills, and resources to protect you that you never had as a child. (Feeling small and little is a sure sign of a flashback.)

Ease back into your body. Fear launches us into "heady" worrying, or numbing and spacing out.

a. Gently ask your body to relax: feel each of your major muscle groups and softly encourage them to relax. (Tightened musculature sends unnecessary danger signals to the brain)

b. Breathe deeply and slowly. (Holding the breath also signals danger.)

c. Slow down: rushing presses the psyche's panic button

d. Find a safe place to unwind and soothe yourself: wrap yourself in a blanket, hold a stuffed animal, lie down in a closet or a bath, or take a nap.

e. Feel the fear in your body without reacting to it. Fear is just an energy in your body that cannot hurt you if you do not run from it or react self-destructively to it. Resist the Inner Critic's Drasticizing and Catastrophizing:

  1. Use thought-stopping to halt its endless exaggeration of danger and constant planning to control the uncontrollable. Refuse to shame, hate or abandon yourself. Channel the anger of self-attack into saying NO to unfair self-criticism.

  2. Use thought-substitution to replace negative thinking with a memorized list of your qualities and accomplishments.

Allow yourself to grieve. Flashbacks are opportunities to release old, unexpressed feelings of fear, hurt, and abandonment, and to validate—and then soothe—the child's past experience of helplessness and hopelessness. Healthy grieving can turn our tears into self-compassion and our anger into self-protection.

Cultivate safe relationships and seek support. Take time alone when you need it, but don't let shame isolate you. Feeling shame doesn't mean you are shameful. Educate your intimates about flashbacks and ask them to help you talk and feel your way through them.

Learn to identify the types of triggers that lead to flashbacks. Avoid unsafe people, places, activities, and triggering mental processes. Practice preventive maintenance with these steps when triggering situations are unavoidable. .

Figure out what you are flashing back to. Flashbacks are opportunities to discover, validate, and heal our wounds from past abuse and abandonment. They also point to our still unmet developmental needs and can provide motivation to get them met.

Be patient with a slow recovery process. It takes time in the present to become un-adrenalized, and considerable time in the future to gradually decrease the intensity, duration, and frequency of flashbacks. Real recovery is a gradually progressive process (often two steps forward, one step back), not an attained salvation fantasy. Don't beat yourself up for having a flashback."

APPENDIX 11

How to Reboot Yourself Using Sacred Feminine Consciousness (Sacred Healing)

—Lauren O. Thyme, essay first published November 2018 in
Awaken The Feminine Anthology, *Rev. Karen Tate, Anthologist*

How can we reboot humanity towards a world permeated with peace, love, and sanity? The question itself leads to an awareness of what is lately referred to as "Sacred Feminine" consciousness. This reference to Feminine does not imply that women are better than men, for all humans are imbued with both feminine and masculine attributes, also known as yin and yang. The Sacred Feminine, also known as Goddess energy, divine intelligence, and spirituality, encompasses qualities that are loving, gentle, and kind. This energy excludes an "us or them" division, eliminating black and white thinking, while bypassing unnecessary, even war-like blame, hatred, and judgment.

A simple solution exists for a complex problem. The answer is that we each focus on our own spiritual, divine and karmic development, without the necessity to change anyone else. To strive to be the best sacred selves we can be.

That's it. There's no one to fix. Only to focus on the heart of ourselves.

This resolution may seem deceptively simple, yet it requires awareness, practice, mindfulness and more practice. Imagine living life in conscious awareness 24/7.

"What this necessitates is to diligently practice the following:

    Willingness
    Noticing without criticism
    Forgiveness of self and others
    Patience
    Unconditional love of self and others
    Mutual support—win/win solutions
    Mutual respect
    Acceptance and allowing
    Detachment
    Blamelessness
    Living in present time
    Open and loving communication
    Trust and surrender to a higher power
    Gratitude
    Defenselessness and neutrality
    Giving and receiving
    Joyful creation—doing what you love and feel com-
    pelled to do—and loving what you do
    Empathy and compassion
    Having fun

Did I say the solution was easy? No, it takes practice and attentiveness.

Everything is perfect no matter what it looks like, for the purpose of learning, growth and evolution" say my Elders. Nothing is wrong in the universe. Focusing on the things or people one perceives as "wrong," "bad," or "evil" only strengthens and expands that energy. We need to worry about absolutely nothing. Worry is a useless activity. In other words, we don't have to blame or judge others, ourselves, or situations. We need only to focus on ourselves. So we can each strive to become peace, love, and sanity within ourselves and around others—friends, relatives, or strangers.

We can focus on those spiritual concerns and when an inharmonious thought comes up, turn it over to the Divine. No need to stop a thought and the attending feeling. No need to figure out a solution to a problem. Simply release it into the care of the Universe. (I say "Here, Goddess" and hand it over.) I find the universe takes care of all those thoughts and feelings and problems— effortlessly—in time.

How to do it?

Ignore the non-stop thought circus. Stop paying attention to all the negative messages outside yourself and those negative messages (from your critic) within. Those are simply fear and worry messages. Whenever you have a problem, upset, or difficulty, give over everything to the care of the divine—goddess, deity, or universal consciousness—whatever you choose to call it.

My Elders tell me "Everything is connected to everything" and "One person can make a difference." The universe consists merely of vibration and consciousness. As one person changes his/her consciousness, and thus his/her vibration, one's life will change.

Lauren's Law #26: "As I transform myself, others transform themselves in my presence." So-called "reality" which includes other people and situations will change along with one's own transformation. Thus the planet and humanity will also change, can change, one person at a time. We can each make a pledge to become that person.

As I transform myself, others transform themselves in my

presence" is known as the Maharishi effect. The higher our emotional vibration, the more people we can affect by simply being our spiritual, transcendent selves. We don't have to "fix" anything or anyone. We only have to become the best selves possible, which then changes vibration and consciousness—and thus "reality."

We need only become "the change we want to see," according to Mahatma Gandhi.

Direct action is no longer the best route. It is outmoded and outdated. With Sacred Feminine aspects, we have come to the intersection where we are conscious co-creators with the Universe. Indeed according to Dr. David R. Hawkins (*Power Versus Force*), Lola Jones (*Things are Going Great in my Absence*), and Abraham-Hicks (*Law of Attraction*), we have no power over anyone or anything else except ourselves. We cannot force change. Instead we endeavor to change our own consciousness. As we would a small, shy kitten, we sit quietly, open, loving, gentle, and detached with ourselves. In its own time the "kitten" will jump on our lap and purr with ecstasy. We create a state of openness, acceptance, and neutrality in which everything is possible, by refining and re-defining ourselves.

Emotions are not bad but are purely vibration of one sort or another. How does an emotion feel and what does that emotion create in our lives? Lower emotional vibrations (sadness, anger, despair, blame, judgment) are ineffectual for creating the kind of positive change we all long for, while that emotion may feel terrible in our bodies and in the atmosphere around us. Higher vibrations such as neutrality, forgiveness, unconditional love, surrender, detachment, and mutual respect are powerful and create a more harmonious space in and around us, which also allows for miracles to happen.

We can bring serenity and evolution to ourselves, and all those with whom we have contact, make life easier and more fun, by rebooting ourselves using Sacred Feminine qualities and actions. Then we can relax and enjoy a new kind of life in which everyone wins.

***

As I have explained, the suffering and illnesses I've experienced in my life led me to discover my past lives, which in turn led me to various healing modalities shown in these appendices, including ones I created. I wrote *Catherine, Karma and Complex PTSD* for those who suffer. If my book helps you or someone you care about, I celebrate.

I wish you blessings and peace.

With loving wishes,
Lauren Olea Thyme

www.ingramcontent.com/pod-product-compliance
Lightning Source LLC
Chambersburg PA
CBHW021044090426
42738CB00006B/173